THE VICTORIAN TOWN CHILD

For many town children the street was their playground. One little girl has even rigged up a swing with the aid of a length of rope, a lamp-post and some railings. (The author)

The Victorian
Town Child

PAMELA HORN

NEW YORK UNIVERSITY PRESS
Washington Square, New York

First published in the U.S.A. in 1997 by
NEW YORK UNIVERSITY PRESS
Washington Square
New York, N.Y. 10003

Published in association with Sutton Publishing Limited,
United Kingdom

C-I-P data available from the Library of Congress

ISBN 0-8147-3575-4

Printed and bound in Great Britain by
Butler & Tanner Ltd, Frome and London

Contents

Acknowledgements

I should like to thank all those who have assisted me in the preparation of this book by providing information and illustrations or who have helped in other ways. In particular, my thanks are due to His Eminence the Cardinal Archbishop of Westminster for permission to quote from the Westminster Diocesan Archives, and to the archivist, Father Ian Dickie, for his help in locating relevant material; to the National Society for the Prevention of Cruelty to Children and the Society's archivist, Nicholas Malton, for allowing me to quote from some of their records; to the University of Essex, for giving me access to their extensive Oral Archives; and to the headmaster of Abingdon School.

I have also received much efficient and friendly help from staff at the various libraries and record offices where I have worked, or who have provided information. These include the Bodleian Library, Oxford; Birmingham Archives; Bristol Local History Library; the British Library; the Church of England Record Centre; Cardiff Central Library; the Greater London Library and Record Office; the Archive Office and Local History Library, Grimsby; Lancashire Record Office, Preston; Liverpool Record Office; Bolton Local History Library and Archives; Portsmouth City Record Office; Manchester Central Library and Record Office; Oxford Local Studies Library; the Public Record Office; and the Tameside Local Studies Library, Stalybridge.

Finally, as always, my thanks are due to my husband for his constant help, support and advice, and for his company on many of my research 'expeditions'. Without him this book could not have been written.

Pamela Horn
November 1996

THE DEPARTURE OF THE INNOCENTS

Take them away! Take them away!
Out of the gutter, the ooze, and slime,
Where the little vermin paddle and crawl,
Till they grow and ripen into crime.

Take them away from the jaws of death,
And the coils of evil that swaddle them round,
And stifle their souls in every breath
They draw on the foul and fetid ground.

Take them away! Away! Away!
The bountiful earth is wide and free,
The New shall repair the wrongs of the Old –
Take them away o'er the rolling sea!

Anonymous verse published in *Our Waifs and Strays*, August 1887, typifying
Victorian views on town children and emigration

Conversion Table: Shillings and Pence

Old money	Decimal	Old money	Decimal
1*d*	½p	1*s* 7*d*	8p
2*d* or 3*d*	1p	1*s* 8*d*	8½p
4*d*	1½p	1*s* 9*d* or 1*s* 10*d*	9p
5*d*	2p	1*s* 11*d*	9½p
6*d*	2½p	2*s*	10p
1*s*	5p	2*s* 6*d*	12½p
1*s* 1*d*	5½p	3*s*	15p
1*s* 2*d* or 1*s* 3*d*	6p	5*s*	25p
1*s* 6*d*	7½p	20*s*	100p, i.e. £1

CHAPTER 1

Victorian Towns

The fact to observe is that the people of England, which calls herself Old, are younger than the people of many other countries, . . . not because life is shorter, but because the births, instead of remaining stationary, are continually increasing, and infusing youthful blood into the people . . . . Villages and small places are rising up to the importance of large towns. Thus Barrow-in-Furness in Lancashire, not long ago an inconsiderable village, is now a municipal borough . . . ; and Middlesbrough in Yorkshire, inconsiderable in 1831, with its 383 inhabitants, has now 39,563 inhabitants, under municipal government.

General Report of the Population Census for 1871,
Parliamentary Papers 1873, Vol. LXXI, Pt II, pp. xiii, xxxi

Victorian society possessed three main characteristics – its youthfulness, the speed with which the population was growing, and its increasing industrialization and urbanization. Between 1841 and 1901 the inhabitants of England and Wales grew from 15.9 million to 32.5 million, and whereas under half of them had lived in 'urban' areas at the earlier date, by 1901 around four-fifths did so.[1] Towns of over one hundred thousand inhabitants rose from six in 1841 to thirty in 1901, although at the beginning of the nineteenth century only London had been so large. Major industrial centres like Middlesbrough and Barrow-in-Furness sprang from insignificance to become municipal boroughs within a few decades, and other communities like Preston were transformed from minor market towns into leading industrial centres. In 1828 Pigot's *Directory of Lancashire* commented on how fifty years before Preston had been 'more remarkable for the residence of independent persons and its claims to gentility, than for the production of articles deemed . . . essentially necessary to adorn the rich and clothe all ranks'. Now the 'rapid strides of science and art, rendered subservient to machinery and manufactures in general' had caused it to be included among the manufacturing centres of Lancashire. A year later, the vicar of St Paul's Church in the town lamented that children of nine years or younger were being employed in the cotton mills. As a result 'the poor that have large young families . . . come and reside in the neighbourhood. . . . At present our streets are perfectly crowded, and present a scene the most deplorable . . . The people are more barbarous and uncivilised than it is possible for anyone to conceive who has not been amongst them.'[2]

It was during the Victorian years that the British became the world's first truly industrialized and urbanized nation. The rapidity with which that transformation was taking place caused anxiety and bewilderment among many witnesses of the process, with the counties of Lancashire, Yorkshire, Cheshire and Warwickshire at the forefront of the changes. 'The south-eastern quarter of Lancashire', wrote James Bryce in the later 1860s:

Families living in overcrowded slums spent as much time out of doors as possible. (The author)

. . . is a district to which it would be hard to find anything comparable in England, or indeed in Europe. . . . From Burnley to Warrington, from Wigan to Stalybridge it is one huge congeries of villages, thickening ever and anon into towns, but seldom thinning out into anything that can be called country . . . Towns have risen so fast as hardly to have yet become conscious of their own existence: they are straggling and irregularly built, handsome piles intermixed with hovels, public buildings extemporised in odd corners, big rambling shops in which, as in a backwoods store, everything is sold, from silks and notepaper at one counter to herrings and potatoes at the other. . . . So too, as in a colony, society is in an unsettled and fluctuating state.[3]

Although in 1843 Robert Vaughan had stressed the importance of cities as centres of intellectual opportunity where 'the more varied association into which men are brought . . . tends necessarily to impart greater knowledge, acuteness and power to the mind than would have been realized . . . in the comparative isolation of a rural parish', such attitudes became rarer as the century developed.[4] Increasingly, contemporaries emphasized the darker side of town life, and the threat the changes posed to the values of traditional society. All too easily working-class neighbourhoods were depicted as disorderly slums which threatened the stability of the wider community, and the overcrowded centres of major cities were seen as a major cause of working-class 'demoralization'. 'When we find father and mother, grown sons, and daughters, and young children all living and sleeping in one room, how can we wonder that there should not be a very delicate sense of morality among them', declared one writer in 1878.[5]

The fact that many poor families moved house frequently, perhaps doing a 'midnight flit' to escape rent arrears, to seek a better home or one nearer their place of work, added to the unease. It was in these circumstances that C.H. Alderson, Her Majesty's Inspector of Schools for Marylebone, in 1874 blamed short-term, short-distance family migrations and the consequent irregular school attendance of the children as two of the major obstacles to efficient elementary education in London.

Constant removals of the home entail constant removals from school . . . The frequency and suddenness with which families appear in a locality, stay some months, and then efface themselves leaving no trace behind, is realized by no-one more fully and sadly than the school teacher on whom the impossible task is laid of teaching their children something *in transitu*.[6]

It was this sense of impermanence which led Charles Booth in the 1890s to claim that it was not in the countryside but 'in town that "terra incognita"' ought to be written 'on our social map. In the country the machinery of human life is plainly to be seen . . . : personal relations bind the whole together. . . . It is far otherwise with cities, where as to these questions we live in darkness, with . . . ignorant unnecessary fears'.[7]

In a population where throughout the Victorian years about one person in three was under the age of fifteen (see Appendix 1), these developments affected the nation's children with especial force: for by the 1890s the vast majority of youngsters lived in towns, unlike the position when Queen Victoria ascended the throne in 1837. This did not mean, of course, that they had a common experience of urban life. Not only were there great differences between the lot of a child brought up in a comfortable middle-class suburb on the fringes of a major city and that of his or her counterpart living in overcrowded, often insanitary, slums at the bottom of the social scale, but there were variations between the towns themselves. The continuing demand in leading textile centres such as Bolton, Blackburn, Bradford, Preston and Halifax for juveniles to work in the mills, and the needs of major ports and commercial centres such as Liverpool and London for boys and girls to run errands, deliver goods, and act as street vendors on a part-time or casual basis, were in marked contrast to the situation in cathedral cities like Winchester and Salisbury, or market towns like Banbury in Oxfordshire and Farnham in Surrey. Although these may have had their industrial enterprises, much of their day-to-day life was governed by the demands of agriculture and the needs of nearby villagers for the goods and services they offered. George Sturt, born in Farnham in 1863, the son of a wheelwright and shopkeeper, remembered its peaceful atmosphere. On market days a few cattle or pigs would be sold, and horses and carts traversed its streets to provide most of its 'slow and spare provincial traffic'. The town was 'easy-going and sleepy . . . , clean-aired yet dingy for want of paint'.[8]

Urban overcrowding and squalor in London: Dudley Street, Seven Dials. (From: Gustave Doré and Blanchard Jerrold, London. A Pilgrimage *(1872))*

This was very different from the impoverished districts of London described by the social investigators Gustave Doré and Blanchard Jerrold a few years later. They were struck by the fact that it was in the poverty-stricken districts that children seemed most to abound, and also: 'that some of the hardest outdoor work should be in their feeble little hands; that infant poverty should be the news-distributor; that, in short, there should be a rising generation hardened in its earliest years to vagabondage, and [allowed] to grow to that most miserable of human creatures, the unskilled, dependent roofless man.'[9]

That did not mean that country towns like Farnham were without poverty and child labour, or that all the streets of working-class London were swarming with what Doré and Jerrold called 'wretched children, covered with . . . rags, bare-footed and bare-headed'. But in the smaller rural centres these harsher aspects were often concealed in isolated enclaves within a broader and seemingly more prosperous whole, like Mixen Lane on the fringe of Thomas Hardy's fictional Casterbridge. This, declared Hardy, was 'the hiding-place of those who were in distress, and in debt, and trouble of every kind. . . . Rural mechanics too idle to mechanize, rural servants too rebellious to serve, drifted or were forced into Mixen Lane.'[10] Casterbridge was modelled on Dorchester in Dorset and a majority of market towns possessed local versions of Mixen Lane.

But even in large cities most working-class families lived in households where they enjoyed the basic amenities of life and where the children were clean, respectable and generally healthy. When Charles Booth published his survey of East London in 1889 he showed that 65 per cent of the population lived in modest comfort, compared to 35 per cent who were in poverty. Within that overall relationship, there were enormous variations between districts. Hackney was

Life in a country town: High Street, Abingdon (then in Berkshire) in the 1890s. Note the boy strolling in the middle of the road. (The author)

notable for its 'well-to-do suburban population' and its core of upper-middle-class residents, while in Mile End Old Town, too, the poverty level was only 24.6 per cent of the population. But in Whitechapel it jumped to 49.1 per cent and in Bethnal Green to an appalling 58.7 per cent. Subsequent investigation revealed that for London as a whole 30 per cent of the inhabitants lived in poverty, and the level of deprivation in certain parts of Southwark, Greenwich and Goswell Road exceeded that of Bethnal Green.[11] The significance of this is underlined by the fact that in 1901 Greater London contained a fifth of the total population of England and Wales, and that during the preceding decade it had absorbed, one way or another, about a quarter of the net increase in population of the entire country.[12]

The failure of contemporaries to appreciate the range and complexity of working-class life became more apparent from the middle of the century, as the better-off began to move in growing numbers to the suburbs, and as those who stayed behind averted their eyes from the insanitary courts and alleys which bordered their own properties. Edwin Chadwick reproached members of the 'wealthier classes' who lived in 'front houses' on the major thoroughfares and yet had 'never entered the adjoining courts, or seen the interior of any of the tenements' which were on their doorsteps.[13]

Areas inhabited by the poor were, indeed, regarded by many members of the middle class as dangerous 'unknown' places into which respectable people ventured at their peril. 'The great mass of the metropolitan community', declared James Grant in 1842, 'are as ignorant of the destitution and distress which prevail in large districts of London . . . as if the wretched creatures were living in the very centre of Africa.'[14] A few years later Joseph Kay wrote of the deteriorative tendencies of urban expansion and warned that if the children of the city were neglected its streets would become the 'training ground for crime and disaffection', and a stimulus to the physical and moral decline of the nation.[15]

It was to counter these fears and divisions and to promote cohesion and order in society that many reformers pressed for the setting up of a network of efficient elementary schools to inculcate such desirable qualities as a respect for religion, an appreciation of the importance of hard work, and a high standard of morality into the rising generation. 'In one street . . . , in the south of London, there now exist 1,500 destitute and criminal juveniles, for whom there is not even a school provided', wrote John Garwood in 1853:

Is it to be wondered at that juvenile crime exists, and even increases, in the metropolis, when the class from which it springs is so often neglected? . . . It ought . . . distinctly to be understood, that there are very many indeed of this class who are willing to be reformed, and brought under Christian instruction and training, and that the means only are requisite to enable them to carry out their desires.[16]

Lord Ashley (the future Earl of Shaftesbury) also saw schools as a means of raising standards in the family as a whole. He claimed to know of 'hundreds of instances' where the example of the children had brought their parents, 'by shame or precept, to habits of decency and order'.[17] In a similar spirit the Royal

THE MOMENTOUS QUESTION.

Paterfamilias (who is just beginning to feel himself at home in his delightfully new suburban residence) interrupts the wife of his bosom. "'SEASIDE!' 'CHANGE OF AIR!!' 'OUT OF TOWN!!!' WHAT NONSENSE, ANNA MARIA! WHY, GOOD GRACIOUS ME! WHAT ON EARTH CAN YOU WANT TO BE GOING 'OUT OF TOWN' FOR, WHEN YOU'VE GOT SUCH A GARDEN AS *THIS!*"

Punch *mocking the pretensions of upper working-class families when they moved to the suburbs.* (Punch, *1871*)

Commission on Popular Education in 1861 argued that 'a set of good schools civilises a whole neighbourhood'.[18] Reformers had a simplistic belief that education would counter social disorder and provide docile and disciplined workers to meet the needs of industry and commerce. Although schooling might benefit the children themselves, by teaching them to read and write and imparting religious truths, for many it was the good of society itself which was the main objective. Just how far schools did, in practice, instil the desired moral message in their pupils is difficult to assess; in many cases they clearly failed.[19]

So, despite the rapid growth of elementary education in the second half of the nineteenth century, the divisions within society remained. Indeed, during the 1880s and 1890s they were sharpened in some respects as improved transport facilities made it possible for many modestly affluent workers to live at some distance from their place of employment, and to sever connections with poorer neighbours in the inner city. The population of Willesden and environs jumped from 16,000 to nearly 115,000 between 1871 and 1901, thus indicating the link between the rail network and the growth of newer suburbs.[20]

Yet the apparently random and divided nature of much of urban society, so disturbing to contemporaries, can easily be exaggerated. As Barbara Finkelstein has pointed out, the complexity and the social mix of individual areas should never be underestimated, nor the cohesive role of families, churches and indigenous neighbourhood organizations ignored.[21] Although people moved house frequently in working-class districts they often did so within a relatively limited locality, and many established close relationships with neighbours. 'The street in which I was nurtured as a small girl had little to boast of, except that in an odd way, we regarded it as Our Street and rich in its own quality of community life', wrote Alice Foley of Bolton during the 1890s.[22] Walter Southgate, born in Bethnal Green in 1890, experienced similar feelings towards the residents in his road. After sixty years he could recall the names and occupations of many who lived close at hand. He also remembered that 'mutual aid was the keystone of existence when difficult times came along'. Sometimes when his parents got into debt the bailiffs would come in. Their presence in the front parlour was, 'in my youthful eyes, . . . a visit of men from the dark regions'. But his mother reacted more practically by going round to neighbours, many of them nearly as poor as herself, so as to secure small temporary loans to save some of the furniture earmarked for removal. One woman even offered Mrs Southgate her wedding ring to pawn.[23]

To Robert Roberts, living in turn-of-the-century Salford, his city, like other industrial centres, was composed of a clutter of loosely defined overlapping 'villages', each virtually self-contained and with its own loyalties and social links.

> Our own consisted of some thirty streets and alleys locked along the north and south by two railway systems a furlong apart. . . . West of us, well beyond the tramlines, lay the middle classes, bay-windowed and begardened. We knew them not.
>
> In the city as a whole our village rated indubitably low. . . . With cash, or on tick, our villagers, about three thousand in all, patronised fifteen beer-houses, a hotel and two off-licences, nine grocery and general shops, three greengrocers (for ever struggling to survive against the street hawker), two tripe shops, three barbers, three cloggers, two cook shops, one fish and chip shop . . . , an old clothes store, a couple of pawnbrokers and two loan offices.[24]

Within each 'village' there were those considered 'respectable' and those who fell short of that standard. Every street had its social rating, and one side or one end of a road was often considered superior to another. End houses enjoyed a high status. Families, too, had their rankings, as did individual members of them:

> Shopkeepers, publicans and skilled tradesmen occupied the premier positions. . . . From their ranks the lower middle-class . . . drew most of its recruits – clerks and, in particular, schoolteachers . . . By entering into any business at all a man and his family grew at once in economic status . . . On the social ladder after tradesmen and artisans came the semi-skilled workers [still a small section] in regular employment, and then the various grades of unskilled labourers. . . . Irish Roman Catholic immigrants, mostly illiterate, formed the lowest socio-economic stratum.[25]

Although there might be disagreements over the conduct of children or other matters, most families in that impoverished district remained 'awesomely respectable', with offspring brought up 'to be decent, kindly and honourable'. People also tried to prevent their children mixing with those of whom they disapproved. It was in these circumstances that London-born Tommy Morgan, who described his parents as 'the two biggest drunkards in Waterloo and Blackfriars', remembered being shunned by more respectable neighbours. They would shout to Tommy and his friends when they were playing in the street: 'Get away from my window, get away from my door, get down further.'[26]

Another youngster, whose father was clerk in charge of a metropolitan railway station, was also very conscious of her family's status. They moved to newly developed Queen's Park in London during the mid-1880s, when she was six and a half. The area catered mainly for postmen, policemen, railway employees, and similar members of the better-off working class: 'it wasn't considered to be a rough quarter'. But over the bridge 'there was a lower class neighbourhood altogether', where there were children without shoes and with which she had little contact.[27]

Her feelings of precarious social superiority were shared by a Bristol girl, born in 1886, one of the ten children of a carpenter and joiner. Although the family was not very affluent they lived in a three-bedroomed house with a parlour, where lace curtains hung at the window and there was 'a proper sideboard with all the best china in'. Her father discouraged her from playing with children from poorer areas and 'we were better than a lot of those down Luke Street way'. She remembered the distinctions between schools, too. Where she attended the pupils never came without boots. Youngsters 'like that' went to a Ragged School instead.

The importance of the second-hand shop and marine store as universal provider and social centre in working-class neighbourhoods, London, 1877. (Greater London Record Office Photograph Collection)

'They sent all the poor little kids there and also there they used to give breakfast tickets. You had to be poor and ragged and have no boots, and you might stink' to attend such a place.[28] In all of these communities, clothing was a clear pointer to social standing, and boys with much darned shirts would nonetheless be encouraged to wear a celluloid collar and a tie to attend school, as a sign of respectability, while those who could not afford footwear were not only looked down upon but were likely to be excluded altogether.

A desire to maintain social differences led to schools wishing to attract better-off children charging higher fees. In the 1870s one of Her Majesty's Inspectors of Schools drew attention to the relationship between fee level and residential area. In Manchester, schools on the outskirts, where the residents were moderately prosperous, charged 6d to 9d per week, as did those in the central areas whose reputation was prestigious enough to attract 'a good class of scholars . . . from considerable distances'. In stable working–class areas there were schools 'of the second grade', where fees averaged around 4d a week. Finally there were those catering for the very poor, where the maximum was 2d or 3d a week.[29]

In considering the lot of the Victorian town child, therefore, these intricate social distinctions and influences have to be taken into account. Also significant were changes in the attitude towards children themselves during the second half of the nineteenth century. Gradually society moved away from an emphasis on the importance of their economic role, as paid or unpaid workers and as providers of services (including looking after younger siblings), to a recognition that they were entitled to regular schooling and leisure time free from family responsibilities. The degree to which this new approach was carried through varied according to the availability (or otherwise) of child employment and the income levels of individual households. Community attitudes were important, too, with many parents in textile towns like Bolton and Burnley continuing to support the principle of child labour to the end of the century.[30] Certainly Jack Lanigan, whose family in Salford was thrown into poverty by the death of his artisan father, remembered the pride with which at the age of ten he passed his school leaving examination and was able to start work. 'I now wanted to tell the world I was . . . a man, working and helping my mother.'[31] For other children, including Walter Southgate, the solution to parental poverty lay in part-time employment out of school hours until they were old enough to take up work full time.[32]

In this process of leaving school and taking a job, class differences were central. 'Many young men in the public schools were receiving full-time education at an age when their poorer contemporaries had been at work for a decade', comments James Walvin.[33] While eighteen was accepted as the normal leaving age for pupils attending leading public schools like Eton, Harrow, Winchester and Rugby, for those at the nation's elementary schools the minimum leaving age did not reach twelve until 1899. Even then, there were problems of enforcement, and the extent to which the state should intervene to protect and sustain its youngest members through labour laws, compulsory education, and anti–cruelty measures remained a topic for debate to the end of the century. For some supporters of *laissez-faire* principles, such measures not only infringed parental rights but fatally undermined family self-dependence.

Among a new generation of 'child savers' there was a firm recognition of the need to accept youngsters as citizens in their own right. Foremost among the proponents of this view was the London Society for the Prevention of Cruelty to Children, set up in 1884. Five years later, it gave as one of its reasons for supporting the passage of an anti-cruelty bill, the need to establish individual child rights: 'Though the property of his parents, a child is not the less a subject of the Crown . . . However small, he is a part of the community to which Parliament is bound to secure at least an endurable life. . . . It is unlawful to work a horse with sores and bruises. To work a child with them is still lawful.'[34] But others took the view that any measure which encouraged parents to 'look to strangers' for the support of their offspring would not only be unjust to responsible parents who were already doing their duty, but would further encourage the evils of 'neglect and dependence'.[35]

These conflicting approaches to child welfare were made clear in a London school board sub-committee report over the provision of school meals to malnourished children. In 1898–9 a survey suggested that 55,000 London pupils habitually attended school in want of food. That was particularly true of the offspring of casual labourers, for whom work was in short supply during the winter months, and of the children of widows. During times of need such youngsters were sent to school in the morning with nothing more than a piece of bread and margarine, and some did not even have that. The sub-committee accepted that certain parents underfed their children through indifference or drunkenness, but saw no way in which their offspring could be excluded from aid except by 'an impossible system of exact . . . house-to-house visitation'. Instead, the pragmatic solution should be adopted of feeding those who needed it, since a starving child was unlikely to benefit from the education provided: 'It is, of course, obvious . . . that this, like all other social evils, may be gradually eliminated by the general improvement, moral and material, of the community. But . . . the prevention of underfeeding in School children . . . is itself one of the potent means of forwarding the general improvement – just as education is itself.'[36]

However bodies like the Charity Organisation Society (COS), which opposed all casual and uncoordinated philanthropy, maintained that this kind of indiscriminate action was likely to encourage the feckless, the neglectful, and the deceitful at the expense of the respectable, the honest, and the self reliant. As early as June 1885, the cautionary tale was told in the *Charity Organisation Review* of youngsters in Liverpool who had lied in order to get penny dinner tickets or who had 'gone without breakfast at the parents' suggestion, or even at their own, in hopes of dinner tickets being given – a chance of raisin pudding in the future being preferred to dry bread in the present – or . . . they had had bread, but having eaten it in the street, did not count it as breakfast.'[37] Men and women who would have been appalled to experience a regime of bread and margarine for themselves apparently saw nothing wrong in prescribing it for younger and poorer fellow citizens, in the interests of promoting family self-dependence.

In the end, it was fear about the future of the nation itself if children were allowed to grow up puny and unhealthy which was to prove a major stimulus to collectivist action. 'Bad food, overcrowded homes, at work for years past on the

British race, have reduced its stamina', warned Robert Sherard in 1905. 'It is a very wretched thing to have conviction . . . that a very large percentage of our poor children are . . . allowed to grow up into miserable men and women amidst the indifference of their parents and the public.'[38]

The rise of foreign competition for British manufacturing industry, most notably from Germany and the United States of America during the 1890s, and the upsurge of imperialistic sentiment which accompanied the outbreak of the Boer War in 1899 led to a good deal of soul searching. The realization that many potential recruits from the major industrial cities were too unfit to join up, fuelled fears about a deterioration in the physique of the working class and underlined the need to tackle weaknesses in the health and welfare of town children if the process were to be reversed.[39] 'In an era of competitive nationhood', comments Hugh Cunningham, 'children were an asset which was neglected at peril'.[40]

Also significant were the reports of medical officers of health and others in the major towns and cities pinpointing the variations in child death rates both within cities and between one town and another. Liverpool in 1893 had an infant death rate in impoverished areas like Vauxhall, St Anne's and Lime Street which was almost twice as high as it was in better off Abercromby and Rodney Street.[41]

Children playing in a London street, c. 1900. (*The author*)

Similarly, while 54 per cent of all deaths in St Anne's and 55 per cent of those in the Scotland division of the city were accounted for by children under five, in Abercromby the proportion was 36 per cent. Eight years later an investigation into the circumstances of over one thousand consecutive child deaths in parts of the·city where infant mortality was very high revealed that in 21 per cent of the cases the families were described as extremely dirty and in 18 per cent the mothers went out to work, leaving the infant in the care of others (often another child) who could not give the requisite attention. In about 11 per cent of the cases families were living in dwellings unfit for habitation, while in over 25 per cent the parents were classed as 'markedly intemperate'. In other instances physical violence and brutality, often the result of excessive drinking, led to much suffering and some loss of life.[42] It was to tackle the high infant mortality attributable to improper or inadequate feeding that the city authorities established a sterilized milk depot, to cater for babies who could not be suckled by their mother.[43]

Apart from these differences within Liverpool itself, there were wide variations between the city's infant mortality levels and those in other urban areas, where incomes were higher or more regular, and housing conditions better. Thus while infant deaths per 1,000 births in 1892 stood at 189 in Liverpool, in London the rate was 155, in Bristol 145 and in Portsmouth 139. But there were towns with an even worse record than Liverpool, including Blackburn, where many of the

Three deprived and dejected waifs on a city street in Newcastle upon Tyne in the 1890s. For a homeless child unable to find work the alternative to starvation was the workhouse or a life of crime. (NSPCC Archives)

womenfolk were engaged in cotton weaving and where the rate of infant deaths was a horrifying 204 per 1,000 births, and in Manchester, where it was 192.[44] In the two latter cases, therefore, about one in five babies born died before reaching their first birthday.

It was to a reduction in these high levels of child deaths that health reformers turned their attention at the close of the Victorian era. Among the measures proposed were the setting up of infant welfare clinics and crèches, and the instruction of older girls attending elementary schools in appropriate domestic and maternal skills.[45] But underlying the debates were doubts over the suitability of the city as a place in which to bring up youngsters anyway. 'Is it possible for children to grow up healthy and strong – mentally and physically – in large towns, or is it as inevitable as it is true that race degenerates with town life . . . ?' asked the social reformer and COS supporter, Helen Dendy. To her, one of the principal drawbacks of an urban existence was its remoteness from nature:

> In the country human nature sinks to its proper insignificance, and preserves its true proportions; in the town its importance is exaggerated out of all proportion, and it becomes the grotesque and even hideous caricature which seems to develop inevitably under the influences of town life, and which is rarely found in the country.
>
> This . . . should be one of the points to aim at in the education of town children; to get them back to a proper reverence for Nature . . . Much can be done . . . by means of books, museums, and public gardens; but all these are tainted by the same leaven of artificiality, and subordination to the little uses of mankind. Perhaps the biggest step in the right direction has been taken by the Children's Country Holiday Fund.[46]

For those unable to visit the countryside, a garden could serve as a partial substitute. The socialist William Morris, with unrealistic middle-class optimism, considered that 'every child should be able to play in a garden close to the place where his parents live'.[47] It was an ideal beyond the reach of vast numbers of children growing up in overcrowded courts and alleys in the larger towns, even at the end of the Victorian era.

The widespread belief in the 'contaminating' moral influence of town life and the superior ambience of the countryside also underlay many of the efforts to promote the emigration of poor children to Canada, especially from the 1870s onwards. As two advocates of the emigration cause wrote in 1902, the scheme was beneficial not only because the moral tone in Canada, 'even in the Cities', was 'much purer than in England' but because the material opportunities for the children sent away would be greater there: 'Canada is . . . a healthy land, and the children rapidly develop into strong, big men and women. If it is a good thing, then, to emigrate any child on account of the better chances it will have in Canada, how much more advantageous must it be to a child whose surroundings in England are likely to degrade it!'[48]

Such views overlooked the hazards and hardships which the large-scale movement of young children created, but they show the importance attached to

Children playing at 'jacks' on the pavement outside a hairdressing saloon in Richmond Row, Liverpool, c. 1895. (Liverpool City Libraries)

breaking the links with town life, and with the threat to the youngsters' religious and moral wellbeing which urbanization was thought to pose. They demonstrate one of the enduring divisions in society's attitude towards young people in the Victorian years, between those who regarded them as innocent 'victims' of an uncaring society that paid little attention to their welfare, and those who considered many of them, especially from the lowest stratum of city society, to be a danger to social order unless they were subjected to strict adult surveillance and removed as far as possible from all temptations.

Even contemporaries like E.J. Urwick, who took a more favourable view of the future prospects of children growing up in towns, were influenced by the widespread anxieties over the health and physique of such youngsters. Urwick conceded that a badly fed town boy 'of the poorest classes' weighed less and was shorter than a country boy reared on more wholesome food, in better air, and under cleaner conditions. He was also more likely to suffer from inherited physical and mental defects than his rural counterpart. But with this he displayed

a remarkable toughness of fibre, a sort of indiarubber capacity of recovery from fatigue or injury or the damage done by his surroundings, as well as an alertness and quickness of movement, which seem to be drawn from the very conditions of his town life. He ought . . . to die early, as the result of all that his stomach and lungs have to suffer in childhood. He ought to lose all his vitality before middle life, as the result of all that his nervous system has to suffer in street and factory. But he does neither. May it not, therefore, be permissible to hope that he is undergoing, slowly and painfully, a process of adaptation to the environment which has become the condition of his existence?[49]

Boys playing leap-frog in London, c. 1900. (The author)

Nonetheless doubts remained as to how far the modern city provided a suitable environment for bringing up children. It was in this context that reformers saw education as an antidote to the worst features of urban life and as a means of drawing youngsters into a world of rules and regulations and of strict timekeeping. This became one of the socializing functions of the teacher – hence the comment by the head of Christ Church Boys' School, Brixton, in January 1863: 'I cautioned the boys as to Regularity and Punctuality', and the repeated warnings given by his colleague at All Saints' School in South London two years later, concerning 'Cleanliness', 'Truant-playing' and 'Lying'.[50]

More positive were the ways in which educational institutions, including Sunday schools, could create a sense of community for youngsters growing up in a rapidly changing environment. In the middle of the nineteenth century the *Morning Chronicle* stressed this aspect when it described the Sunday schools in Manchester as

not only a vast educational instrument, but a great social fact. Nearly every school has its library, and many their benefit societies. At Whitsuntide, the yearly week of rest, every school has its country trip. . . . Sunday-schools act also as powerful agents in binding different classes together. Men in the middle ranks of life very commonly act as teachers; and acquaintanceships formed in the school-room not unfrequently lead to life-long business connections. Families are for generations connected with the same school; a great proportion of the children at any given time, are the offspring of old scholars . . .[51]

A sherbet seller offering her wares at a halfpenny a glass at the entrance to Greenwich Park in 1888. (Greater London Record Office Photograph Collection)

A similar role was played by the Band of Hope, established in 1847 to discourage youngsters from falling victim to the 'demon drink'. It, too, sought to recruit the children of the poor in towns and cities. Among them was Walter Southgate, who joined in 1900, at the age of ten. He soon became a captain and was given a blue sash as a mark of his authority:

> . . . at these weekly gatherings of . . . abstainers, who paid a halfpenny a week for under 12s, . . . we had songs and recitations coached by a dramatic youth who had come all the way from Oxford University in need of experience in slumming in the East End.
>
> [The] gatherings were held in a mission hall run by the Church of England at the end of our street. . . . My function was really to see that the kids kept quiet and obeyed orders from Big Brother. . . . Punching kids on the nose I quickly learnt was not the best method of persuasion as I was very small for my age and the bigger boys could easily have made mincemeat of me. I threatened, therefore, that I would blot their copy book when the annual outing to Epping Forest came around. This annual treat, the only outing in the year, when, as a child, I was able to see the open country, was given . . . free by the church people to all total abstainers under 12 years old. We had a long ride in four-horse brakes, a free tea of bread and strawberry jam and dollops of seedy fruit cakes. What we couldn't eat at the time we secreted in our pockets, which crumbled long before we got into the horse brakes to come home. Bad manners, of course, but what do half-starved kids care about etiquette? The church effort was a valuable one because it got the children young enough to learn the lesson about the evils of over-indulgence in alcohol.[52]

Many children also derived pleasure and stimulus from the sights and sounds of the town itself, with its constant stream of street entertainers and vendors, and the lively tunes of the hurdy-gurdy man. There was always something happening – something to watch. In Bolton, Alice Foley remembered that even the rag-and-bone men were colourful, with their hand-carts festooned with strings of balloons, 'and the balloons, together with white or yellow "rubbing-stones", were exchanged for empty jam-jars or a handful of rags . . . We also had a pale, stuttering boy who hawked muffins from door to door, whilst on wintry nights the hot-pea man came along, swinging his bell and inviting custom for his mushy-green peas, giving off a savoury smell on the chilly air.' On dark evenings Alice and her friends flocked to a nearby piece of spare ground where 'Pot Bailey', a well-known local character, auctioned his store of crockery 'from chamber-pots to fine glass ware . . . illuminated by flickering paraffin flares'. While the adults made their bids, the children played 'tig', flitting in and out of the 'magic circle and revelling in the warmth and smells of milling humanity'.[53]

These pleasures were enjoyed primarily by the children of the working class, who formed the vast majority of the juvenile population in any town. It is to the lives and prospects of their more prosperous, and perhaps more fortunate, counterparts in the middling ranks of society that we must now turn.

CHAPTER 2
Middle-class Children

The social influence at work was the class spirit . . . The 'middle' class, and especially the newer element in its composition, was sensitive on the point. It did not wish its children to mix with all and sundry – at least, not with all and sundry of a lower social grade . . . It was not an exalted principle, and it expressed a typically Victorian belief in the enduring character of contemporary class-distinctions.

K.E. Kirk, *The Story of the Woodard Schools* (1937), p. 16

It was in the nineteenth century that the real importance of the middle class within British society became clearly established. As a result of the increasing complexity of the nation's economic life, not only was there an expansion in manufacturing production and the extractive industries but in the service sector, including retail distribution, banking and insurance. In many occupations, such as engineering and construction, new and specialized skills were developed, while in the larger undertakings, especially after the passage of the 1862 Companies Act, there was a growing need for accountants, lawyers and other experts. Lower down the social scale, the number of clerks, shop assistants, commercial travellers, teachers, and business people of all kinds increased. The demand for clerks, particularly in London, was so great that their national total jumped by 273 per cent between 1841 and 1881 – well ahead of any increase in the overall population.[1] And in the smaller towns of the north of England in the mid-1860s parents were said to be so anxious to set their children 'in the way' of becoming rich that they sent them 'into the works or put them to an office at 13 or 14, each fearing lest the sons of others should distance his own in the race'.[2]

As a result of these changes, by 1867 R.D. Baxter estimated around a quarter of the families in Britain could be called middle class, although within that broad category their income, aspirations and living standards varied widely. A professional man enjoying solid success could secure £1,000 a year or more, while a clerk or minor factory manager might have to settle for £150 or £200.[3] However, no matter what their precise earnings, virtually all of them were concerned to maintain their social standing and to instil a similar spirit into their offspring. There was what William Marsden has labelled 'a compulsive, individualistic quest to achieve or preserve status'.[4] That included, in most cases, a desire to keep at least one domestic servant, to live in an appropriate style and location, and to observe the 'intangible rules about who spoke or bowed to, called on, dined with or intermarried with whom'.[5]

A professional middle-class family. The Revd Benjamin Waugh with his children by the summerhouse in their North London garden, c. 1889. Waugh was founder and first director of the National Society for the Prevention of Cruelty to Children. (NSPCC Archives)

There was also an emphasis on the importance of the male head of the household as the family breadwinner. Katharine Hopkinson, whose father was the managing director of a large engineering firm in Manchester, described him as 'living in the world of affairs', while her mother inhabited a domestic sphere, running the home, keeping the household accounts and holding herself ready 'to give tranquillity and comfort and sympathy' to her husband when he returned tired or depressed.[6] Such gender attitudes inevitably led to daughters being regarded as of less importance than sons, and that applied not merely to expenditure on their schooling but to other aspects of their lives. This was made clear in Charles Dickens's novel, *Dombey and Son*, when Mr Dombey's daughter, Florence, was dismissed as 'merely a piece of base coin that couldn't be invested' in his firm's business affairs; by contrast, his son was expected 'to accomplish a destiny'. 'Girls,' declared Mr Dombey, 'have nothing to do with Dombey and Son.'[7]

Outside the pages of fiction, Molly Hughes, whose stockbroker father had mixed fortunes on the London Exchange, discovered from an early age that it was 'Boys first'. As the only girl in the family she claims to have accepted this without resentment:

> I came last in all distribution of food at table, treats of sweets, and so on. I was expected to wait on the boys, run messages, fetch things left upstairs, and never grumble, let alone refuse. . . . I was never taken to anything more exciting than a picture gallery, not even to a pantomime at Christmas. . . . My father's slogan was that boys should go everywhere and know everything, and that a girl should stay at home and know nothing.[8]

Even though few families carried female subordination to quite these lengths, the general principles underlying Molly's upbringing were widely applied.

In professional circles there was concern to train children to accept Spartan living conditions. Gwen Raverat, whose father was a don at Cambridge University, remembered the austere meals that were served. For breakfast, there was porridge with salt, not sugar, and milk to drink. Jam was regarded as a 'dangerous luxury', as was butter. 'There was only bread-and-butter and milk for tea, as Jam might have weakened our moral fibre; and sponge-cakes when visitors came.'[9] Margaret Fletcher, whose father taught at Oxford University, had similar memories of her own strict upbringing: 'Children must be hardened early . . . Children must not sit by the fire, or loll in easy-chairs. They must have cold baths every morning . . . They must not eat sweets, that would ruin the teeth, or cakes, though a plain bun without currants might grace a festival. . . . They must lie upon very hard mattresses, over which the coverings must not be excessive.'[10]

On winter mornings Margaret awoke to see the bath of cold water standing ready. In strict order, she and her brothers and sisters 'leapt upon the little stool, the only concession to softness, and flung the water over your shoulder, regaining the dry land whilst there was enough feeling in your fingers to negotiate buttons and strings. Cotton went next the skin, for the days of woollen vests and "combinations" were yet to come.' After dressing, she went briefly into her mother's room to say her prayers, before sitting round the table in the day nursery, at 'a respectful distance from the tall fender at the . . . fire' to eat 'things you often did not like but which there was no possibility of refusing', and drink cold milk.[11]

It was part of the process of teaching youngsters stoicism and good behaviour, and of instilling discipline. 'Keeping up appearances' was an important tenet in the middle-class creed, and that included accepting discomfort without making a fuss. It could also encourage less well-off members of the middle class to keep themselves to themselves, because they were anxious to conceal from neighbours just how modestly they had to live. The son of a Manchester clerk remembered his mother telling him: 'No use being poor and seeming poor, always put on a good face outside . . . Always give people a good impression.'[12] However, at least corporal punishment was becoming less acceptable as a penalty for bad conduct by the middle-class young during the second half of the nineteenth century, although other sanctions were imposed. One boy remembered being perched on a chest-of-drawers as a punishment. Other children were deprived of a favourite food or banished to a room on their own when they misbehaved.[13]

Concern for status influenced the kind of schooling the children received. As late as 1895 the Royal Commission on Secondary Education conceded that although 'social mixing' was becoming more widely accepted, nevertheless: 'A parent who has reason to think that his children, if sent to a certain school, will run the risk of acquiring habits of speech or behaviour which might be disadvantageous to them afterwards, is entitled to decline such a risk.'[14]

One of the main reasons behind the middle-class flight to the suburbs in the Victorian era was the desire of families to escape the 'contaminating' influence of the urban environment and seek what they hoped was a more harmonious and healthy situation on the rural fringes, where they would have congenial neighbours. But even here residence was affected by the ability to pay. 'Highgate and Hampstead on their salubrious hills were socially superior to Camden Town and Maida Vale, just as the Manchester suburbs of Altrincham and Alderley Edge were a cut above Wilmslow and Hale.'[15] Edgbaston in Birmingham kept its desirable status by a determined application of private planning controls, and the newer London suburbs of Clapham, Forest Gate, Wandsworth, Peckham and Finsbury Park were recommended for modestly off clerks employed in offices in the City of London and Westminster.

Among those migrating in this way was John Cadbury, the Birmingham cocoa manufacturer, who in 1835 moved from the city centre to leafy Edgbaston. The new Cadbury home, unlike the family's previous dwelling, had a children's playroom, later converted into a schoolroom, as well as a nursery and extensive grounds. Each child had a garden to cultivate and there was a large lawn on which to play games. Maria, the only daughter, remembered her father measuring round the lawn twenty-one times for a mile, and each day before breakfast the children would run round with their hoops, one after another, 'seldom letting them drop before reaching the mile . . . how rosy we were when seated round the breakfast table, ready for the basons [sic] of milk provided for each child with delicious cream on the top, & toast to dip into it, afterwards bread & butter, & coffee, to part of our milk'.[16] At nine o'clock the school room bell rang, but before that the children generally had another run in the garden, or, in the case of the boys, played games on gymnastic poles of various kinds, one as high as a ship's mast.

USEFUL, IF NOT ORNAMENTAL.

Master Alfred (an ingenious boy). "LOOK HERE, WALTER! SEE WHAT A JOLLY TARGET OLD AUNT BETSY'S ROUND HAT MAKES."

Archery in the suburbs. (Punch, *1855*)

As the towns expanded, the better-off moved still further out, to escape the encroaching bricks and mortar. Katharine Hopkinson's parents at first lived about six miles from Manchester, but then migrated to Alderley Edge in Cheshire. Quick rail transport made this exodus feasible, and Katharine recalled the snobbery engendered, especially among the women. In their circle it was axiomatic that 'socially speaking, no good thing would be likely to come out of Wilmslow, the neighbouring village nearer Manchester. On the other hand, Peover, a village deeper in Cheshire than Alderley Edge, . . . was regarded by most of our ladies with equal though different scorn as the preserve of people who liked to be "in with" the county.'[17]

Geoffrey Brady, the son of a cotton manufacturer from Stockport, similarly remembered that although the parental circle included professional people, there was no attempt made to mix with families higher or lower on the social scale. The county people of Cheshire steered clear of the professional families and mill owners in the towns, and 'although we were perfectly polite and friendly towards local shopkeepers, and respected them immensely as "honest tradesmen", we didn't ask them to come and play whist or tennis. . . . They were just that grade lower down.'[18]

Religious snobberies were important, too, with members of the Church of England regarding themselves as superior to Nonconformists or Roman Catholics. Katharine Hopkinson claimed that her mother knew very few Wesleyans socially, and chapelgoers who wished to rise in the world often drifted from chapel to church.[19] Robert Graves, whose father was one of Her Majesty's Inspectors of Schools, recalled how as a child he looked down on one of the maids employed at his Wimbledon home when he learnt she attended chapel.

Robert was, indeed, to confront the whole vexed issue of social status at the age of four, when he contracted scarlet fever. Because a younger brother had just been born, he could not be nursed at home and so was sent to a public fever hospital. There he shared the ward with 'twenty little proletarians' and one fellow member of the bourgeoisie, who was the small son of a clergyman. These two were given special treatment both by the nurses and their fellow patients. Robert accepted the kindness shown to him as his due, but was astonished at the respect shown to the clergyman's son:

> 'Oh,' the nurse would cry after he had gone, 'oh, he did look a little gentleman in his pretty white pelisse when they took him away!' 'That young Matthew was a fair toff,' echoed the little proletarians. On my return from two months in hospital, my accent was deplored, and I learned that the boys in the ward had been very vulgar. I did not know what 'vulgar' meant; it had to be explained to me. About a year later I met Arthur, a boy of nine, who had been in the ward and taught me how to play cricket when we were convalescent together. He turned out to be a ragged errand-boy. In hospital, we had all worn the same institutional night-gowns, and I did not know that we came off such different shelves. But I suddenly realized with my first shudder of gentility that two sorts of Christians existed – ourselves, and the lower classes. . . . I found that the servants were the lower classes, and that we were 'ourselves'.[20]

Middle-class girls' education in London at the turn of the century. Pupils at a private school out for a walk. (The author)

Anxiety to maintain social distance was especially acute among the humbler ranks of the middle class, for, as the Royal Commission on Secondary Education put it, 'the resolve to avoid contact with social inferiors is usually most inflexible where the social distinction is narrowest'.[21] That remained the case even when the barrier between the lower middle- and the upper working-classes proved 'highly permeable', with some family members employed as clerks or in minor professional posts, and others working as skilled artisans. Stella Spencer's father, for example, held various lower middle-class positions, including acting as manager of several Cooperative Stores and working as a commercial traveller, while various members of his family were operatives in a textile mill.[22]

Katherine Bowie, the daughter of a ship's officer working out of Liverpool, remembered that her Scottish-born mother 'didn't understand the people round about her', and so the children were forbidden to enter neighbours' houses, or to play in the street. For this family, Liverpool's cultural and social diversity was beyond their experience. 'The social system . . . was conceived by them simply in terms of those who were "nice people", and those who were not.' Apart from Katherine's teachers, the music mistress and the dressmaker were regarded as 'nice', but she and her two sisters had to steer clear of unsuitable characters like the coal man and the bin men, in case they heard swear words.[23]

Some children resented these parental restrictions, although disobedience was rarely contemplated. Stella Spencer was one of them. She lived in comfortable circumstances at Crumpsall near Manchester, although her father's business career had had its ups and downs and he himself was of humble origin, being the illegitimate son of a Lancashire millgirl. Perhaps for this reason her mother was unduly sensitive on the issue of status. Stella and the other Spencer children were forbidden even to speak to youngsters in a neighbouring working-class street, let alone play with them. Meanwhile, on the other side of the house the son of a wealthy Manchester merchant lived with his family. His three children were looked after by a nursemaid and contact was prohibited between them and the Spencers. 'We used to stand on the flat top of our summer house and look at both lots of children and say how daft it was that we could not all make up a game of rounders', wrote Stella, years later.[24]

These class distinctions could lead to rivalry and ill-feeling between the different groups of children. In Oxford during the late 1860s and early 1870s, Margaret Fletcher remembered having to run the gauntlet of the children of local shopkeepers when she took a short cut along a narrow thoroughfare flanked on either side by shops. The youngsters who lived in this street usually played on the pavement, and if any 'university children' went by without an adult escort they would jump about with excitement and point with their fingers as they shouted 'gentry' after them. This was done with 'such scorn and contempt', wrote Margaret, 'as almost to imply *à la lanterne!*' The young victim's response was to call out 'Cads', and then sprint breathlessly for safety.[25]

Another girl, the daughter of a Tunbridge Wells grocer, had similarly unpleasant memories of the daily walks she and two friends took to a select private school about two miles away. During the journey they passed what her mother called 'the ragged school', attended by poor Roman Catholic children: 'this was a terrifying point . . . especially in the afternoons when we came back from school because just at that time the ragged school children would be coming out and they would surround us and . . . jeer at us . . . of course we had to wear gloves and be extremely respectable. . . . One of the school regulations was that you mustn't be seen in the street without gloves.'[26]

Great store was laid on the children acquiring the appropriate social graces, so as to distinguish them from the rougher elements in society. In Geoffrey Brady's case this meant learning proper table manners: 'My parents would insist on what they considered the correct way to hold your knife and fork, waiting until everybody had finished before there was a second round of things, not talking as a small child unless I was myself spoken to, and not using your table implements the wrong way.'[27]

Even more detailed rules were drawn up for Margaret Gladstone, the daughter of a professor of chemistry at London University. Margaret's mother had died soon after her birth in 1870, and her four older half-sisters took on something of a quasi-maternal role. On her twelfth birthday, two of them, Isabella and Elizabeth, provided her with lists of 'do's and don'ts' regarding her general conduct. Elizabeth's included 'Notes on etiquette':

Walk. Take short, firm steps, keeping the body upright & steady. Lift each foot clear off the ground so as not to shuffle or drag, & go along in a straight line not waggling from side to side of the path or pavement. Do not swing more than one arm at a time, & do not work that one like a windmill. When carrying an umbrella do not break, bend, or lose it.

Behaviour at table. Do not begin to eat before other people. Do not cut off all the fat, gristle &c. before you begin to eat. Wait until you come to it, & then quietly remove it if you feel that it is too distasteful for you to touch. Do not take large mouthfuls. Chew your food thoroughly (at least 20 bites) before swallowing. Do not hold your knife or fork up between the mouthfuls, put them down on the plate. Never take a second mouthful before you have finished the first. Do not finish to the last crumb or spoonful, or scrape your plate. When finished do not clutch your knees.

General remarks. Do not read much. Do not eat too much butter or jam.[28]

Isabella's list was longer but more succinct, and included such strictures as 'Don't eat too much, especially of pastry'; 'Say your prayers'; 'Keep your hair in order'; 'Keep yourself very clean'; and 'Go to bed early and have plenty of sleep'.[29]

Although most comfortably off families employed nannies or nursemaids, parents and older siblings normally took a more active part in the upbringing of the children than applied in aristocratic or landed circles. That included giving

TRULY CONSCIENTIOUS.

Toyshopman. "BEG PARDON, MISS, BUT HERE'S YOUR CHANGE, WHICH YOU'D FORGOTTEN—ONE-AND-NINEPENCE!"
Little Maid. "OH, THANK YOU VERY MUCH! BUT WE'RE NOT ALLOWED TO TAKE MONEY FROM ANYBODY BUT GRANDPAPA!"

Some virtuous middle-class children. (Punch, *1891*)

lessons and keeping a careful eye on their health and welfare. This was true of Elizabeth Gaskell (whose husband was a Manchester Unitarian minister), who was later to achieve fame as a novelist. After the birth of a still-born daughter in July 1833, she became deeply involved in the progress of her next child, Marianne, and from March 1835, when the baby was six months old, until October 1838, she kept a detailed diary of the little girl's development.[30] In all, Mrs Gaskell was to have five children, one of whom, the only boy, died at the age of ten months. Years later she confessed that the wound of his loss would 'never heal on earth, although hardly any one knows how it has changed me'.[31]

From an early stage older daughters were expected to help look after younger brothers and sisters. Hence in 1845, when Marianne Gaskell was about eleven and Meta, the second girl, eight, their mother described how the former had to give supper to the third daughter, Florence, and to be 'answerable for slops, dirty pinafores and untidy behaviours while Meta goes up stairs to get ready and fold up [the baby's] basket of clothes while he is undressed (this by way of feminine and family duties). Meta is so neat and so knowing, only, handles wet napkins very gingerly.'[32] Later, when Marianne had returned from boarding school, she took over the teaching of her two youngest sisters, in succession to the governess, while Meta went to a boarding school in Liverpool. Mrs Gaskell was much concerned in getting Meta's clothes ready for this latter event. In typical middle-class fashion, she expressed anxiety about the friends her daughter might make in her new surroundings. 'I cannot trust Meta with her new silk at school', she told Marianne: 'I don't care what she wears at Liverpool, provided only it is clean and whole. Except Helen & Miss Martineau [the school principal] I had rather (from what I have seen of Liverpool people) that she knew as few as possible in after-life; . . . I always regret when I hear of Helen having taken her out or introduced her to any of their acquaintances, such as the Bensons, Rathbones &c.'[33]

In some cases, as with Molly Hughes, a mother might take over the entire education of her daughter, partly to save school fees or a governess's salary, but also because the maternal influence was considered very important. Molly remembered that there was 'no nonsense about a time-table'. Lessons began with a session on the Old Testament, when she 'read aloud the strange doings of the Patriarchs. No comments were made, religious or otherwise, my questions were fobbed off by reference to those "old times" or to "bad translations".' After her stint at reading she had to parse every word in one of the verses, and then while her mother pursued her hobby of water-colour painting, Molly continued reading, sewing, writing, or learning by heart. Instruction was given in French and Latin while English history was gleaned 'from a little book in small print that dealt with the characters of the kings at some length'. Geography was studied sketchily from a large atlas and a small geography book, of which she could recall only the opening sentence, 'The Earth is an oblate spheroid', followed by the statement that there were 'seven, or five, oceans. I never could remember which.' Dr Brewer's *Guide to Science*, written in the form of a catechism, was used for science lessons, and for sewing she made endless pocket-handkerchiefs for her brothers. Her mother, like Molly, took little interest in arithmetic and when in her twelfth year, it was decided to send her to an 'Establishment for Young Ladies' about a mile from home, this proved an initial embarrassment. But soon she and a friend managed to be almost always top of the school. They 'shared a hearty contempt for [the] teachers. The only things they taught us quite thoroughly were the counties and chief towns, dates of the kings, French irregular verbs, and English parsing.'[34]

The preoccupation with good conduct and discipline led to much emphasis being placed upon the inculcation of proper religious and moral values. In the case of girls, this included training for their likely future role as a 'Lady Bountiful'. Margaret Gladstone and her sisters played a major part in supporting philanthropic ventures like the Latymer Road Mission in Notting Hill. When still in her early teens, Margaret helped with one sister's Sunday school classes, and some of the pupils from these were invited to tea and sweets at the Gladstone home on the Sabbath. Other regular Sunday duties included attendance at church with members of the family and 'doing Scripture answers to *Our Own Magazine*'. The reading of suitably improving books, like Charlotte M. Yonge's *The Daisy Chain* was also permitted.[35] Other activities including visiting a crèche and making pen wipers for a bazaar.[36]

Significantly, when the new High Schools for Girls were set up in the 1870s and 1880s, they, too, established Dorcas Societies to make clothes for the poor, and Flower Missions to supply flowers to local hospitals. Sometimes money was raised to endow cots at nearby children's hospitals or homes. At Oxford High School, for example, a Guild of Charity was founded in 1884. Its members paid a minimum subscription of 2s 6d per annum and undertook to make at least three garments for the poor each year. Amelia Wright, a ten-year-old orphan in a Home for Waifs and Strays, was adopted in 1885 by the guild, and her clothing was supplied by members at a cost of £3 a year.[37]

Maria Cadbury, at a Quaker boarding school in Lewes during 1853, likewise reported that she and fellow pupils had begun their 'poor work meetings'. In her home, religious teaching began at an early age, when her mother gave 'the first simple Bible instruction, from "Mamma's Bible lessons", . . . & afterwards, "Line upon Line," the latter being a great favorite [sic]; later on, Richard [an older brother] read it to George [another brother] & myself & never can I forget those sweet times together.'[38] Richard clearly took his role as older brother seriously, for in 1846, when Maria was eight and he was away at a boarding school in Hitchin, he wrote to remind her 'to pray always every night and . . . not do any thing wrong out of sight that thou would not like persons to see for if no body sees God sees.'[39] Subsequently he and George took on charitable duties in connection with the temperance cause in Birmingham. In 1855, Richard confided that he and fifteen-year-old George had made their 'accustomed calls' after attending the Quaker meeting-house on the Sabbath. They had left a Band of Hope leaflet at each house on their round: 'we found the Bath chair man's family seated round their comfortable blazing fire and seemed pleased with their band of hope . . . we distributed the rest of the bands of hope up the court and particularly remembered to leave one at the carpenter's at the bottom . . .'.[40]

Even some of the national charities established youth sections to appeal to the children of the well-to-do. The Royal Society for the Prevention of Cruelty to Animals, for example, set up a Band of Mercy, and the National Society for the

Prevention of Cruelty to Children followed suit in 1891 with the Children's League of Pity. It called for ten thousand volunteers to support the venture, and its monthly magazine recounted the ways in which young members raised funds by organizing entertainments, holding sales of work, and saving pocket money. A twelve-year-old girl described how she had decided to hold a children's bazaar. One brother had run the flower stall, another had looked after the bagatelle stall, and she and two friends had kept stalls for the sale of fancy goods and refreshments. 'Everyone thinks the Bazaar was a great success. We intend to have one every year.'[41] The League's avowed object was 'to enlist the happy children of the land in the service of the unhappy', and its members received collecting cards on which they recorded acts of self-denial. Such a scheme had long-term advantages, too. Middle-class children were not only effective canvassers but, once committed, were likely to become NSPCC supporters in later life.[42]

The role of the middle-class child as a 'ministering angel' was a feature of much of the 'improving' literature of the day. It was an important theme in Silas Hocking's popular novel, *Her Benny*, which was set in mid-Victorian Liverpool. The eponymous hero was a street child who gained the sympathy of nine-year-old Eva Lawrence, the daughter of a 'well-to-do man of business' in the city. Inspired by her Sunday school teacher 'telling us that we ought to be little missionaries, and lend a helping hand to the needy . . . and do all the good we can', Eva appealed to her father to give the lad a job. Mr Lawrence agreed and Benny was appointed an errand boy, and to do minor tasks around the office. Once at work, he learnt to write, with the help of one of the clerks in the office, and Mr Lawrence lent him books to increase his general knowledge. After some misunderstandings and hardships, he eventually became a partner in the business and married Eva. They moved into a large house and in later life he told his children how 'by being honest, truthful, and persevering' he had overcome adversity and had succeeded, with the 'blessing and mercy of God'.[43]

The young Katharine Hopkinson was one of many children expected to read similarly improving texts, like *Jessica's First Prayer*, *Little Meg and her Children*, and *Teddy's Button*. She commented acidly on the 'aroma of sentimental Victorian piety which they exhaled from every page', but admitted that one of the books, called *Pilgrim Street*, gave her some insight into the life of a Manchester slum.[44] In her case an awareness of the lives of the labouring poor in the city where her father earned his living was gained very much at arm's length.

These stories appealed not only to sentimentalists who wished to stress the redeeming power of the innocent child, but to many who wanted to teach the importance of honesty, goodness and hard work in the achievement of material prosperity. Both aspects were significant components of mainstream Victorian views on childhood.

Parents were also aware of their personal obligation to guide their children. The Quaker brewer, William Lucas, doubted his competence as a father in this regard, writing in his diary on one occasion: 'Often do I pray for more ability to guide and influence the dear dispositions of our dear children.'[45] Another time he admitted that the 'good example of parents when they can gain their children's affections' was much more important 'than all systems, rules or nostrums of education'.

So far, emphasis has been placed on the superior social status and the normally comfortable living standards enjoyed by middle–class children, compared to those lower down the scale. However, experience showed these could quickly be placed in jeopardy if the breadwinner died or failed in business. In 1879, when Molly Hughes was twelve, her father was killed in an accident, and although she continued to attend her private school it was a struggle to make ends meet. Concern to conceal poverty became a major preoccupation and she often felt humiliated because of her shabby clothing.[46] Still more traumatic was the experience of the Levy family of Manchester. Mr Levy had been a speculative builder and surveyor and when he died his wife not only had to give up her home but to withdraw her three sons from a Margate boarding school. She opened a small grocer's shop and when that failed, she was reduced to factory work.[47]

Similar misfortunes befell some of the pupils attending Howell's School at Llandaff, Cardiff, which was opened in 1860 by the Drapers' Company. It admitted two kinds of boarder – ordinary fee-payers and orphans, who received a charitable education. Among the children entering in the first year was Olivia Denroche, whose Irish father had come to seek his fortune in Wales; he had died, leaving his wife and two children almost penniless. Mr Denroche came from a family of barristers and landowners in Ireland and until she was four the little girl had lived with her parents in an elegant house in Cardiff. She was an intelligent child, but without charitable aid she could not have received the kind of education her family desired. Another victim of parental misfortune was ten-year-old Eliza Francis, the daughter of a Monmouth apothecary. Her mother had died before she was nine and when her father became insolvent, Eliza was cared for by an aunt, until she entered Howell's School.

Some of the first orphans to be educated at Llandaff came from as far afield as London, Brighton and Bath, since the benefits of being on the foundation were considerable. They included the provision of clothing, and board and lodging for ten out of every twelve months, until the girl concerned was seventeen. While there she received an education designed to fit her to earn a living as a governess, and when she left, she was entitled to a dowry of £100, providing her character and conduct had been blameless.[48]

Such opportunities as these were rare, however, and for this reason a few fathers sought to make arrangements for their offspring in the event of their death. 'I have sought by insuring my life, and by a careful investment of the payments I receive for my exertions in business, to lay by a suitable provision for my family', wrote the Quaker civil engineer, Edwin Tregelles, in 1842. 'This has cost me much toil and some anxiety at times; but I have acted from a sincere desire to do right, and not from the love of accumulation.'[49]

However, most bereaved families, like Molly Hughes and her mother, had to struggle on as best they could, relying on the help of relatives, or perhaps upon the mother or older siblings setting up in business. Ironically, one of the most famous public schools for girls, Roedean, was established by three sisters when their barrister father was prevented by an accident from continuing to practise. They and their mother began the school partly to teach the younger sisters but also to take in pupils to provide an income, and their venture soon prospered.[50]

It was, indeed, in the sphere of education that anxiety to maintain status and social distance from those perceived as inferiors was most acute among the middle class. For boys, especially the sons of professional families, this could mean avoiding contact with the offspring of shopkeepers and small businessmen, hence the prohibition at mid-Victorian Kensington Proprietary School upon the admittance of tradesmen's sons. Islington Proprietary School was also 'socially exclusive', but it did allow the children of tradesmen not resident in the locality to enter, although those from nearby businesses could not. Presumably this was to avoid possible embarrassment for the parents and children of professional families who might have to meet socially the shopkeepers, plumbers and builders they dealt with on a commercial basis.[51]

Even at the end of the century a similar attitude applied. One visitor complained of the petty snobbery which characterized society in Leamington Spa:

I suppose that the higher air being laden with it, it descends like the sooty particles in more active centres of industry. I was informed by the proprietor of a private boys' school . . . , which draws its day pupils mainly from the smaller tradesman class, that his numbers had sensibly increased . . . because parents were objecting to send their boys to the Warwick middle school, where they would meet with half a dozen boys a year (perhaps mostly schoolmasters' children) who had passed on with scholarships from the elementary schools.

Pupils at Abingdon School, Berkshire, in the early twentieth century. With its grammar school roots it attracted the sons of professional men and the more substantial business people. (Abingdon School)

And I was also informed (but not by the proprietor) that from the same private school one boy had been practically drummed out because the tradesmen's sons would not be contaminated by the presence of an artisan's son.[52]

For girls, 'social exclusiveness' might mean being educated at home by a governess, at any rate until they were old enough to be sent to a select boarding school at a distance from home, perhaps at the seaside. During the 1860s and 1870s the number of private schools at Southport and Birkdale, for example, proliferated, with pupils drawn from the towns of industrial Lancashire as well as from affluent households in the locality. Even in the mid-1890s Southport was described as a 'happy hunting ground' of private education. One visitor claimed there were 'Brass plates on more gates than I could count. The private schools are legion . . . All of which I saw or heard of were of the expensive . . . type, consisting chiefly of boarders.'[53]

According to the Cambridge don's daughter, Gwen Raverat, in her family there was 'a strong theory that day-schools for girls were Bad', though 'boarding schools for older girls might sometimes be allowed'. So she and her sisters were condemned 'to the dull confinement of the schoolroom at home, under a series of daily governesses'. Her brother, by contrast, went at an early age to a nearby private school.[54]

Education thus became a means of quarantining children from undesirable contacts. But, unlike the situation for working-class children who attended publicly supported elementary schools, no effective network of middle-class provision existed. In the mid-1860s a writer in the *Saturday Review* described the educational facilities available to them at 'a vast tract of howling wilderness and imposture'.[55] Even at the end of the century the situation remained chaotic with schools varying widely in quality, as well as in the fees charged, the curriculum covered, and the leaving age of the pupils.

Boys were catered for in three main types of establishment. At the top of the scale were the great public schools and the most prestigious endowed grammar schools, where education was primarily classical in content and the anticipated leaving age was eighteen or nineteen years. Such establishments as Eton, Harrow, Rugby and Winchester provided principally for the children of the aristocracy, gentry, clergy, and the upper ranks of the armed services, although boys from professional and business families were entering in increasing numbers towards the end of the Victorian era.[56] At Winchester, boys whose fathers were in business or the professions rose from 2.9 per cent of the intake for those born in the 1820s and attending in the 1830s and 1840s to 7.2 per cent for those born in the 1850s and entering in the 1860s and 1870s. By the end of the century, 13.7 per cent of scholars born in the 1880s and entering Winchester in the 1890s and 1900s were from a business or professional background, with 4.7 per cent of fathers in manufacturing industry alone. That compared with a derisory 0.4 per cent from the manufacturing sector in the early Victorian years.[57] Among those attending these élite schools were the descendants of some of the pioneers of the Industrial Revolution, such as the grandsons of Matthew Boulton and Richard Arkwright. Both went to Eton, while John Marshall's grandson went to Rugby. Interestingly, the leading Birmingham businessman and radical Liberal politician, Joseph Chamberlain, sent both of his sons to Rugby School, despite its pervading atmosphere of Conservatism and muscular Christianity. He himself had attended private schools in London before studying at University College School for two years, between 1850 and 1852. He then went straight into the family business, but his plans for his two sons were clearly very different.[58]

Some newer public schools, like Cheltenham, Wellington and Marlborough, experimented with 'modern studies' to meet the demands of the business and professional classes for a more practical curriculum than the classics. But all of them were concerned to encourage feelings of corporate identity, loyalty, obedience to authority, and a sense of fair play through the development of team games. In 1864 the Clarendon Commission, in its report on the leading public schools, claimed that the cricket and football fields were 'not merely places of amusement; they help to form some of the valuable social qualities and manly virtues, and they hold, like the classrooms and the boarding house, a distinct and important place in public school education'. 'By the 1860s,' comments James Walvin, 'published guides to the public schools gave almost as much space and emphasis to the role of sports and games as to learning. Boys who passed through these schools developed a commitment to team games and to the social values they were thought to express.'[59]

In the late 1860s James Bryce underlined the way in which the élite establishments were used by the *nouveaux riches* to assist in the upward social mobility of their offspring. He described how Lancashire manufacturers at the commencement of their careers were content to live simply and to send their children to local schools, but once their income began to exceed £1,000 a year they were anxious to sever links with the class from which they had risen. Instead they strove to attach themselves to those they regarded as socially superior and as a first step sent their children to boarding schools some distance away,

nominally to get rid of the dialect, but really to get rid of their cousins, to form genteel connexions, and acquire manners more polished than those at home. The older manufacturing families are . . . not wholly exempt from similar feelings. They . . . are anxious that their [son] should make no acquaintances among their . . . inferiors in their own town; they fear that he may learn vulgar phrases at school, and that his health may suffer in the smoke of a town; . . .[60]

For families whose children were intended to leave at the age of about sixteen there were what were labelled 'second grade' schools. These included reformed grammar schools, some proprietary schools, and the better private establishments. Their pupils came mainly from the sons of all but the most senior members of the medical and legal professions, and of larger businessmen. Parents from a commercial background often demanded a curriculum which covered such 'modern' subjects as mathematics, modern languages and the sciences.[61] 'It may be said, that in education of this grade a certain amount of thorough knowledge of those subjects which can be turned to practical use in business . . . is considered by the parents absolutely indispensable', concluded the Schools Inquiry Commission in 1868; 'and . . . they will not allow any culture, however valuable otherwise, to take the place of these.'[62]

Sport became increasingly important in boys' schools. Here pupils from a private school make their way to cricket. (The author)

For many, especially in the mid-nineteenth century, the better private schools could offer the desired flexibility, and could also reinforce a family's religious commitment, as with the Cadburys and Rowntrees, who chose Quaker schools for their children. During the 1880s Seebohm Rowntree attended the same boarding school in York as his father had entered over thirty years earlier. When he first arrived he was one of the youngest of the seventy-two pupils and as his home was just opposite, he did not board, but had his meals and spent all his leisure hours at home. Years later he regretted the arrangement: 'I was one of five day boys . . . and we never really entered into the life of the school.'[63]

Edward Muspratt, the son of a Liverpool chemical manufacturer, attended private schools, too, ending up at Dr Heldenmaier's boarding school at Worksop. Edward's father had selected this because of its emphasis on modern languages and science. That included the use of a chemistry laboratory, a rare provision in schools during the 1840s and 1850s. Gymnastics and games also featured prominently, and there were long walks during which wild flowers were gathered and butterflies caught, so as to provide practical lessons in botany and entomology.[64]

The proprietors of the larger private schools, for their part, extolled the virtues of this kind of independent institution. 'We are not hampered or interfered with by people who know practically nothing of education, nor can any Government inspector dictate to us what our curriculum of teaching shall be', declared the Revd F.W. Aveling, founder of Christ's College, Blackheath, soon after its opening in 1894. 'Private schools represent the free life of England. That freedom we value greatly. At the same time we hope to cultivate all the "esprit de corps" of public schools. Our football record will show the public spirit of our boys. And we hope that ere long our University record will do the same.'[65]

Elsewhere proprietors responded to parental desires to prevent the corporal punishment of their offspring. An advertisement for the Hyde Side Academy, Edmonton, in 1840, promised that 'young gentlemen' who attended would be 'kindly treated and comfortably boarded', the aim being to 'awaken and exercise the powers of the mind and to make memory subservient to judgement'. The master 'never degrades the mind or lowers the spirit by the infliction of corporal punishment'.[66]

But many private schools failed to meet these standards. Even in the mid-1890s an assistant commissioner for the Royal Commission on Secondary Education could divide the private sector into five broad categories. This ranged from large establishments, probably with some boarders, which were run along public-school lines, and smaller schools catering for backward or delicate boys and offering a mixture 'of the mental and physical sanatorium', to academies which had been set up only because 'the lady's husband has died, or the gentleman's proper venture in life has failed'. Almost anyone who settled at a suitable seaside resort, such as Southport, could get pupils. Well-meaning friends would canvass for children to attend, and in one case the assistant commissioner was told of the principal of a school, not previously a teacher, who had had an accident and lost his memory; 'so his friends set him up as a schoolmaster'.[67]

Finally, there were 'third-grade' institutions intended for boys who expected to begin working at about the age of fourteen. These were patronized by the sons of tradesmen and small business people and were intended to give 'a clerk's education'. That included arithmetic and an ability to write a good letter. 'It cannot be said that this is aiming at much,' declared the Schools Inquiry Commission in 1868, 'and it is to be wished that parents even of this rank should learn the value of a somewhat higher cultivation.'[68] But it acknowledged their right to insist that 'what they wish for shall be secured before anything else be added'. It was in this area of 'third-grade' education that the commission believed the deficiencies in middle-class schooling were most acute. One assistant commissioner commented on some third-grade schools in London that 'to anyone who has been used to good primary schools under Government inspection, the interiors of . . . smaller grammar schools are most repulsive'.[69]

Dissatisfaction with the existing arrangements did lead to action being taken in some towns. In Liverpool, the Collegiate School, set up in 1843, was constructed on three floors, one for each of its three divisions. In the upper section the curriculum was mainly classical and mathematical, the middle school catered for the children of the better class of shopkeepers and clerks, and the third division gave commercial instruction to the offspring of small shopkeepers, clerks and the 'better class of mechanics'. Fees ranged from £23 2s per annum for the upper school to £5 5s for the lowest grade. A similar strategy was adopted at another Liverpool school, the Institute. In this way they catered for what James Bryce called the 'whole social area of what is called the middle class'.[70]

However, when the residential district around the Collegiate School deteriorated in later years the better-off families migrated to the suburbs and it experienced recruitment difficulties. Some boys had to walk up to eight miles a day to and from school. As a result the headmaster persuaded the railways, the

Mersey ferries and the omnibus proprietors to offer concessionary fares to children. He also 'showered south-west Lancashire with maps marked by circles concentric on the Collegiate'.[71] This phenomenon of the schoolboy commuter was even more evident at the prestigious Manchester Grammar School, located near the polluted Irk and Irwell rivers. Its unfavourable location led to the decline of its boarding facilities, but it was conveniently situated for the city's railway stations. In the mid-1890s two-thirds of its pupils lived outside the city limits, thirty coming from places over twenty miles from Manchester.[72]

Schools in London encountered similar problems, and as early as 1865 one commentator noted that boys attending the Stationers' School in Fleet Street came in from Staines and Gravesend. As a result of transport improvements he considered there was 'scarcely any part of London to which a parent who can afford the annual ticket may not send his son in the morning, and receive him back in the evening'.[73] But this solution had its critics. Irrespective of the cost involved, which excluded many, there was the tiring journey, with the children 'wasting in a railway train the hours that should be given to air and exercise'. Discipline lapses could also occur when youngsters were left unsupervised on a lengthy rail journey.[74]

Some schools reacted to the social deterioration of their immediate neighbourhood by moving to the area where most of their clientele resided. That happened with Preston Grammar School in 1844. It left declining Stonygate for well-to-do Winckley Square, from which many pupils came.[75] But for most contemporaries the only solution was the creation of an effective network of secondary schools. The 'great educational movement of the last fifty years which has done so much to elevate the labouring and artisan classes, and has affected . . . the highest classes of all has scarcely visited the intermediate region', lamented *The Times* in 1861.[76] Even in the mid-1890s the incidence of these schools remained patchy, varying from about 16 secondary pupils per 1,000 of the population in 'tolerably well-to-do' Leamington Spa, to 10 per 1,000 of the population in 'overwhelmingly artisan' Birmingham. In Oldham a derisory 1 in every 1,000 boys and girls attended secondary schools, and in Bolton about 3 per 1,000 were so educated.[77] Not until the new century were steps taken to begin the construction of an efficient national network. In the interim provision remained hopelessly inadequate to meet demand, especially from those at the lower end of the middle-class economic and social scale.

For some less affluent parents one solution was to send their offspring to carefully selected elementary schools, where the fees were high enough to exclude 'undesirable' elements. This applied to a number of Nonconformist and Anglican elementary schools in the more salubrious districts and, after the 1870 Education Act, to a minority of those set up by school boards. That applied to Tindal Street School, opened in Balsall Heath, Birmingham, in 1880. A year or two after it started children from more prosperous areas were said to be passing other board schools in order to attend Tindal Street. The local school board had decided that it was to be the preserve of middle-class children living in and around Balsall Heath, and so successfully was this strategy implemented that in 1882 HM Inspector reported attendance to be 'almost solely by the children of the middle class . . . There are few, if any, poor children in attendance . . . [T]he Board have recognized the social superiority of the children by refusing to admit into the school any of their numerous free scholars all of which are in the neighbouring board schools.'[78] So single-mindedly was this policy pursued that middle-class children were transferred to Tindal Street from nearby schools. Such blatant discrimination did not, however, survive the furore that followed its disclosure, although, as Carl Chinn points out, by then it had served its purpose. Henceforth 'Tindal Street . . . was indelibly associated with "respectability", and thus with a good education, and so it became entrenched as the "best" in west Sparkbrook and Balsall Heath'.[79]

Fleet Road board school in East Hampstead, London, also enjoyed a high reputation for success in preparing children for scholarships to secondary education during the 1880s and 1890s. Its academic success led to its being labelled 'the Eton of the board schools' and it soon attracted a substantial middle-class clientele. In 1896 it won the London County Council's top two scholarships for both boys and girls, out of about 2,500 pupils who had entered.[80] On prize days the atmosphere was compared to that at many secondary schools, with scholarships and other successes proudly proclaimed.[81]

Yet if elementary schools like these went some way to meeting the demand for 'third-grade' education, they were no true substitute, not least because their pupils were normally expected to leave at the age of thirteen (or less) rather than the fourteen minimum desired for 'third-grade' schools proper.

Furthermore, there were strong reservations among some as to whether schooling intended primarily for the lower orders and supported partly out of government grants and, in the case of board schools, out of the rates also, should be used by those who could afford to send their children to more expensive establishments. In the late 1850s a witness to the Royal Commission on Popular Education complained of the way in which the middle class was taking advantage of 'state-aided schools' and was forsaking private academies. If this could be done, he argued, then 'let us all assert our moral and equitable claim to be supplied, at the public expense, with broughams and horses, fine houses and furniture, . . . and nothing inferior to hock at lunch and champagne at dinner'.[82]

The objections to middle-class consumption of state-supported education grew louder in the 1870s when some of the boards in the major industrial towns sought to meet the gaps in 'third-grade' provision by setting up higher grade or central schools to cream off the more affluent or more academically advanced elementary pupils. Bradford was one of the pioneers, opening its first higher grade school in 1876, with a broad curriculum and relatively high fees. A second followed a year later but it was in 1879, when the new Belle Vue Schools were opened in the city, that a storm of protest arose. Typical of the objectors was the view of the *School Guardian* that, 'The State may require that all children should be taught the rudiments of learning; but there it ought to stop.'[83] Nevertheless, Bradford persisted and by 1900 there were six higher grade schools in the city. Other towns followed, and in the mid-1890s there were sixty of these schools established outside London, thirty-five of them concentrated in the three counties of Durham, Lancashire and Yorkshire. Eight Midland and eastern counties had nineteen between them, and in twenty-three counties there were none at all.[84] Higher grade schools offered a means, through the scholarship system, for a small

Higher Grade schools attracted a considerable number of lower middle-class pupils. Model drawing class at a London Higher Grade school, c. 1900. (The author)

number of elementary pupils to enter the secondary sector proper. But their uneven provision and the legal confusion about their precise status made it impossible for them to meet the real needs of the lower middle class. This difficulty was compounded when in 1899 they were invalidated by a government auditor who successfully contended that the London School Board had acted illegally in spending public money on education beyond the elementary stage.[85] In the new century higher grade schooling disappeared, as a new system of secondary education was set up under the 1902 Education Act.

Meanwhile, for middle-class girls, educational arrangements for much of the period were even less satisfactory than those available to their brothers. At the humbler end of the social scale they might be sent to elementary schools or small private academies, where instruction was interspersed with spells at home, carrying out household chores. 'Mothers belonging to what is called the lower middle-class are able to make their daughters useful at home', commented James Bryce in the 1860s. They 'can help in the house-work and mind the baby . . . Hence it often happens that girls are not sent to school till long after the age when systematic instruction ought to have begun, and . . . they are kept away upon slight grounds.'[86]

For the daughters of better-off families the choice usually lay between education at home (as in the case of Molly Hughes in her early years) or attendance at a small private school, where the main emphasis was on the acquisition of 'accomplishments', such as French, music and drawing. These were designed to give a little superficial polish and to attract a husband in later life. In 1873 the advertisement for a Halifax school indicates the kind of instruction provided, with 'Pianoforte, Singing, Drawing, Painting etc.' listed as part of the 'ordinary course' of lessons.[87] According to one mid-Victorian critic, the average schoolgirl devoted 640 hours of her school life to arithmetic and 5,520 hours to music![88]

Even the better type of private establishment, like that attended by Margaret Gladstone in the 1880s, placed much emphasis on these traditional aspects of girls' education, with weekday afternoons and Saturday mornings devoted to music, painting and drawing, as well as preparation for more academic lessons. In the spring of 1885, when Margaret was fourteen, her diary shows that the weekly timetable included three arithmetic lessons, two in French, two in geography and two in history, plus grammar, 'Shakespeare', reading and literature, and, of course, scripture. In addition, two half-days were devoted to drawing and painting and one to music and singing. She also spent a great deal of time at home practising on the piano.[89]

However, reforms were already in hand. Pioneering establishments like Miss Buss's North London Collegiate School, set up in 1850, aimed to wean girls from 'accomplishments' and prepare them for more intellectual pursuits. For Miss Buss and fellow innovators, like Miss Beale, the head of Cheltenham Ladies' College, a careful course had to be steered between the academic studies they considered necessary and the 'accomplishments' which most parents still demanded for their daughters. This became particularly evident from the mid-1860s, when in a pioneering move girls were allowed to enter the Cambridge Local Examinations on the same terms as boys. For the first time an objective academic yardstick could be applied to girls' education. The Schools Inquiry Commission in the same decade had its effects on female schooling, too, by drawing attention to its weaknesses and, in a minor way, encouraging a transfer of educational endowments to create girls' grammar schools. By 1894 the Royal Commission on Secondary Education estimated there were eighty endowed schools for girls in England, compared to a mere twelve thirty years earlier.[90]

An elaborately dressed little girl in a suburban garden. (The author)

Still more important was the move to establish proprietary girls' high schools under the aegis of the non-denominational Girls' Public Day School Company and the Anglican Church Schools Company, with thirty-eight schools associated with the former and thirty-three with the latter set up in the last thirty years of the century.[91] Nonetheless, the pioneers were aware of the need for caution. Miss Beale, for example, argued that better schooling would mean that 'a wise and right-minded woman' would be less likely 'to make a foolish, an inconsiderate marriage' and 'that if girls were more accustomed to weigh and consider, there would be less of extravagance and folly, homes better ordered, servants more honest and contented, children happier'.[92]

As one writer has pointed out, 'the Beales and Busses of the second half of the nineteenth century' succeeded by diversifying 'content rather than fundamentally restating customary social objectives of female education'.[93] Significantly, Miss Buss, despite her academic ambitions for her girls and her emphasis on the importance of examinations, also stressed the centrality of family responsibilities. In an address to girls leaving school she advised each to remember that she must 'take up all necessary domestic duties – above all, she must be ready to help her mother, and not to be a burden to her. She has to remember that there is domestic work for duty; . . . each must do humbly and faithfully the first, small, humble, quiet duty that lies close to her.'[94]

Some critics argued that the intellectual strain associated with serious academic work might cause the girls physical damage and harm their reproductive system. Margaret Fletcher, who attended Oxford High School during the 1870s, recalled the lengthy debates on the effect of advanced schooling upon female health and brains:

> Whole shelves in libraries began to be filled with books on the subject . . . Skulls were measured, brains weighed, nerves tested, and conclusions were usually accompanied by warnings. . . . I remember one kind of argument in favour of preserving the *status quo*. It ran, a particular woman might be endowed with great gifts, but she was merely a trustee of these, she must not trade with them, but keep them in a napkin that she might one day hand them on unimpaired to a possible son. This theory did not commend itself to girls, for although the claim 'To live my own life' in its full meaning had not appeared, that of 'Let me learn what my brothers learn' could everywhere be heard . . . .[95]

Similar objections were raised against games at many of the early girls' schools, although by the 1880s and 1890s a more relaxed attitude prevailed. They were said to overtax the girls' strength, as well as being unfeminine. Miss Buss herself, on seeing hockey played for the first time, is supposed to have called for more balls to be fetched, in case the children hurt themselves.[96] Her North London Collegiate School was the first to introduce formal medical inspections of pupils in 1882, and initially gymnastics were carried out under the supervision and sometimes in the presence of a doctor.[97]

But apart from the need to secure a proper balance between school work and female duty in the home, the new proprietary establishments had other problems. Some parents were reluctant to allow their daughters to make lengthy train or tram journeys to reach school, and at Notting Hill High School this was occasionally mentioned as a reason for pupils leaving. 'The high schools that sprang up in leafy London suburbs like Blackheath, Putney, Streatham, Dulwich, Clapham, Sydenham and Wimbledon reflect this Victorian need for girls to be able to walk to school', comments Gillian Avery. However, some did make lengthy trips and were as proud of their season ticket 'as any girl of later years with her latch-key'.[98]

Another parental fear was that by drawing pupils from a wider spectrum of the middle class than was customary in most old-style élite private schools, these new establishments would encourage the forming of undesirable friendships. Hence the emphasis placed on proper conduct by head teachers and governors. The first number of the Oxford High School magazine, issued in 1879, four years after the school was opened, included a piece on 'Behaviour in the streets' in which the anonymous author warned of the need to maintain high standards:

> One of the complaints made against the High School is, that it does not teach manners, that it makes girls rough and boyish. The behaviour of some of our girls in the street often justifies this complaint. Girls stand waiting outside the school, walk arm-in-arm stretching right across the pavement, rush to school in a most disorderly way. Many of them put on their gloves in the street, and some wear *no* gloves . . . We ought to remember that when going to and from school we . . . have its honour to maintain, and we ought to be all the more careful to do so because we are then not under the eye of our mistresses, and our behaviour is trusted to our honour.[99]

Some pupils objected to the sterility of the daily round, as teachers, often poorly qualified, sought to prepare pupils for the all-important examinations. Molly Hughes, who attended Miss Buss's North London Collegiate School in the 1880s, complained about its rigid discipline and the way in which every moment had to be accounted for:

> Even when we got home we were not free. There were little printed time-tables on which we had to enter the hour at which we began to work, the hour we finished, and the total time taken. . . . Marks were the life-blood of the school. No work whatever was done without them, so that a large proportion of time was consumed in assigning them, counting them . . . To be deeply pleasing to a husband, and widely pleasing to other men, seems to me as good an ideal as a woman can have. But instead of facing squarely the real needs of future wives and mothers, as the vast majority of girls were to be, Miss Buss seized the tempting instrument at her hand – the stimulus to mental ambition afforded by outside examinations. . . . And thus, for better or worse, the education of girls became a feeble imitation of what the boys were doing.[100]

Lower middle-class respectability in Gloucester. (The author)

Although Molly completed her course successfully, she had to rely on her brothers for help in classics and mathematics.

Helena Sickert, daughter of the artist, had similar reservations. She attended Notting Hill High School in the late 1870s, when she was thirteen. She railed at the shortage of well-trained teachers and the fact that the curriculum was closely allied to that at boys' schools: 'My brothers spent eight years grinding at Latin to arrive at Matric standard, which I had to reach in three', she commented acidly. At home she also resented the fact that when her brothers had completed their homework they were allowed to play while she, once she had completed her allotted tasks, 'very often had to mend their clothes; sort their linen and wash their brushes and combs'.[101]

Despite these doubts, however, most early high school pupils recognized the importance of their pioneering role, if middle-class females were to progress in the intellectual sphere. 'We were the first to write ourselves down High School girls', noted Ruth Mayhew, of her attendance at Oxford High School, after its opening in November 1875, 'and we bore ourselves bravely, feeling ourselves indeed the elect, proud of our School, sacrificing ourselves willingly for its fair name, full of hope, energy and determination.'[102]

Others accepted the policy of class mixing, so long as parents could pay the fees. 'The girls were of all social conditions in my time', remembered a pupil at Notting Hill High School during the 1870s. 'I sat between the daughter of a publican and the daughter of a laundress, and I never succeeded in beating the former. The daughter of a viscount was at the bottom of the class.'[103] Over the period 1873 to 1900, the children of merchants dominated at Notting Hill, contributing 374 to the total, compared to 219 coming from a legal background and 195 who were the daughters of clergymen. A few parents had far humbler occupations, with a cabinet maker, a watchmaker, a dairyman, a stationer and a Poor Law relieving officer among the fathers recorded during this period.[104] Even Margaret Fletcher, a pioneer entrant at Oxford High School, overcame her doubts about mixing with tradesmen's daughters on terms of equality. 'There was no cheating; . . . We really wanted to play up in every detail.' In her case there was also a stimulus to effort over and above 'that great vague glorious crusade of showing what women could do. It had been explained to us that we must all look forward to doing something for ourselves. There would not be enough money coming to us for each one to live independently.'[105]

The new schools broadened the scope of middle-class girls' education, especially in families where it was intended that daughters should subsequently be able to earn their own living. At the same time efforts were made to retain the ideals of service and domesticity which had traditionally characterized female instruction. It was said that 'Miss Buss's school became popular with parents in spite of, not because of, her intellectual ideals. . . . [P]arents "forgave her for Latin and Mathematics because they valued so highly her general work and influence for her girls".'[106]

The lives and aims of urban middle-class children, therefore, varied widely not merely on account of parental circumstances or place of residence but on gender grounds, too. For girls even in the mid-1890s private academies continued vastly to outnumber the reformed day schools, with between ten thousand and fifteen thousand of them estimated to be in existence in 1894, each averaging about forty to fifty pupils. By contrast there were thirty-six Public Day School Company schools in that same year, catering for just 7,111 girls.[107]

Among the children of the smaller tradesmen, meanwhile, it was common to expect them to lend a hand in the family business when necessary. Charles Marks, born in 1888, the elder son of a Ramsgate butcher, was often sent by his father to a village a few miles away to collect 'a couple of calves' which his father wanted to slaughter: 'I could kill and dress a sheep when I was twelve and could help on beef quite a bit . . . I never had any time like other boys to go out to play. . . . As a mater of fact I often got in trouble because I wasn't able to do my homework.'[108] One regular chore was to deliver meat on horseback to a large boarding house in Broadstairs. 'That went on for a long time before this landlady came over and told my father he'd have to send somebody else instead of sending a little boy like that. Then instead of riding over I had to put the horse in the cart and drive over. I didn't like that as much.' This continued until his father's death in 1902, when Charles was fourteen.[109]

Ella Bryan, whose father was a fruiterer and greengrocer in Chatham, also helped in the shop from an early age. When she was six her father taught her to chop firewood, which was sold in halfpenny bundles. Yet, although their income was small, her father considered himself middle class, and mixed 'with the élite of the town at the time, the mayor and leading tradesmen'.[110] He always impressed on his children the need to keep up appearances. 'If you've only got 2*d* in your pocket, don't tell anyone.'[111]

Ella's experience was very different from that of her upper-middle-class contemporary. Katharine Hopkinson, living in a comfortable Cheshire suburb. For her, education at home by first an Italian and then a French governess was followed by a spell at a Folkestone boarding school, where the main emphasis was on accomplishments and 'ladylike' subjects. To ensure pupils' insulation from the harsher realities of everyday life, newspapers were not allowed in the school and all discussion of politics was discouraged.[112]

CHAPTER 3

Working-class Home Life

Most of the houses were the two-bedroomed type; if you were lucky there would be a small parlour with a horse-hair suite, . . . and you might also have a cellar . . . Children often slept 4 in a bed, two at the top and two at the bottom. On freezing nights the beds were warmed with the oven shelf or a brick kept in the oven for the purpose . . . Our staple food was bread and dripping, nearly every mother baked her own bread . . . Broth was another popular meal; sheep's heads could be bought for one penny or twopence . . . One could get bones free from the butcher – pot herbs free from the greengrocer – these with a little barley would make a dinner for the hungry children. Porridge too was cheap, always made with oatmeal and a little treacle added . . . Saturday was an anxious day for many mothers, wondering if Dad would come home with his wages intact. Alas, many couldn't resist the pull of the strong beer and the company at the pub . . . Their punishment came on Sunday. Instead of going off for a jaunt with a pal, they spent a day indoors . . . Their Sunday suit was missing. It had found its way to the pawnshop.

Reminiscences of Mrs H. Jones of Orrell, Lancashire, born c. 1887–8[1]

The home life of most children was dependent on factors over which they had no control, such as the time and place of their birth, the amount of parental income, the size of the family, and their precise position within it. During the Victorian years the birth rate gradually declined as economic pressures and growing information on contraception led many married couples to limit their fertility. Whereas in the 1860s and 1870s the average number of babies per completed family born to each married couple varied between five and six, by the end of the century this had fallen to between four and five.[2]

Within that overall trend, there were major class differences. While women from the professional and upper classes marrying in the early 1880s had families about a third smaller than their predecessors marrying in the 1850s, among unskilled labourers the fall was only about a seventh, and in mining communities family size dropped by just one-tenth.[3] These figures do not indicate the number of offspring living at home at any one time, or the overall size of households, since not only did many children die in the first months or years of life, as a result of disease or malnutrition, but elder brothers and sisters might well have left home by the time the last babies were born. At the same time, grandparents and other more distant kin, or lodgers, swelled the size of individual households, as family circumstances dictated. A survey of Preston in 1851 suggests that almost a quarter of householders had relatives living with them, while the payments made by lodgers helped to meet weekly outgoings, including the rent.[4]

All of these factors affected the individual child's day-to-day experience, and where families were large, mothers could become worn down with the burdens of maternity. Mrs Lizzie Layton, born in Bethnal Green in 1855, the seventh of fourteen children, recalled her mother as almost always 'either expecting a baby to be born or [having] one at the breast. At the time there were eight of us the oldest was not big enough to get ready to go to school without help.'[5] In such circumstances older children (especially daughters) took responsibility for the care of their younger siblings from an early age. In his survey of east London in the late 1880s Charles Booth quoted the case of a carman and his wife with two daughters aged seven and thirteen. The wife drank heavily and did little within the house, so the older girl carried out many of the chores, preparing the breakfast and taking her sister (and herself) to school: 'The little sister was the pretty one and the pet of her parents', wrote Booth; 'the elder one was the drudge, and twice this child had run away and stayed out all night before or after a beating.' When the landlady took pity on her and gave her a second-hand dress, to replace her own worn-out clothes, it was immediately pawned; 'the poor girl never wore it'.[6]

A one-room tenement in the East End of London – overcrowded, untidy, and with little furniture or comfort. (The author)

A Bristol youngster, the eldest of a family of ten, had similar responsibilities when she returned from school at midday and in the afternoon. She was expected to perform such household tasks as laundering the baby's napkins, doing other washing, preparing vegetables and helping with the cooking. 'I started cooking when I was ten.' The washing up was done outside in the yard, which was bitterly cold in winter and led to 'chapped hands and chilblains'. At meal times the older children had to feed the younger ones and the general parental philosophy was, 'He that doth not work doth not eat'. In later life she confessed that if she had been a boy she would have run away to sea, as she had heard other children did, because of her resentment at the domestic duties heaped upon her.[7]

Nevertheless in most families relations between children and their parents, especially their mothers, were close (if not particularly demonstrative). Mothers, for their part, often sacrificed their own wellbeing in order to feed their children or protect them against the anger of violent fathers. Alice Foley, whose Irish father frequently fell into frightening rages after a drinking bout, felt a deep affection for her mother. Once, in a fit of exasperation, Mrs Foley threatened to leave home, and for weeks afterwards Alice 'moved around in terror and heaviness at the threat of desertion. . . . Pathetically, I tried to find ways of pleasing mother in the hope that she would not leave us, and on quiet evenings by the fire when we played Ludo or Snakes and Ladders, I cheerfully manoeuvred to send my counter down a long snake so that mother's could reach "home" safely.'[8] Early in her childhood she arranged a small altar on the mantelpiece in her bedroom and, with a candle illuminating a cheap statuette of the Virgin Mary, she prayed long and hard that her father would renounce his drinking habits so that her mother could shed her burden of care and responsibility. But it was in vain.

Parental occupation and the size of families were major factors in deciding the kind of home that children had. The fact that most workers, mindful of the early start they must make each day, liked to live near to their place of employment meant that those with similar occupations tended to congregate together and their children would play with one another. However, there could be rivalries, too. In Burnley it was said that employees at one factory might refuse to associate with those at another, even if they lived in the same street, while the womenfolk competed with their neighbours to have the cleanest doorstep or the best array of flowers at the window.[9] Sometimes, as in parts of Birmingham, occupants of houses with a bay window considered themselves socially superior to those without this addition.[10]

In the early years of industrialization, the rapid growth of the urban population often outstripped the provision of new housing, and the living conditions of many families deteriorated. In 1849, a contemporary compared cellar dwellings in Bolton, inhabited by people 'fully as squalid and dirty in appearance as the worst classes are in the worst districts of Manchester', with comfortable cottages built by Messrs Arrowsmith and Slater for their mill workers in the Gilnow district of the same town. There was a similar contrast at Ashton-under-Lyne between Charleston, a 'labyrinth of noisome courts and small airless squares, formed generally of houses of a fair size, but miserably out of repair', and the 'snug little colony' belonging to Messrs Buckley's mills at Ryecroft, where the owners lived among their employees and were 'in the habit of familiar intercourse with them'.[11]

At Hyde, near Manchester, another mill owner, Thomas Ashton, provided water to the 320 houses which he owned. Prior to that tenants had had to fetch it 'from various wells and places in the neighbourhood', or had relied on collecting rainwater for washing in tubs. 'For a family of six or eight persons the labour of fetching water for washing and culinary purposes was very great', declared Ashton. 'There were formerly water-carriers. The poor people used to pay a penny per day for the smallest families; some of them paid 1s a-week.' As a result of his improvements this was no longer necessary and water was readily available.[12]

However, most working-class families lacked this kind of paternalistic provision, and unpaved streets and inadequate sanitation were the lot of many. In 1861, *The Builder* condemned dwellings in Kirkham Street, Preston, near to one of the Horrocks's mills, where some families lived in cellars and the yards were 'so confined that the people must hang their clothes to dry in the street, at the doors, on the stairs, over the beds, or else in the terrible choked offal-pits that are within a pace of the back doors'. Even in the market place the gutters ran with slops thrown out of houses in the surrounding courts, and with the overflow from urinals.[13] Likewise in Todmorden at around the same time there were no drains or collective arrangements to remove the accumulations of filth in ashpits, middens and privies. The roads and streets were unpaved and unlit, and there was no covered market. As a result the working people had to shop on Saturday evenings at stalls in the open air – a miserable situation during wet and cold weather.[14]

'[O]ur industrial armies are cut down by the camp diseases which are generated by . . . inadequate house accommodation, and by the want of sanitary arrangements', complained the Registrar General for Births, Deaths and Marriages in 1866. 'Impure water, impure air, their own exhalations, kill men, women, and children on the spot, and breed the leaven which devastates the towns and valleys in the vicinity.'[15] In addition, poverty and the shortage of accommodation often forced families to share a house, as was the case in Kirkham Street, Preston. In larger towns and cities the situation was aggravated by the fact that population expansion was accompanied by the clearance of much low-rented and slum property to make way for road improvements, railway building, and commercial development, without adequate replacements being constructed. In Bethnal Green, where overcrowding was severe even in the 1880s and there was a large number of children (with 15.26 per cent of the population under five in 1881), the situation had been made worse by large-scale house demolition in 1867–8 to construct Columbia Market and Square. In 1876 further demolition took place to extend and widen Bethnal Green Road, and between 1877 and 1884 for the construction of the Bishopsgate Goods Station, as well as the alteration and widening of the railway in connection with this.[16]

Despite investigations by royal commissions and official committees, and the implementation of piecemeal reforms, even at the close of the Victorian era the situation in many districts remained unsatisfactory. In 1891, 16 per cent of the national housing stock comprised dwellings of one or two rooms only, and there were slum areas in all large towns where the masses of back-to-back houses,

Spartan living conditions in an overcrowded home in a London slum, c. 1900. The beds on which some of the children were sitting show that the family slept as well as ate in this room. (The author)

courts and alleys were little improved from the position half a century before.[17] 'After twenty years of inquiry [into] the housing of the working classes . . . and endless meetings, and floods of ink and eloquence', complained the chief sanitary inspector for Bethnal Green, in 1901,

> this, the most important of all sanitary questions, stands just about where it did at the commencement. All shades of opinion and all parties appear to agree that the matter presses for immediate settlement, and yet no one has even introduced a measure that would in practice provide machinery less intricate, less costly, and much more capable of speedy application than any of the so-called Housing Acts yet in force.[18]

The previous year he had criticized the unwillingness of landlords to provide homes for the poorest class of tenants, such as dock labourers and other casual workers, whose income was uncertain and who found difficulty in getting rooms they could afford.[19] Hence the situation at Digby Walk, Bethnal Green, in 1891, where almost two-thirds of the families shared a house – sometimes with two or three others – and where 56 per cent of all dwellings had four children or more living in them, as well as adults. In one case, where three families shared, there were ten children and six adults in residence. None of the children was old enough to work, all but one being aged eight or less.[20] Fifteen of the thirty-six heads of household in the Walk worked as labourers, hawkers or costermongers, while other occupations included paper stainer, boot riveter, umbrella frame maker, metal case maker and French polisher.

These conditions of overcrowding were blamed by contemporaries for encouraging precocity and immorality among older children. In the mid-1880s, the rector of Christchurch, Spitalfields, claimed to know of 'a "great deal of incest" . . . attributable to overcrowding', as well as cases of juvenile prostitution.[21] Not until 1908 did incest become a criminal offence.

The primitive cooking facilities in many homes meant that diets had to be restricted to what could be boiled or fried, with soups, potatoes and perhaps a little bacon featuring prominently on the menu. Prior to the passage of legislation in the 1870s to control and ultimately outlaw adulteration, much food was very impure. Bread frequently contained alum, while oatmeal was cheapened with barley-meal and trade refuse known as 'rubble'. Milk was diluted with dirty water, a practice likely to cause illness among consumers. In Portsmouth the medical officer of health, who also acted as the public analyst, found examples of charcoal and rice in tea, chicory in coffee, and water in milk, as well as much unwholesome meat and fish offered for sale. In 1875, he noted drily that over the surrounding countryside there was a common saying that 'any meat is good enough for Portsmouth'.[22]

Queuing for cheap meat in London at the turn of the century. (The author)

Other cities shared these problems. As a result, poor children suffered not only from a shortage of food but from the effects of adulteration. Families could be cheated by the giving of short weight, too. Mrs Layton in Bethnal Green remembered that when she began serving in a nearby shop at the age of ten she was told by the owner that if she added a piece of bread to the loaf as a makeweight she was 'to be sure to press it down, so that the scale went down'. Articles of clothing and household goods were regularly brought to the shop and left, rather like at a pawnbroker's, only food instead of cash was given in return for them. The practice was illegal, 'so all articles had to be brought in when no one was about, and I was trained to help to smuggle things in'. She saw 'a pair of children's boots left in pawn for a loaf of bread and a small quantity of butter. Babies' pinafores, frocks, saucepans, candlesticks . . . have been brought to hold for food.'[23] Mrs Layton only stopped giving short weight when an aunt came in to the shop and saw what she was doing. She told the little girl in no uncertain terms what she thought of such cheating, which might rob a poor child of a slice of bread. 'I felt so thoroughly ashamed of myself . . . that I was days getting over it. I was too young to tell my mistress about it, but I never gave short weight again.'[24]

In Rowntree's survey of conditions in York in 1899 he drew attention to the role of children in shaping the life-cycle of families. When none of the children was old enough to work, the household would probably be in poverty, but as some of them grew up, their earnings might be sufficient to allow a move to be made to a better home. This was the case with the Foleys. Alice, the youngest of six children, was born prematurely in 1891, when her parents moved from Bolton to Dukinfield in search of employment. Soon after they arrived, Alice's father lost his new job. They already owed rent, and with local shopkeepers unwilling to extend credit to strangers, the parents decided on a midnight flit. Mr Foley hired a cart and he and the three boys left with their few sticks of furniture piled precariously upon it, to return to Bolton. His wife and daughters travelled by train and on foot, but the stress of the journey was so great that when Mrs Foley reached a friend's house she gave birth to Alice.[25] The family then settled in a single cramped room, since Mr Foley was more interested in politics and gambling than in getting regular employment. Until Alice was three the household was largely supported by her mother's earnings as a washerwoman. Then the eldest girl got work as a 'setter-on' in a spinning mill. With her income they were able to move into a two-up, two-down terraced dwelling, with a cobbled yard, a privy midden and an earth closet.[26]

There was modest comfort in this house, with the flagged floor of the living room meticulously sanded, and gleaming fire-irons at the hearth.

Over the fireplace was a false cornice, a wooden shelf with a faded brocade pelmet. This served to hide a string stretched across the range from which hung damp stockings and handkerchiefs. On top of the mantelpiece stood a pair of china dogs with golden neck-chains, an old clock, and the family tea-caddy. Above father's armchair hung a pink-backed copy of the 'Racing Handicap' which was daily consulted by him . . . On the same hook also dangled a stout leather strap with five thongs which provided an occasional clout for the noisy, or gigglesome ones.[27]

A few shabby pictures hung on the walls, and among the scanty furniture was a much treasured red dresser, a sewing machine, and an ancient horsehair sofa, which the younger children claimed as their own. Cups and saucers were not used, 'just blue and white ringed basins. Our diet was mainly milk, porridge, potatoes, and "butties" of bread and treacle with a little meat at weekends. At tea-time our parents shared a savoury tit-bit from one plate, father getting the lion's share, for mother doled out tiny morsels from her portion to the younger children. We usually stood at the table and were forbidden to chatter or giggle if father was in a bad mood.'[28]

If a mother lacked the energy and determination of a Mrs Foley to keep the house clean and the family fed and clothed, conditions could easily deteriorate. House-flies and bluebottles swarmed in kitchens during the warm weather, but most demoralizing of all was the perennial struggle waged against nits, lice and bugs, since these quickly infested rooms and children if there were any lapse of vigilance. Even in careful houses, problems arose. George Hewins, a Stratford-on-Avon building worker, recalled that however much his wife scrubbed the floor and he limed the walls, it was impossible to keep the house vermin-free. 'Bugs and fleas, it was one long battle, and we was on the losing side.'[29] In their tiny two-bedroomed cottage, he, his wife and his mother-in-law shared one bedroom, together with the latest baby, while the remaining children shared a bed in the other. 'If one of them got measles or a fever the missus would say: "In you go! You can *all* get it together and I'll know where you is!"' They also had to stop in bed while their clothes were being washed and dried, because they 'only had one change'.[30]

Bad housing and associated economic deprivation damaged youngsters' health not only by encouraging the spread of epidemic disease, as in the Hewins household, but more permanently, too. In the early 1860s John Hollingshed described the poor as 'half human rats' with 'weasel-like offspring', who were crammed into 'rookeries'.[31] Such comments revealed his own prejudices, but it was no accident that forty years later Liverpool boys from two-roomed homes were, on average, 11.7 lb lighter and 4.7 inches shorter than those of similar age from four-roomed houses. Similarly girls living in one-roomed homes were on average 14 lb lighter and 5.3 inches smaller than those who came from four-roomed dwellings.[32]

In cramped accommodation it was also easy for small children to suffer death or injury as a result of clothing catching fire or pans of boiling water being overturned on them. In mid-century Portsmouth, seven-year-old Sarah Passingham and four-year-old Charles Buckland both died when their clothes caught fire while they were left alone in the house, and Emma Sedgley was drowned when she fell into a large pan of water.[33]

The conditions experienced by the offspring of casual workers crammed into one or two rooms, with low incomes and little security, differed very greatly, therefore, from those enjoyed by the sons and daughters of skilled artisans and craftsmen, at the upper end of the working-class scale. Their father would probably rent a property of his own, perhaps with a garden, and there would be a varied diet, including meat every day instead of once a week, for Sunday dinner,

Father and daughter in a fishing port.
(The author)

as was the case with their less fortunate brethren. In the mid-nineteenth century several long-serving employees of the Ashworth cotton firm, for example, had sheets, blankets and quilts on their beds, strips of carpet on the floor, and curtains at the window. 'Some had mahogany chests. Books, Bibles, and clocks were all prominent. The inside walls were papered, while the outside walls were whitewashed every year, and the woodwork painted every two years.'[34]

Half a century later the status symbols aspired to were a separate parlour with a piano, an overmantel covered with ornaments, and an upholstered suite. Many failed to attain their goals but a 'velvet plush cover with tasselled ends might conceal a cheap, deal table-top', and a pair of American rocking-chairs would serve as substitutes for the upholstered suite. 'The bedding and underclothes which often had to be strung across the street to dry should be as good as possible because they were a public demonstration of one's economic position.'[35]

Even in Walter Southgate's home where 'mother's parlour', as the children called it, became a bedroom at night, a pot holding the aspidistra was placed on a table in front of the street window, as well as a Bible and a brassbound album of family portraits. The window was carefully draped with lace curtains and antimacassars hung over the backs of the chairs and the sofa. On the Sabbath there was a fire in the parlour grate, 'but we could never escape the odour of camphor, camphor balls hung above each picture frame as an antidote against mildew and bad smells'.[36]

One girl, whose father was a mule spinner in a Bolton cotton mill, remembered that her mother was able to afford a washerwoman to help with the laundry once a week, though she herself did not work, and the father purchased two houses which he rented out. As she grew older, it was one of the daughter's tasks to collect the rent. Once a year she, her five brothers and one sister went on a brief holiday to Blackpool.[37]

Another youngster, whose father was a dyer in the Nottingham lace trade, spent his late-Victorian childhood in a largish suburban house, for which the substantial rent of 6s a week had to be paid. 'Course we'd got a big garden back of the house . . . and we used to grow all us own vegetables.' His mother made jams and pickles, and there were herbal remedies produced from garden plants, such as rue and wormwood for digestive disorders. In the summer his mother made dandelion beer, and they kept a few fowls. Meat or fish was eaten daily, and although there were few books, the local evening paper and a Sunday newspaper were purchased. The boy helped cultivate the garden, and during school holidays he and his friends wandered for miles gathering blackberries.[38]

However, a sudden depression in trade could adversely affect the position of even prosperous families. During a recession in the cotton industry in the early 1840s, many formerly comfortably off workers were driven into debt and poverty. Thus a Dukinfield family of five headed by a skilled spinner saw their total weekly income plummet from £1 1s 6d in 1836 to 14s 4d five years later, at a time when food prices were rising. At the later date 31.4 per cent of their total income had to be spent on bread, compared to 16.3 per cent so expended at the earlier period. Even then the family was overspending its income by 33.8 per cent; in 1836 they had *underspent* by 21.8 per cent. In 1841, they, like many of their neighbours, were in serious debt.[39] (See also Appendix 2.)

The situation in Lancashire was even more parlous during the American Civil War, when supplies of raw cotton were drastically reduced between 1861 and 1865. Although some of the larger enterprises, like the Fieldens of Todmorden, paid their workpeople at least half their normal week's wage, whether they worked or not at the height of the recession, and helped employees with gifts of food, fuel and clothing, smaller enterprises could not afford these concessions. Many, especially on the weaving side, had to close their mills. As a result large numbers of textile workers were unemployed, with almost fifteen thousand people out of work and forty factories closed in the Preston area alone in March 1863.[40] Public works were instituted and Poor Law provisions were supplemented by charity on a mass scale. This included the setting up of soup kitchens and the provision of fuel and blankets. Many families had to move into cheaper homes in the 'more pestiferous quarters of the town', where they congregated in extreme penury, having sold most of their possessions.[41] Some emigrated or moved elsewhere within Britain in search of work. Perforce the children shared in these misfortunes alongside their parents, as they hung on waiting for the return of better days.

Even in the 1890s unemployment could cause serious distress. Joseph Stamper, whose father was a foundryman in St Helens, Lancashire, remembered how children whose parents were out of work would wait at the factory or foundry gates at the end of the day, pleading with the men who came out to give them any surviving remnants of the sandwiches they had taken with them. One of Joseph's friends had the alarming experience of having his home sold up three times because his father was unable to pay the rent through unemployment. Joseph himself witnessed the third occasion. On the wall of the house a notice was written in chalk: 'Owing to Arrears of Rent and by Order of the Landlord. Sale this day at 2.30.' His friend's mother stood watching the proceedings weeping silently, while her children clustered disconsolately round.[42]

Other problems arose where wives had to work in order to make ends meet, perhaps because their children were too small to earn. As a result they had little time to cook or carry out domestic chores. Women who worked in textile mills were often condemned as poor housewives because they could not sew or cook very well. 'In the larger proportion of cases, a properly cooked dinner is a luxury only seen once a week', claimed one critic in 1882.[43] Others emphasized the need to teach domestic skills to the girls while they were still at school.

In reality, however, most mothers (probably two-thirds or more of them) did *not* engage in paid employment, although a number, like Mrs Foley, might take temporary jobs, washing or charring, if funds were tight. In the case of laundry work this might be carried out either at home or on the premises of an employer. In the latter case, the youngest children would probably have to be left in the care of neighbours or relatives while the mother was away. In 1844, Dr Southwood Smith drew attention to the threat this posed, especially when they were given opiates like Godfrey's Cordial or Atkinson's Infant Preservative to keep them quiet. He quoted the case of a small girl who had asked a chemist for a dose of Godfrey's to give to the baby the next day, as her mother was 'going out to wash'. According to the Nottingham coroner, there were instances of opiates being given to a baby on the day of its birth. With such persistent dosing large numbers of infants died or grew up to become 'pale and sickly children, often half idiotic, and always with a ruined constitution'.[44]

Where clothes were dried in the laundress's own house, this could mean the misery of wet washing hanging in crowded rooms, especially during the winter. The children might also have to help with the mangling and ironing, or with delivery of the finished articles. But even this was preferable to other domestic trades, where the home became a cluttered workshop and the children began lending a hand as soon as they were able. In 1885 the Royal Commission on the Housing of the Working Classes fiercely condemned the many 'noxious trades' carried on in a domestic setting:

Rag-picking is a powerful means of conveying disease owing to its filth. Sackmakers and matchbox makers often do all their business in the room in which their families live and sleep. The latter have to keep their paste warm, and the smell of it is most offensive. The most pernicious of the trades, however, is rabbit pulling, in which the fur is pulled from the skins, making the atmosphere most offensive . . . and the fluff-laden atmosphere has the most harmful effect upon the lungs. Haddock curing and smoking are perhaps more disagreeable than dangerous, but the practice of costermongers storing in their rooms and under their beds their unsold stock, watering it in the morning to give it an appearance of freshness, must be the means of bringing into the house large quantities of decomposing matter.[45]

What the effect might be on the health of those who consumed vegetables and fruit treated in this way, the report did not state.

In the case of matchbox making, children began to help their mother from a very young age. Toddlers were set to place sandpaper on the boxes, since this early involvement was considered necessary to promote manual dexterity in later life. According to a mid-Victorian commentator, children from eight to ten years were generally the quickest operators. 'The most expert [boxmaker] known to me, a girl of ten years . . . , can earn four shillings and twopence weekly . . . Her mother and the younger ones help either in cutting the paper, folding, making boxes, . . . sanding, drying, counting, or tying up for [the] shop.'[46] Yet even these formidable efforts could not guarantee a livelihood, and for some, the only solution was to sell their meagre possessions to buy food, when trade was bad. 'I have seen a room in which nothing was left except a table at which the children were making their matchboxes, and the one little pillow for the mother's head at night. The four children slept on the bare floor.'[47]

The Crooks family in the late 1850s. Will is the second child from the right, looking over his father's shoulder. (From: George Haw, From Workhouse to Westminster *(1911))*

Will Crooks's mother had to take on the role of principal breadwinner during the mid-1850s, after her husband, a ship's stoker, lost his arm in an accident, when the little boy was three. At first, 'with the aid of some good friends', the father tried to earn a living as a carter, but the venture failed and his horse had to be sold to pay the rent. Almost the only work Mr Crooks could get was as a watchman:

> I don't know what we should have done but for mother. She used to toil with the needle far into the night . . . Many a time as a lad have I helped . . . to carry the clothes she had made to Houndsditch. There were no trams running then, and the 'bus fare from Poplar to Aldgate was fourpence, a sum we never dared to think of spending on a ride.
> My elder brother was as clever with the needle as many a woman, and often he would stay up all through the night with mother, helping her to make oil-skin coats. . . . We were so poor that we children never got a drop of tea for months together. It used to be bread and treacle for breakfast, . . . for dinner, . . . for tea, washed down with a cup of cold water. Sometimes there was a little variation in the form of dripping. At other times the variety was secured by there being neither treacle nor dripping.[48]

Bread was strictly rationed, so that the three eldest children were restricted to three slices apiece at each meal, while the four youngest had two and a half slices.

Mrs Crooks made and mended the family's clothes and acted as shoe repairer as well. 'She was everything to us', declared Will, '. . . I owe it to her that I was saved from becoming a little wastrel of the streets, for, as a Christian woman, she kept me at the Sunday School and took me regularly to the Congregational Church where I had been baptised.' When he was eight Will got a job helping with milk deliveries at 6d a week, but despite these efforts Mrs Crooks could not pay her way, and for a short time Will, his brother and three sisters, as well as their father, had to enter the much-hated workhouse. But as soon as she could hire a cheaper room, the family returned home. Will then obtained a post as errand boy at a grocer's shop for 2s a week, and with their combined earnings, they were able to stay together.[49]

If these female domestic trades were poorly paid and caused a good deal of discomfort in the home, at least mothers were on hand for most of the day to care for their children. That was not the case when they worked in factories, and arrangements had to be made to look after the youngest children. Michael Anderson suggests that in Preston during 1851 around 11.5 per cent of youngsters under ten years of age had mothers working in a cotton mill. Sometimes an older child would be kept from school to take care of the infants, or a 'nurse girl' of nine or ten would be hired for the purpose, if there were no suitable sibling. In other instances an otherwise unemployed grandmother would be in the house, and would combine domestic chores with caring for the children, or perhaps a lodger would perform a similar function. Anderson estimated that about 17 per cent of the factory working mothers in his Preston sample had a grandmother at home.[50] A further possibility was to rely on the help of neighbours or of kin living in the vicinity, to whom a small payment in cash or kind would be made, or, in the case of young babies, these might be left with a paid child-minder. For the smallest infants that solution was particularly hazardous because it meant the mother was unable to suckle her baby. Instead it was fed artificially, with all the dangers from poor hygiene and unsuitable food that this presented. If the baby became fractious, opiates might be administered. In 1874, the Medical Officer of Health for Bolton blamed working mothers for the town's high level of infant mortality:

> Female operatives too soon return to labour after their confinement. . . . [I]n some cases mothers return to work within the week, and it has been stated to me by a gentleman, that he has known several instances of women confined on a Friday, returning to work on the Monday of the following week . . . As a result the mother's health suffers, and the influence on the health and mortality of the children is most baneful. The infants thus deprived of maternal care are left in charge of the younger children, who are scarcely able to take care of themselves, or carried to some elderly female to nurse during the day. Occasionally the mother will return to suckle her infant at breakfast and dinner time, but this is exceptional, for, as a rule, they are fed artificially in lieu of their natural food. . . . Children are too frequently fed with sop, which, from long standing on the hob, has become sour; with milk out of a bottle imperfectly cleansed or encrusted with curdled milk, or with food similar to that eaten by adults, such as tea, potatoes, cheese, &c. Under such treatment can one be surprised when they suffer from diarrhoea, become restless, or fall into ill health?[51]

He called for the setting up of 'Infant Nurseries' where the babies would be properly cared for, clothed, and given suitable food while their mothers were at work. Such institutions would be self-supporting, so as to avoid encouraging habits of dependence in parents, or relieving them of the responsibility for bringing up their offspring. But such initiatives were not popular. Working mothers preferred to make their own arrangements or to rely on family support. So when in the middle of the nineteenth century the Essex silk manufacturers, Courtaulds, set up a nursery for the children of married women employees with infants aged from one month to two years, at a fee of 4*d* a day, the workers refused to use it, and it was closed after three years. They seem to have disliked the nursery's insistence on the unfamiliar practice of overall bathing of the baby and the compulsory changing of clothes. They preferred their own childcare methods, such as paying a young nurse girl about 1*s* 6*d* a week, or leaving their infant with an older female relative or neighbour.[52]

Before the extension during the 1860s of factory legislation restricting child labour in a wide range of industries, some mothers, particularly widows or deserted wives, took their children to work in order to avoid having to pay for a child minder. This was true of Mrs Waring, a press woman at a Birmingham button factory, in the early 1860s. Her husband had deserted her six years before, and she had brought her son, aged six, to work alongside her in the factory. 'He saves me the 1*s* a week that I should have to pay for a girl [as an assistant], and the 6*d* or 8*d* a week which I should have to pay for sending him to where he could be cared for in overhours, i.e. all beyond the regular school-time while I am here at work.' She had one other child, a little girl, who earned 1*s* a week at another button factory.[53]

Nevertheless, most children did *not* have mothers who worked away from home in factories, even in such counties as Lancashire and Cheshire, where female employment in the textile mills was widespread, or in Staffordshire, where women and girls were occupied in pottery manufacture. A survey of children aged eight to twelve living in the Potteries in 1861 suggests that only 17 per cent had mothers who were in employment. As might be expected those without a father at home were most likely to have a working mother.[54] Similarly, it has recently been estimated that not more than a quarter of female employees in the cotton industry were married. Of these, many were childless or had only one child. Probably not more than one in ten wives in a mid-century cotton town like Preston worked in the mills; almost four-fifths were 'plain wives and mothers undistracted by any paid work'.[55]

Some females reacted to the need to earn extra income or to compensate for the loss of the major breadwinner by opening a small shop. A widow from Leigh in Lancashire whose husband died when her daughter was a few days old adopted this solution. The shop was open from 7 a.m. to 11 p.m., and when it closed the mother stayed up to carry out household chores, such as washing and ironing. As her daughter grew older, she, too, had to help in the business and around the house, although there was paid domestic help. When she returned from school each day the little girl was never free to go out and play. 'You'd to pass your time weighing lbs of sugar . . . quarters of tea, cutting soap in blocks, . . . weighing peas, currants, and all like that . . . 'Cause, me mother couldn't get through on her own.' Even so it was a struggle to keep solvent: 'if everybody would've paid their way it wouldn't 've been so bad, but you see, if they knocked out . . . at the pit the men had to come back, then the wages were gone and it all dropped on me mother. "I can't pay this week, he's got no money, like." They didn't think we had to live.'[56] Mrs Morris's mother in Barrow was another 'parlour' shopkeeper. She set up in business so that she might pay for her children to have a secondary education.[57] But most female shopkeepers, like the widow in Leigh, ran their business purely to provide a basic income.

Another alternative for impoverished mothers was to apply for help to as many charities as they could. Normally that was an option only available in the bigger towns and cities where there were large numbers of philanthropic organizations. In the late nineteenth century Charles Booth quoted the case of Mrs Park, who lived in Shelton Street, off Drury Lane, in London. Her husband, a former soldier, had been invalided out on grounds of ill-health, and according to Booth, the wife worked for her children by attending every mothers' meeting she could manage, as well as every mission hall gathering. In this way she obtained supplies of soup three or four times a week, and sometimes a loaf of bread as well. 'At Christmas she may contrive to get two or three Christmas dinners from different places.'[58]

Children queuing for free meals in London, c. *1900. (The author)*

In Portsmouth there were boot and clothing clubs and during the winter coal charities and soup kitchens were organized. The Ladies' Committee of the Southsea Coal Society, for example, provided approximately a thousand hundredweight of coal each year free to the poor, while the Portsea Free Ragged Schools not only supplied soup dinners to the pupils but to local families as well.[59]

In order to maximize these benefits, worldly-wise applicants learnt to use various stratagems. According to Arthur Harding, who began life in the Nichol, a notorious slum on the fringes of Shoreditch in London, the main thing was to have your poverty 'well known to the people who had the giving of charity'. His mother made sure that those in a position to help understood that she herself was crippled, and that she had a feckless husband and several children to support:

> The whole idea was to get your nose in . . . The clothes you wore had to be something that didn't fit – so that they would give you some, . . . for your Sunday best. But you had to be clean and that was easy – soap and water didn't cost a lot of money. . . . My mother . . . didn't much care if we went to school or not. But she knew it was the law of the land . . . and she liked to be well in with the Mission. There was always a few bob to be got from them, provided you were well behaved.[60]

For critics like the Charity Organisation Society and its supporters, such casual philanthropy failed to tackle the root causes of a family's poverty. It merely alleviated the symptoms, thereby encouraging parents to continue on their thriftless course without ever achieving self-dependence. 'My governing principle in this work is to help the parents to help the children, not to help the children to help the parents', declared one advocate of a more stringent approach. 'If the parents were utterly worthless, I would help the children in spite of the parents; but as long as a child has one parent who can do anything for it I would not interfere with it except by helping the family as a friend, and from individual knowledge.'[61] Similarly, in September 1891, the *Charity Organisation Review* declared that the question to be posed in respect of any charitable agency was: 'Will it work towards the enforcing of parental responsibilities or towards the undermining of them?'[62]

A REGULAR CUSTOMER.

"HA'PENNY CANDLE, PLEASE, AND BE QUICK, FOR MOTHER WANTS HER TEA."

"OH, YES! OF COURSE, MISS; COULD WE SEND IT ANYWHERE FOR YER?"

Running errands for mother was a regular chore for many children. (Punch, *1852*)

This debate over the proper function of philanthropy continued, unresolved, to the end of the Victorian era. In the new century the establishment of the first elements of the welfare state turned the discussion in a fresh direction, as collectivist ideas began to undermine the commitment to *laissez-faire* principles.

Meanwhile a number of youngsters from the poorest families showed their ingenuity in securing food. A Bristol girl went to the local slaughterhouse to collect bags of bones: 'We'd go up . . . with a big pillowcase and thruppence, and the man would fill 'n up with bones from the pigs . . . Take them 'ome to my mother and granny and my aunty. They'd share it between them and make stew.'[63] She also ran errands for slices of bread and butter, and took goods to the pawnshop for neighbours, standing in a queue at the pawnbroker's at seven in the morning. Each of the neighbours gave her threepence and her mother waited for her to hand over the money. 'I used to take for four neighbours. . . . I used to put the four bundles on the counter, give the names of each one. They used to charge a ha'penny interest for the ticket. Then I'd come back to each one . . . My mother used to give me a penny and keep the elevenpence . . . I used to get thruppence when I went up on the Saturday and fetched it out.' People would pawn anything they had which was surplus to their immediate requirements, including clothing and bedding. Some families, living in overcrowded homes, made a regular practice of pawning their 'Sunday best' clothes each Monday morning because they had nowhere to store them. Certain pawnbrokers in London even set aside special accommodation for a best dress, charging a halfpenny fee for the service.[64] When Saturday came round the pledge would be redeemed, only to be returned the following Monday, when its owner returned to the ordinary daily round.

Elsewhere youngsters went to baker's shops to collect stale and broken loaves, offered free or at a small charge, while in central London a number went to restaurants and cookshops where they begged unwanted food. In most working-class households children were regarded as their mother's errand-goers, and would be sent on time-consuming tasks, like standing in the queue at a soup kitchen or going to distant shops where goods were sold at low prices. One boy, the son of an Edmonton watch repairer, not only had to carry out household chores, like cleaning the steel knives and forks and the boots, or supervising the cooking of the Sunday joint while his parents attended chapel, but he went by tram to the newly opened International Stores to buy cheap groceries. It was a penny fare on the tram but if he cared to walk both ways he could keep the penny.[65]

Those who were slightly more affluent than their neighbours might also provide help in times of need, not only by giving or lending items of food and clothing, but in a more substantial fashion. A Salford girl, whose father had charge of the corporation horses, recalled that during one very cold winter he went to local shopkeepers to get scrap meat, bacon, bones and the like, as well as peas and beans. He had plentiful supplies of carrots and oatmeal for the horses and with these ingredients and some free loaves from a baker he and his wife prepared bread and soup for poor families in the area, using the wash-boiler in the cellar: 'I can remember seeing the people come – they had to come at a certain time on a certain day twice a week – they came for two or three weeks that winter and me mother gave them soup. They had to bring their own utensils . . . and . . .

the children running about barefoot.'[66] On other occasions the little girl was sent with food to poor neighbours, including one woman with four children whose husband had deserted her, and who confessed her main aim in life was to get enough cash to stay in the one-roomed home they rented.[67]

Although the vast majority of children lived with their parents, some were unable to do so for one reason or another. Apart from the special position of those who grew up in a workhouse or other institution, whose situation will be discussed in Chapter 8, there were youngsters whose parents had died or who were 'shared out' among relatives for other reasons. Perhaps the parental home was overcrowded or the relative needed help from someone young and active. One estimate suggests that in 1861, 11 per cent of children had lost a father and 11 per cent a mother by the age of ten, while 1 per cent had lost both parents. Even in 1891, when mortality levels had improved, 9 per cent of children had lost their father by age ten, and 8 per cent their mother.[68] Most of these parentless youngsters were brought up within the family circle by grandparents, aunts and uncles, or siblings.

Illegitimate children, too, were often brought up by grandparents, perhaps as one of their own children, with uncles and aunts (and their own mother) treated as brothers and sisters. In this way their true status was disguised. In March 1871, for example, court proceedings at Braintree, Essex, against Emily Ray for the desertion of her illegitimate child were suspended when the infant's grandmother collected it from the workhouse and promised she would care for it.[69] Even more common was the arrangement whereby a girl came home to have her baby and then left again to return to her employment, possibly as a domestic servant, with the infant remaining in the care of relatives. George Hewins from Stratford-upon-Avon was brought up by a great-aunt, when his maidservant mother abandoned him. He later went to live with the great-aunt's daughter for a time and helped the latter's brother by working out of school hours as a lather boy in his barber's shop.[70]

Kinship links were particularly strong among Irish families who had settled in England, and there were cases like that of Mary Connor, who sent her eldest daughter to a sister after the death of her husband in 1864, while she and her ten-year-old son entered the workhouse. Then there was Margaret Hearn, a second-generation migrant, who was deserted by her husband in the winter of 1862. She and her five children went to live with her mother-in-law until the Poor Law authorities decided they must all be sent back to Bristol, where the husband had been born.[71]

Sometimes, as with two young flower-sellers encountered by Henry Mayhew in mid-nineteenth-century London, help was given by friends. The two girls, aged fifteen and eleven, had lost their mother seven years before, and had never known their Irish-born father. Since the mother's death they and their brother, who was a costermonger, had lived with an unemployed Irishman and his wife, sharing their single room and paying a rent of 2s a week. The couple slept in a recess in a corner of the room, which was curtained off, and the wife washed and mended the children's clothes. With the self-possession which characterized many of the street children interviewed by Mayhew, the elder girl claimed that since her mother's death, she had earned 'a bit of bread' for herself and her brother and sister, and had 'never had any help but from the neighbours'.[72]

BAD GRAMMAR, BUT GOOD PLUCK.

"NOW, THEN, FATHER, JUST LET ME *KETCH* YER A 'ITTIN' O' MOTHER, THAT'S ALL!"
"I AIN'T A 'ITTIN' OF HER, DRAT YER!"
"NO ; BUT YER WAS JUST AGOIN' TO! LET ME *KETCH* YER, THAT'S ALL!"

[*Seen and heard by ye Artist.*

The casual brutality of some working-class fathers is pinpointed by Punch. *(1875)*

Even more fortunately placed children could find life in an overcrowded home uncomfortable. A Bristol docker's son remembered that he and his five brothers had to sleep in a single bedroom and this led to frequent fights and arguments. At meal times there was neither sufficient room nor sufficient furniture for them to sit round the table together. Some ate standing up, while others had their meal at a different time.[73]

Conditions in the roughest families were still worse. One family, from the Blackgate area of Salford, spent much of their time either fighting with one another or being beaten by their drunken father, who worked as a blacksmith's striker.

None of the family ever went to church or to Sunday school. The children bathed in a canal, warmed by discharges from the boilers of a factory, rather than at home. Their patched trousers were 'hanging out at the back' from fights. If they had any decent clothes, for most of the week they would be in pawn. . . . Their meals were eaten without knives and forks, and the children were allowed to chatter and even to read comics while they were eating. . . . Bread, tea, and kippers were the staple, with potato pie the Sunday special. Because there were so many children the youngest were forced to eat from a ledge underneath the table, while their parents and elder brothers sat above. . . . The children got into the habit of petty thieving when money was short. 'We couldn't see the old woman short . . . We'd . . . go together . . . outside the shops . . . We'd perhaps take a couple of taters out of that bag . . . and get onions, . . . We'd get a dinner that way and take it to the old woman and let her stew it up. She'd know where it came from.'[74]

Even more parlous was the plight of George and John Strugnell of Portsmouth. At the ages of thirteen and twelve, respectively, they were caught stealing cabbages and enquiry revealed that they were usually turned out of their home at night to sleep under an archway. The two boys had never attended school or any place of worship, and both were illiterate. Their father 'pitched into them when drunk' and 'sometimes they had victuals and sometimes not'.[75]

Happily such unfortunates as these were very much in the minority. Most parents did their best to care for their children and to instil the basic tenets of good behaviour and morality. Thus a Salford family from the Blackgate area, although very poor, succeeded in maintaining their standards. The father was a strict disciplinarian and meals were eaten in silence. Although the parents were not 'dressed up over the etiquette', the children had to eat their meals properly with a knife and fork.[76]

In large households the weekly bath could present a problem. It usually took place in the kitchen on Friday or Saturday night, with the children washed in relays. In Alice Foley's family she and another sister were put into a huge cream and brown mug, in which the family dough was kneaded, by the eldest girl, Cissy. This was filled with hot water and the two youngsters took it in turns to stand in the mug while they received their weekly scrub-down. Their hair was fine-toothcombed, to guard against nits, and then it was neatly braided. While this was going on the rest of the family went out.[77]

In more affluent or hygiene-conscious families care was taken to have a fresh supply of water for each bath, but for the majority it had to be shared. Indeed, a Bristol girl remembered that on Saturday nights her mother not only washed all the children in the same bath water, in front of the kitchen fire, but she would then 'tip all the clothes in and wash 'em'.[78] The wet washing would be hung across the room overnight and be dry for Sunday. In her family, clothing was always obtained second-hand, with the Salvation Army providing some winter outfits. Shoes were bought for a penny a pair: 'You had to pick 'em in the shop and try them on.' They rarely fitted properly and the result was blistered feet.

In such homes it was difficult for children to read books or to engage in hobbies which required the use of a table. The son of a bricklayer's labourer in Oxford found it 'too noisy . . . too crowded' to read in the living room of his home. Instead he used to take a book to bed and on summer mornings awoke at 4 a.m. so that he could read.[79]

Some illiterate adults, like Will Crooks's mother, encouraged their offspring to read to them when opportunity offered. Mrs Crooks borrowed magazines and invited the children to read aloud to herself and the neighbours. 'I was about ten or eleven when *The Leisure Hour* and *The Sunday at Home* were started, and mother and the neighbours used to get these and ask us boys to read the stories to them.' Will also made purchases from an old man who went round poor people's homes selling books. 'From him I got some of Dickens's novels. I suddenly found myself in a new and delightful world.'[80]

Public libraries became established on a widening scale from the 1860s, and at the end of the century one of Alice Foley's duties was to take a bag of heavy books each Monday evening to exchange at the branch library some distance away. When she returned, the borrowed books were divided out, but sometimes her illiterate mother found this exasperating. Once she jumped up and exclaimed that she 'met as weel goo eaut, for this place is nowt but a deaf an' dumb schoo'.' Alice was reading *Alice in Wonderland* at the time and she offered to read aloud to her mother. To her surprise Mrs Foley agreed and from that time she became her mother's 'official reader'. Almost every day when the little girl returned from school her mother would ask for another chapter. 'When I stumbled over big or unknown words, she would say encouragingly "O, ca' it Manchester" and so it was until both spelling and reading ability improved.'[81]

Some parents were openly disapproving. In a cash-conscious world where earning wages was considered more important than leisure pursuits, the reading of books was regarded as a waste of time. This was true of the Rann family, who lived in a late Victorian London mews. Mr Rann was a navvy and Mrs Rann worked as an unqualified midwife. Their poverty was great, and the children were sent out to 'pick up firewood' or earn a few pence running errands and the like. Both parents were illiterate and they refused even to allow books or newspapers into the home, perhaps because they feared these might be a challenge to their authority. Card playing was also banned. Yet the children were carefully brought up, with the boys taught to 'raise the hat to the ladies'. Grace was said at meals and there was no talking: 'you had to sit right and you had to hold your knife and fork right.'[82]

Generalizations about the home life of working-class children are, therefore, difficult. For the offspring of the better-paid artisans it might mean living in a comfortably furnished house, with a back garden or yard where they could play, and with opportunities to go on outings and to play with toys and board games. One boy from such a home wrote an account of his doings for a week at the end of the Victorian era:

After tea I do my home-lessons. Then I go to a club at seven o'clock and play draughts, dominoes, gymnastics, etc., and then we come out at eight o'clock and from eight till about a quarter past I get errands for mother and at about half-past eight I go to bed. On Tuesday I go to a Band of Hope [temperance meeting] at half-past five and I come out at six, and if it is a wet week I go to a library on Monday dinner time and borrow a book and read it. On Wednesday I have a game with the boys in the street and if it is a wet night I take in a friend of mine and play at ludo, draughts, dominoes, race game, etc. On Thursday I go to the Happy Evenings and play at hockey, painting, etc. On Friday I do some of my work instead of doing it on Saturday and after I have finished I go in the streets and play with my friends. On Saturday I finish the rest of my work, look at the boots and the knives and forks, and do the windows. On Sunday I go to church at half-past two and come out at a quarter to four, then I go out for a walk or for a ride in the country.[83]

Children gathered around the Byrne fountain, Scotland Place, Liverpool, in 1895. Some had bare feet and may have been playing truant from school, but they were evidently enjoying themselves. (Liverpool City Libraries)

Other families, like the Foleys in Alice's early days, might have to share a house but nevertheless brought up their children to be well behaved and orderly. At the bottom of the economic and social pile were those whose main breadwinner was either a casual worker or unemployed, or like Dicky Perrott's father in Arthur Morrison's graphic 1890s novel, *A Child of the Jago*, lived on the edge of criminality. The book was set in the half-dozen streets on the boundary of Bethnal Green and Shoreditch known as the Nichol, and from an early stage the eponymous hero, Dicky, realized that his father only secured a livelihood by breaking the law. Unless he made a 'click' the family did not eat. Eventually Mr Perrott stabbed to death a receiver of stolen goods when a burglary went wrong, and he was hanged. Dicky himself died from stab wounds in a fight with another lad.[84]

Arthur Harding was a real-life product of the Nichol and he shared its lawless attitude, graduating from petty theft and pickpocketing to involvement in armed hold-ups and 'protection' rackets. As a child he foraged for potatoes in Spitalfields market, dragged home boxes to chop up for firewood, and stole coal from the coal vans. 'It was something which made a mother happy, when a child brought something home: instead of a bashing they'd get an extra lump of pudding at dinner.' Stealing from vans was easy, because they moved at a very slow pace. 'Sugar came in big cases . . . but if you made a hole in them you could scoop the sugar from the road. They'd leave a trail of sugar till somebody drew . . . attention to it.'[85]

Even without such illegal activities, however, the daily routine in an over-crowded, multi-occupied dwelling could be uncomfortable and insecure, involving as it often did midnight flits to escape rent arrears, and perhaps ill-treatment of youngsters by brutalized and drunken parents or other adults. Yet it must be emphasized that such unfortunates were a small minority of the total child population. In large measure, even when parents and children lived in unpleasant surroundings, they had a good deal of strong, if rough and ready, affection for one another. The children were anxious to help in the home or to find casual employment so as to supplement household income.

When Charles Booth conducted his survey of life in east London in the late 1880s he concluded that although many men and women could be 'very bad' in their personal character, they normally loved their children and wanted to make them happy. He quoted the case of a carman who would take two of his offspring with him during the summer months when he made deliveries in the country. Equipped with supplies of bread and butter and with 2*d* to buy fruit, they set off early in the morning and returned at night, tired and dirty, but full of the day's adventures. 'I see nothing improbable', added Booth, 'in the general view that the simple natural lives of working-class people lead to their own and their children's happiness more than the artificial complicated existence of the rich.'[86] Nonetheless he had to admit that financial uncertainty was the major threat to this favourable picture among vast numbers of working-class families. If the breadwinner were sick, or unemployed, or laid off during a lengthy labour dispute then the precarious comforts they enjoyed could be lost. According to the Anglican cleric, Robert Dolling, in his parish at Landport, Portsmouth, one week's sickness of the main wage earner meant 'a fortnight's living upon the pawning of clothes and furniture, with nothing before them but the workhouse' for the majority of local residents.[87]

Another commentator noted that among casual labourers in London the underfeeding of children quickly became apparent when there was unemployment because few earned more than the bare amount needed to provide for their family when they were working. If they did have anything in hand they would purchase extra furniture or other household goods so as to have something to pawn when in difficulty. 'Their home is the bank on which they draw in time of trouble', she declared.[88] But such resources quickly drained away and then parents and children had to rely on charity and such earnings as the mother and her offspring could secure, if they wished to avoid recourse to the hated Poor Law. As in the case of Will Crooks's mother, that could mean a very hard struggle.

Even those, like Alice Foley, who avoided the worst rigours of poverty, nonetheless knew what it was to be humiliated by a family's lack of means. Alice never had new clothes but always wore an older sister's 'hand-me-downs':

> my school attire was not unlike Joseph's coat of many colours, but the patch-work effect was scrupulously hidden by a large white pinafore. One luckless day, whilst artlessly pirouetting in the school-yard, pinafore lifted high . . . , the joy of life was suddenly darkened by . . . a group of well-dressed girls chanting in unison the coloured sections of my frock. Down came the pinafore like a drop scene and a dismayed child slunk away conscious of not being quite like other people.[89]

The fall in food prices in the final quarter of the nineteenth century, as a result of growing imports of foreign grain and frozen and chilled meat, plus a larger production of milk and vegetables in Britain, helped to improve diets by the end of Queen Victoria's reign. But sharp class differences persisted. In 1889, Board of Trade returns demonstrated that on a low income of £28 to £40 per annum, the proportion spent on food was more than 87 per cent, but on a higher income of £70 to £80 per annum that proportion fell to 56 per cent. Whereas a skilled engineer with a weekly income of 30s would spend 2s to 5s on meat, the comparable weekly outlay of an unskilled labourer would be only 1s 3d to 3s. And most of that was likely to go to the father of the family rather than his wife and children.[90]

CHAPTER 4

The Growth of Mass Schooling

I left school at the age of twelve . . . Children went to school from the age of 2½ years and they had to pay school money – a penny or twopence a week. They were sent so early in order to 'get from under the feet' whilst the newer additions were coming into the world or crawling about the place . . . If you passed an infants' school whilst lessons were on, you would hear children's voices chanting CAT spells cat, DOG spells dog and so on. . . . Many teachers were never seen without a cane in their hands . . . For good attendance one received a framed certificate. The walls of our house were covered with the things.

Reminiscences of Mrs H. Jones of Orrell, Lancashire, born c. 1887–8[1]

During the Victorian years the perception of mass schooling changed. No longer was it regarded as an optional luxury which, nonetheless, most youngsters experienced at some period in their lives, but rather as an integral part of their daily existence. The legal minimum working age, first established under the Factory Acts of 1833 and 1844 for children under thirteen working part-time in textile mills, was extended progressively by new factory and education legislation during the 1860s and 1870s. Eventually under the 1876 and 1880 Education Acts, compulsory attendance was required for all children aged between five and ten, and thereafter to thirteen or fourteen, according to local by-laws, unless they could pass a leaving examination or gain exemption in some other way. Further legislation in 1893 and 1899, respectively, raised the minimum leaving age from ten to eleven, and then to twelve (except for many living in country areas, for whom eleven still applied).

In this way a gradually advancing legal boundary of childhood dependency was established. Whereas under the Factory Act of 1844 and the factory and workshop legislation of the 1860s young workers in the industries covered could be employed from the age of eight, that minimum became ten during the 1870s, and, as we have seen, it was raised yet again during the 1890s. School thus became a bridge between the years of infancy and the sterner duties of late adolescence,

Girls carefully posing in their pinafores: Class 3, Standards V to VII. (The author)

with its expectation of regular full-time employment. In the eyes of some, indeed, one of the school's principal tasks was to prepare youngsters for the world of work by instilling the virtues of obedience, cleanliness, punctuality and diligence. Schooling, it has been said, 'defined and regulated childhood and youth as discrete, sequenced phases of preparation for adulthood'.[2]

Children, meanwhile, came to be accepted as special cases who needed state help in gaining protection against exploitation by adults, since they lacked the intellectual and physical powers to do this for themselves, especially in the spheres of education and welfare. That applied to the early factory legislation, since the requirement that young workers aged between eight and thirteen attend school for half a day was proposed as a means of combating excessive child labour and as a desirable educational innovation in its own right. Not only did the mixture of lessons and paid employment enable poor children to gain both instruction and an income, but a half-day stint of three hours in school was considered the maximum period a working-class child could concentrate on academic subjects. Some contemporaries, admittedly, pointed out that half-timers who had spent the morning in a factory were so tired in the afternoon that they fell asleep at their desks. Others complained that their intermittent attendance disrupted the routine of the schools. There were also claims that their 'depraved' conduct undermined the moral standards of full-time fellow pupils. They 'become clever at repartee and in the use of "mannish" phrases, which sound clever when they dare use them', declared one critic. 'They lose their childish habits . . . some of the boys commence to smoke and to use bad language.'[3]

Nevertheless, it was only in the 1870s that dissatisfaction with the half-time system became widespread, at a time when the increased provision of ordinary elementary education and the accompanying decline in child employment highlighted the deficiencies of part-time instruction. It began to be seen less as a 'rescue' agency to save youngsters from overwork and more as a device for legitimizing continued juvenile labour.[4]

Parental opinion of the value of education likewise changed over these years. At the start of Victoria's reign most parents wanted their children to learn to read, but by the middle of the century writing, too, was recognized as important. Schools which failed to offer this became less popular, even though as late as 1851 more than a third of pupils attending public elementary schools did not learn to write and about half were not taught arithmetic. In private schools the situation was still worse, with less than half of the scholars taught either writing or arithmetic. Girls fared particularly badly in this regard, since for them success in sewing was considered more important than in sums.[5]

Industry, too, which in the initial phases of mass production had operated with an illiterate and often very young labour force, began to require efficient adults able to read notices and instructions and operate complex machinery. It was recognized that better education would facilitate the smooth running of an increasingly complex urban society in which letter writing, newspapers, advertisements, and the drawing up of legal documents all played an important part. Occupational incentives might have a role, too. The directors of the Great Northern and the London and North Western Railways refused to employ boys who were unable to read and write, and it is noticeable that in the area around the London termini of the two lines many working-class parents kept their sons at school so that they could acquire these skills. A post on the railways was valued because of its security and respectability.[6]

Great differences nonetheless remained between the attitude of skilled workers, many of whom were anxious to promote their children's education, and the unskilled, for whom economic survival was the main priority. 'No one has so impatient a contempt for the uneducated working man as has the educated working man', declared Thomas Wright, a journeyman engineer, in 1871.[7]

Skilled workers not only sent their offspring to school regularly but often kept them there until they were thirteen or fourteen. By contrast, the children of poor labourers had little formal instruction and left at an early age. In 1872 over 55 per cent of all pupils on elementary school registers in England and Wales were aged between four and nine years; a further 6.5 per cent were under four.[8] Just 27.14 per cent were over ten.

Family circumstances and background thus helped determine whether and for how long children attended school. Another difficulty in the early nineteenth century was that education provision in the rapidly growing industrial towns of the north of England failed to keep pace with the rise in population. Many children were unable to attend school long enough to learn to read and write properly. This was especially true where there was a strong demand for juvenile labour. Literacy in such districts slumped. In Ashton-under-Lyne, for example, the ability to write, as shown by couples signing the register when they married, dropped sharply from 48 per cent for those marrying in 1823 to 10 per cent in 1833 and 9 per cent a decade later. In 1844 a local commentator gloomily observed: 'if writing . . . is to be considered a criterion of the education of a people, verily the inhabitants of this town are in a pitiable condition: and what makes the matter worse and improvement almost hopeless, is the remarkable fact that we are in a state of rapid retrogression.'[9]

Around the middle of the century the situation improved, but even in 1870 the industrialized West Riding of Yorkshire had an average *illiteracy* rate of 28 per cent. This ranged from the position in Hunslet, Leeds, where 35.9 per cent of those marrying could not sign their name, to Sedbergh, a market town, where a mere 3.7 per cent were unable to do so.[10] On a national scale in 1871, 19.4 per cent of males and 26.8 per cent of females were still unable to sign their name when they married, but that was a major improvement on the position thirty years before, when the respective failure rates had been 32.7 per cent for men and 48.9 per cent for women.[11]

Many youngsters snatched a breakfast on the way to school at a coffee bar, if they had the requisite pennies. (The author)

Apart from the availability of school places, the willingness of parents to forego their children's labour long enough for them to get an education was another factor influencing literacy levels. Included in this was the need to pay fees at most schools up to the 1890s. Indeed, despite a special government fee grant in 1891 to allow free schooling, even in 1894 more than three-quarters of a million elementary pupils still made payments.[12] The result of this 'subservience' of education to the needs of the family economy was clear. Not only was the amount of time a child could devote to learning strictly limited, but up to the 1870s no particular period of life was set aside for formal education. Family size inevitably influenced the decision, as did the willingness of parents to supplement school instruction themselves (see Appendix 3(a)). While older children perhaps started work at an early age, to boost household income, the youngest members, benefiting from the earnings of their elders, could stay at school longer.

The frequency with which the urban poor moved home, in order to escape rent arrears or to get better or more convenient housing, added to the difficulty. According to one of the first of Her Majesty's Inspectors of Schools, reporting in 1845 on densely populated Bethnal Green, children who began their education at the age of three or four might pass through four, six, or eight schools before they left five or six years later: 'in a school of 200 boys it not seldom happens that from 100 to 160 boys have entered within twelve months . . . in London we not only lose our children at a very early age, . . . but . . . a fearfully large proportion of poor children either do not enter our schools at all, or remain in them so short a time, that any expectation of their receiving real benefit from the instruction therein given must be a mere illusion'.[13]

Throughout the 1850s and 1860s about two-fifths of children in government-inspected schools remained at a given institution for under a year.[14] In the early 1860s the general position was summarized by an assistant commissioner for the Royal Commission on Popular Education when he admitted it was impossible 'to state with precision how long the children . . . "usually" stay at school': 'There seems to be no conventional standard accepted amongst parents, either of instruction to be acquired or of the length of time that ought to be spent at school. A child is taken away . . . not because he has been to school so long, or knows so much, but because he is old enough to work.[15]

Yet the Royal Commission itself, although anxious to promote an efficient system of 'sound and cheap' elementary education designed to fit the offspring of the poor for their future station in life, remained reluctant to exclude the possibility of child employment. It concluded that compulsory schooling was 'neither attainable nor desirable', since,

> Independence is of more importance than education; and if the wages of the child's labour are necessary, either to keep the parents from the poor rates, or to relieve the pressure of severe and bitter poverty, it is far better that it should go to work at the earliest age at which it can bear the physical exertion than that it should remain at school.[16]

With such official ambivalence concerning the rival merits of school and paid work, it is not surprising that attendance in many areas remained poor. Sometimes, too, periods of schooling were interspersed with lengthy spells away. 'Sarah A. Venters returned to School after having been absent three years assisting her Mother', noted the headmistress of the Beneficial Girls' School, Portsmouth, in November 1865. Some months earlier she had commented on the return of another girl 'after an absence of 13 months', and there were many cases of pupils having shorter spells away, usually because the girl concerned was helping at home or minding a baby.[17]

The small amount of knowledge some youngsters acquired before they began work was exemplified by interviews carried out in 1863 in connection with the Children's Employment Commission. One eight-year-old employed alongside his father in a Birmingham brass casting workshop, claimed to have attended a day school for twelve months before starting work. But on being asked to name letters of the alphabet he was unable to do so.[18] Then there was twelve-year-old William Homer, occupied at a large brass foundry in the same city. He had attended a day school from the age of four until nine, but when asked to read simple words he pronounced 'for' as 'of'. His general knowledge was equally shaky: 'The Queen is the Prince of Wales; is the Prince Alexandra'.[19] Clearly such youngsters had benefited little from the tiny amount of instruction they had received. The Assistant Commissioner who conducted the interviews was himself surprised at the ignorance he found:

> Considering . . . the plentiful means of secular and religious instruction provided in Birmingham where most were examined, including Sunday, day, and evening schools, libraries, &c., . . . it is . . . not a little remarkable that the evidence should disclose such a low state of education or rather practical absence of it . . . It is not too much to say that to many God, the Bible, the Saviour, a Christian, . . . are ideas entirely or all but unknown. 'I've heard that (Christ), but don't know *what it is*.' . . . Heaven was heard of only 'when father died long ago, mother said that he was going there.' . . . An analysis of 80 girls of from 7 to 16 at one large factory may give some idea . . . Of these 72.5 per cent admitted that they could not read, 13.75 practically could not, 12.5 could read a little, and the remaining 1.25, i.e. one girl, could read effectively.[20]

The scanty schooling most of the young workers had received was blamed for this dismal record, but even some who professed to have attended for relatively long periods had learned little. That might be due to poor or inexperienced teachers: 'It's only a lad of about 14 that teaches; he used to hit us', said one youngster. But persistent truancy and the lack of any strong moral and religious influence were also considered factors. 'Some have never been in a place of worship.'

It was to counter such ignorance and to stem the worrying rise of urban crime and political unrest that the churches and other voluntary bodies began to set up schools in the early nineteenth century. The most important of the providers were the Church of England's National Society (formed in 1811), the non-sectarian British and Foreign School Society (established in 1814 and largely supported by

Nonconformists), and the Roman Catholic Poor Schools Society (set up in 1847). The Church of England was by far the most active of the participants. In 1860 it owned around nine-tenths of all the public elementary schools and enrolled about three-quarters (76 per cent) of the pupils. A further 10 per cent were educated in British and Foreign schools, and just over 5.5 per cent by the Roman Catholics. The remainder were largely accounted for by various Nonconformist bodies, of which the Wesleyans and the Congregationalists were the largest.[21]

State aid to build and later run the schools became available from 1833, and six years later the first of Her Majesty's Inspectors of Schools were appointed to examine the organization and efficiency of the state-aided establishments. Over the years the government's contribution to elementary education rose sharply, jumping from £20,000 in 1833 to £193,000 in 1850 and £669,000 eight years later.[22] The scale and speed of the increase led to the appointment of a Royal Commission on Popular Education in 1858, to investigate the effectiveness of the elementary system thus promoted. Out of its deliberations came the 1862 Revised Code, which introduced a 'payment by results' system, making state grants to schools contingent on the level of attendance of pupils and their success in annual examinations conducted by HM Inspector in reading, writing and arithmetic (the three R's), plus needlework for the girls. These were arranged in six 'Standards', linking the age of the child to the anticipated level of attainment. For the first time an academic 'norm' was established related to age and based upon a national curriculum. However, the irregular attendance of many pupils and the deficiencies in the teaching and equipment of large numbers of schools frustrated the anticipated progression of the children. In 1877–8, for example, of 1,335,118 scholars examined, 655,435 were over ten years of age and should have been presented in Standards IV to VI. But over half (i.e. 390,575) were tested in Standards suited to children of from seven to nine years of age, including 72,125 who were presented in Standard I, which was intended for seven-year-olds.[23]

The shortfall in achievement was confirmed by the comments of individual inspectors, especially from the industrial districts. Of the Wigan area of Lancashire, Mr Scott Coward complained: 'The very large proportion of children in Standards I and II of advanced ages must leave the upper standards small and attenuated. . . . It is no uncommon thing in manufacturing districts to be told by teachers of admitting half-timers of 10 years who are ignorant of even the alphabet.'[24]

Over the years the system was modified, with extra grants awarded for English grammar, history and geography in 1867, and for foreign languages and the sciences from 1871. But 'payment by results' remained the cornerstone of government aid to elementary education into the 1890s. 'Reading, writing and arithmetic were the foundation, with history, geography, music and art as embellishments', recalled one youngster educated in the late 1880s. Occasionally, as at Maud Clarke's school at Tipton, in about 1900, the 'embellishments' were omitted. In her case the girls learnt no history or geography, but were instead instructed in cookery, dressmaking and domestic science, since these were considered relevant and practical. 'We were groomed as future housewives and mothers.'[25]

Schoolroom interior with elaborate religious paintings on the wall. (The author)

The system of rote learning encouraged by the Revised Code and the concentration in the schools on the examination subjects overshadowed the lives of children for over thirty years. Although teachers had to pay attention to all pupils, not merely the brightest, since all had to succeed in the annual examination if the maximum grant were to be earned, this often meant the school routine degenerated into a sterile, repetitive regime. Ill-feeling arose between teachers and parents when the former tried to pressurize mothers into sending their children to school regularly in preparation for the examination. 'Ellen German sent for several times', noted the headmistress of the Beneficial Girls' School, Portsmouth, in 1868 of one persistent truant, 'her Mother came, said she had a cold . . . said that it was no benefit to the children to be at the Examination – it was the Mistress & Master who reaped the benefit'.[26]

Discipline was normally severe, as the teachers, many of them young trainees or pupil teachers under the age of eighteen, sought to instruct and control large and sometimes unruly classes. At St Clement's Boys' School, Liverpool, the staff in 1862 comprised one adult male head and five trainees. Three were pupil teachers of between thirteen and eighteen years, and two were stipendiary monitors aged between thirteen and seventeen. As such, they were little older than the children they were endeavouring to teach. 'John McDonald [stipendiary monitor] disobedient in playing with the pupils about the premises – thus encouraging them to loiter about the building after having been forbidden to do so', commented the headmaster of St Clement's sourly in October of that year.[27]

At the Beneficial Girls' School parents intervened when the mistress kept children in as a punishment. 'Mrs Hoskins came very angry after her girl – told her she had to stop to say her lesson', wrote the headmistress on one occasion. The mother replied that 'she did not care anything about lessons, she wanted her to take her brother's dinner – told her that her girl had told me several falsehoods but she said she had not, and would not allow the girl to come to me when I called her that she may hear what the girl would say, but hurried her out of School in a passion'.[28]

The excessive use of corporal punishment created other problems. 'Sent after several boys who are eligible for examination', declared the master of St Peter's National Boys' School, Burnley, in February 1873. 'The answer returned was that they had left in consequence of PT [pupil teacher] Baldwin striking them. Found that a system of punishment had been followed without my knowledge.' A written apology was obtained from Baldwin, who promised 'in future to try my best to refrain from striking them'. But it was to little avail, for on 1 May came the entry, 'Gave Tom Baldwin an imposition of 1,000 lines for striking John Layfield.'[29]

Some of the older boys reacted by hitting out at over-strict teachers, to the approval of fellow pupils. The son of a Bristol labourer blamed his unsuccessful school career on the severe discipline:

I couldn't concentrate . . . It was fear of the teachers, they were brutal in them days . . . [There] was a big strapping man, he was over six foot tall . . . I was sat in my desk one day with me copy book in front of me, writing what the teacher was dictating. And I was conscious of a blot on the paper, but I couldn't do anything about it. But all at once, . . . I felt a hand wham . . . right across my ear. Well it stunned me for a minute, but I got out of my seat and I kicked him right in the shins. After that he sent me to the headmaster. But he didn't do much about it . . . just reprimanded me.[30]

Often, though, it was the inadequacy of the school premises and the lack of equipment that inhibited progress. At an infants' school in Edmonton one pupil remembered the room was so cold during the winter that the teacher made the children march round, holding hands, and singing a hymn, until they had warmed themselves up,[31] while at St James's National School, Bolton, the head complained in March 1865 of a shortage of writing materials: 'There has been a great want of slates for three months, the work of the school could not have been carried on, if the slates belonging to the night school had not have been used. The three lower classes have neither a book nor a card to read from – the reading lessons are chalked upon the black board.' Despite promises from the managers, ten days later the slates had still not arrived.[32]

The Beneficial Girls' School at Portsmouth had even greater problems with poor premises. In January 1870 it moved to a new site over a stables, where the mistress was soon complaining of the noise from the horses and dogs, and the bad language of the stable lads, as well as the offensive smell from a dung heap just under the schoolroom window. This attracted swarms of flies and she had to send for supplies of chloride of lime to scatter around the room. Despite repeated protests and threats by HM Inspector to withhold the grant unless these 'utterly pestilential' premises were vacated, more than three years elapsed before the move was made. Even then difficulties persisted since the new schoolroom was the vestry of a nearby church.[33]

This school was located in an area notorious for prostitution and drunkenness, and both mistress and pupils were harassed by some of the local residents, including the keeper of a nearby beerhouse and her friends, as well as by 'idle girls' and the stable lads. On one occasion a lump of sausage meat was thrown through the street window, shattering the glass and hitting one of the pupils. On another, 'several very dirty boys' came up the stairs and shouted for the teacher. When she asked what they wanted they spat upon her and were 'very rude'. She reacted by sending for a policeman.[34]

With such situations in mind it was not surprising that HM Inspector Stokes should comment in 1872 that bad school buildings were 'a great obstruction to success in teaching'.[35] It became the task of the state and the school providers to remedy these weaknesses during the final thirty years of the nineteenth century, and to build new schools where necessary.

Meanwhile, a large minority of children, perhaps a third of those attending school in the early 1860s, went not to public elementary schools but to private 'adventure' or 'dame' establishments run by their proprietors. These varied greatly in both the quantity and the quality of instruction offered. In Bristol, where nearly two hundred working-class private schools operated during the 1850s, they included one kept by Jane Porter. It was run in an overcrowded dwelling-house occupied by seventeen people. Equally unsatisfactory was the ramshackle building in Church Lane, where Elizabeth Cole kept her school. It was home to five families and Elizabeth's eldest son, aged thirteen, was already working as an errand boy. Three of her remaining children, aged between five and ten, attended the school, along with other local pupils.[36]

Many of these places were little more than child-minding institutions, where an elderly woman or 'dame' perhaps taught her young charges to read and, in the case of the girls, to sew and knit, while she herself continued with the household chores. Fees were normally higher than in the publicly funded elementary schools, though facilities were almost certainly poorer. Thus the widowed Mrs Maria Busby of Hasker Street, Chelsea, conducted a class in her kitchen, where she combined the mangling of washing with scholastic instruction. In the early 1870s ten children, mainly aged about five years of age, were attending, each paying 4d or 5d a week. Only one, a girl aged over seven, could read reasonably well, and one pupil could write. Mrs Busby, who was in her early fifties, had been teaching for four years.[37]

Not all of these private schools were to be condemned. Charles Shaw, who went to 'Old Betty's' dame school at Tunstall, Staffordshire, in the late 1830s, before starting work in a pottery at the age of seven, felt great affection for her and her methods. On fine days the pupils sat outside, working at their books or their knitting, while the old lady, 'knitting herself incessantly, marched backwards and forwards, hearing lessons and watching work'. To Shaw, such teachers as she were invaluable because 'they made night schools possible for those who wanted to go further, say, to learn writing and arithmetic; and they made it possible for Sunday school teachers to have less elementary drudgery'.[38]

It may be asked why parents patronized the private schools, especially when public elementary schools were available with lower fees. Part of the attraction seems to have been their informality – their willingness to accept pupils' attendance on an intermittent basis, with parents paying when they could and feeling at liberty to fetch a child out to run an errand or do a job.[39] Their domestic setting and the small number of pupils gave them an intimacy which appealed to younger children, and which was very different from the impersonal atmosphere and 'barrack-room discipline' of their elementary counterparts. When HM Inspector Brodie questioned some Lancashire mothers about their preference for private schooling they gave various answers: 'better taken care of there'; 'looked after separately'; 'don't get infectious diseases'; 'don't get so rough'; 'don't learn bad language'.[40]

The Royal Commission on Popular Education in 1861 considered part of their appeal was the feeling of parents, who were paying the fees, that they were more in control of what was taught than applied in schools provided by the voluntary societies. Their higher fees, too, gave some the impression that they were more 'select' than elementary schools, and that by making this choice they were showing their independence, rather than accepting a favour from their social superiors.[41]

Some of these motives certainly applied to the daughter of an Essex foreman patternmaker, who was born in 1879. Initially she had attended an ordinary school but when she discovered that a neighbour's daughter was being privately educated she wanted to follow suit. 'I talked my mother round to let me go there . . . but I didn't learn a thing.' Yet, despite the school's academic shortcomings, she considered it worthwhile, and remained about two years. 'It was nice going to a private school, 'cos you felt you were a little . . . ahead of the ordinary . . . When you went to the other children's schools they weren't too clean – my mother had to comb our heads every night, when we were young.'[42] That was to guard against nits.

Ultimately, as public elementary provision increased in the last thirty years of the nineteenth century, the number of private schools dwindled. With much emphasis being placed on the reformist role of education, their lack of a firm moral message made them unpopular in official circles. By the 1880s only a handful remained, these being allowed to function as a stopgap until the education authorities could build new schools of their own.[43]

In the meantime, by carefully graduating fees to cater for different classes of pupils and, in some cases, by providing neighbourhood schools for better-off areas, public elementary education was increasingly able to meet the needs of various categories of scholars. Fees became a device for social differentiation so that the lowest charges of 1*d* or 2*d* a week were aimed at those who, as the *School Guardian* delicately put it in 1876, would 'not feel comfortable among the more orderly and well-dressed children who are found in most of our Primary Schools'.[44] In 1872, fees in the British and Foreign schools in Finsbury, for example, were higher in order to attract the offspring of 'small tradesmen and others' who could afford to pay for a more select education.[45]

From the outset, one of the main aims of the voluntary societies in building schools had been to reduce crime and political unrest in the larger towns. Education was seen as exerting a civilizing influence, with the teacher acting as a parental substitute to inculcate discipline and good order in children whose own parents were not able to give proper guidance. 'I have found the hopes of all enlightened men to rest, as the great hope of staying to some degree this flood of evil, upon education', wrote Henry Moseley, one of the first of Her Majesty's Inspectors, in 1845. He then added drily that men had taken refuge in this hope 'in despair of any other solution', rather than on firm evidence.[46] Efficient schooling was seen as an 'insurance' for the respectable majority against the depredations of the destitute and the criminal and, in the long run, as a possible means of reducing expenditure on the penal system. If children were taught to keep out of gaol in later life, it was a worthwhile investment, as well as a desirable end in itself.[47]

Boys learning woodwork at a London manual training centre, c. 1900. (The author)

In the 1830s and 1840s these anxieties about crime and destitution were intensified by the findings of the newly established statistical societies, which linked areas of social deprivation with high juvenile delinquency. At the same time the work of Evangelical missionaries in the larger cities, especially London, revealed the indifference of large sections of the poor towards religion. In the capital, the City Mission, set up in 1835 to spread the gospel message among the poorest elements in society, soon branched out into educating destitute children in what became known as Ragged Schools. In 1844 nineteen of these united to form the Ragged School Union, catering for those whose filthy condition and inability to pay fees led to their exclusion from other elementary schools (at any rate before the passage of the 1870 Education Act). By 1870 average attendance at Ragged day schools in London had reached 23,052, with a further 29,778 attending Sunday schools. Night classes were held for those youngsters who worked during the day, with attendance at these reaching almost 10,000 in 1860 and remaining at around that level for a further decade.[48]

Although the Ragged School contribution to the education of young Londoners was modest, at a time when about 319,000 youngsters were attending the capital's elementary weekday schools in the early 1870s, it was the *nature* of their constituency which gave them significance. Thus the tenth annual report of the Church Street Ragged School, Chelsea, claimed success because of the number of children

> rescued from a position of poverty and vice, and brought under the influence of kind, wise religious instruction. . . . The Ragged School is . . . for the children of those parents who through insufficiency of means, or what is worse, through a careless indisposition [*sic*] as to what becomes of their offspring, leave them to run wild in the streets, if no efforts are made by the Benevolent to take care of them.[49]

Self-interest was undoubtedly one motive for this initiative to help youngsters derogatively labelled 'street arabs' or 'guttersnipes'. It was feared that without such provision they would become lawless drifters and a threat to social order. But there was a humanitarian purpose as well, which found expression in the promotion of welfare schemes. Refuges were set up for some homeless youngsters, school meals were provided for the hungry, and clothing clubs and savings banks organized to promote thrift. 'There are', declared Lord Ashley, president of the Ragged School Union, '. . . amongst the children, guilty and disgusting as they are, many thousands who if opportunities are given them, will walk in all the dignity of honest men and Christian citizens.'[50] It was a comment which underlined the attitude of many towards the youngsters they were seeking to help.

London had pioneered the Ragged School movement but other towns and cities followed suit. In Hull, where a school was opened in 1849, food, clothing and training were supplied to neglected and vagrant children. Shoemaking, joinery, and tailoring were taught to the boys while the girls learnt housewifery skills. A similar step was taken in Portsmouth in the same year, and by 1852, forty-one towns (including London) had Ragged Schools, 110 of them in the capital and 70 in provincial towns and cities. In 1861, Liverpool alone had 64 such schools and it and Manchester had established unions along the lines of that in the capital.[51]

At Portsmouth great stress was laid on the need for pupils to be clean and orderly, while soup dinners were given to them twice a week during the winter. 'It was a great advantage that in the very bitter weather, when they had not a bit of fire in their homes, they were enabled to give the children food . . . and it was . . . a great thing to get the very young in from the gutters, and to give them a home, at least for a time, free from bad language', declared the 1877 annual report complacently.[52]

CAUTION.

Prosperous Shoe Black. "YOU DON'T KETCH ME PUTTING MY MONEY INTO ANY O' THEM BANKS, I CAN TELL YER!"

Two members of the London shoe-black brigades pioneered by the Ragged School movement. (Punch, *1855)*

The schools' rehabilitation programme included finding work for some pupils. The migratory way of life of many of them made this difficult, but between 1853 and 1874 the London Union claimed that its local committees had helped more than 34,000 youngsters to gain paid employment. For the boys, this was often in the armed forces and for the girls in domestic service. To encourage settled habits, prizes were offered to those who stayed in their post for at least a year. From 1851 some of the boys were given temporary work in shoe-black brigades, cleaning the footwear of passers-by. Six years later there were nine of these in London alone. Each member received a uniform and some shoe-cleaning equipment to enable him to earn a modest income and amass some savings. These were then used for the boy's benefit when he left the brigade.[53] At Portsmouth, where a shoe-black brigade was formed in 1863 from eight of the senior boys in the day schools, half of them worked alternate weeks for an average weekly income of 7s. One-third of this was given to them in cash, and the rest was set aside for clothing and footwear. On 18 February 1865, for example, two boys had two shirts apiece, at a cost of 4s 4d each, while two had clogs, at respective prices of 6s and 3s 6d.[54]

The Ragged School movement hailed the brigades as a valuable means of giving youngsters healthy and remunerative employment, but in practice they were a blind alley which did little to prepare the boys for worthwhile work in later life. For this reason they gradually faded away.

Ragged Schools were not the only organizations catering for working children, or those needing moral guidance. From the late eighteenth century Sunday schools had been concerned with saving souls and winning back an irreligious urban population to Christianity. They, like the Ragged Schools, charged no fee and the fact that they gave instruction on the Sabbath, when working children were at liberty, increased their appeal. In them youngsters were taught, largely by volunteers from their own social background, the elements of reading, writing, religion, and, occasionally, other subjects. By 1850, two million children were in attendance and that figure almost trebled in the next fifty years, to reach 5.9 million in 1901.[55] 'Through the Sunday school', writes Thomas Laqueur, 'children were inundated with the printed word. The Sunday School Union alone sold some 10,000,000 reading and spelling books in the first half of the century. . . . Tracts, books, testaments and Bibles were distributed in tens of millions.'[56]

Nonconformists were particularly active in promoting the schools and in 1858 they accounted for more than half of all Sabbath day scholars, compared with the Church of England's 45.8 per cent share, and the Roman Catholics' 1.5 per cent. Often church weekday schools had a Sunday school associated with them which pupils were expected to attend, at any rate until the 1870 Education Act granted freedom of conscience in the matter. Among the Dissenters, the Wesleyans made the largest single contribution, with 19 per cent of the total, followed by the Congregationalists' 11.2 per cent, and the Baptists' 6.7 per cent.[57] The fact that they were inexpensive to run doubtless appealed to communities with limited resources, and the sense of religious solidarity they encouraged helped to make them popular.

But it is not easy to decide how successful they were in sustaining a Christian culture among working-class children. For youngsters weary after a long working week and lacking any solid educational background, the religious instruction given could easily lead to confusion and error. Some of the teaching was extremely lurid, especially when it dealt with the question of hell and eternal damnation. One former pupil remembered learning to recite in the 1840s:

> There is a dreadful hell,
> And everlasting pains,
> Where sinners must with devils dwell
> In darkness, fire, and chains.[58]

Nonetheless, many youngsters enjoyed the social and recreational facilities offered at the larger urban schools, and they also benefited from the religious message conveyed. The importance of Sunday school in the life of Charles Shaw, the young pottery worker, was made clear in his autobiography:

> Whatever the weather on other days, Sunday always seemed to me a sun's day. It gave me the only gladsome morning of the week. I got a washing that morning such as I had not time to get on other mornings. I had poor enough clothing to put on, but my eldest sister always helped me in my toilet on Sunday morning, and my hair got brushed and combed and oiled (with scented oil), so that I always carried a fragrance with me. . . . The Sunday school . . . leavened my life from my sixth to my tenth year, and this determined all my future. I had temptations afterwards . . . [but] the influence of the Sunday school stood me in good stead. . . . Sunday brought sweetness into my life, and lifted me out of the demoralising influences of the working days.[59]

In later life, Shaw became a Methodist minister, but most Sunday schools failed to boost the adult membership of the churches and chapels that promoted them, in the way intended. They did, however, disseminate values of respectability and refinement which appealed to large numbers of working-class families. Some children, though, were too poor to attend. Jack Lanigan and his brother, the sons of a Salford widow, were unable to join 'because we never had any decent clothes to go in. You were considered posh if you could attend Sunday School, but we went to Gravel Lane Ragged School on a Sunday evening. You never saw such a bunch of scruffy kids . . . If we had been bunched together you could not have made a suit from the lot.'[60]

By the late 1860s, therefore, many organizations were providing working-class education. In addition, for youngsters confined in a prison or workhouse, schooling was given under the terms of the 1823 Prisons Act and the 1834 Poor Law Amendment Act, respectively. Reformatory and industrial schools (whose role will be considered in Chapter 8) also grew up in the 1850s to cater for children who had broken the law or were deemed likely to do so and had been given a period of detention as a result. Yet there remained a minority of boys and girls in the slums of the larger towns who continued to fall through the school net. Liverpool, Ashton-under-Lyne and Barrow-in-Furness were just some of the towns where provision lagged behind need, while in London itself about a quarter of a million extra places were required at the beginning of the 1870s. It was to meet these needs and to create a national network of efficient elementary schools that the 1870 Education Act was passed. Its importance can be exaggerated, since most children already attended school for at least some part of their lives. But what it did ensure was that the speed with which literacy had increased during the 1850s and 1860s was maintained. 'Had the state not intervened at this point', comments Professor Altick,

> it is likely that the progress of literacy would have considerably slowed . . . simply because illiteracy was by that time concentrated in those classes and regions that were hardest to provide for under the voluntary system of education. In short, the . . . Act was responsible for the mopping-up operation by which the very poor children, living in slums . . . were taught to read.[61]

At the same time, in the nation at large there was a realization that Britain's industries were falling behind their German and American competitors. W.E. Forster, in introducing the 1870 Act to Parliament, underlined this international aspect, when he emphasized there must be no delay in implementing it: 'Upon the speedy provision of elementary education depends our industrial prosperity. It is of no use trying to give technical teaching to our artisans without elementary education; . . . and if we leave our workfolk any longer unskilled, notwithstanding their strong sinews and determined energy, they will become over-matched in the competition of the world.'[62]

In districts where the voluntary schools could not cater for all the children living in the area the deficiency was to be met by the election of rate-aided boards. These were empowered to build schools and to introduce compulsory attendance for children between the ages of five and ten, and thereafter to twelve or thirteen, according to local by-laws, unless the youngsters could gain exemption. The principle of compulsion – although at this stage 'permissive' compulsion only – was thus extended beyond children in factories, workshops, Poor Law institutions, prisons, reformatories and industrial schools, to the wider juvenile population. In 1876 these provisions were extended to areas not covered by school boards, with the setting up of school attendance committees. Finally in 1880, compulsory schooling was unequivocally applied to all youngsters within the relevant age range, since some boards and attendance committees had failed to act under the earlier measures.

Initially, despite the employment of special attendance officers (sometimes euphemistically called 'visitors'), compulsion was difficult to enforce. This was partly because in large cities there was a need to construct additional school buildings. Even at the end of the century London had many temporary structures in use, and in Bradford, the imposition of compulsory by-laws was delayed until 1872, so that sufficient temporary accommodation could be acquired to make it a realistic proposition.[63]

A posed picture of a London school attendance officer (known as a 'visitor') interviewing a truant. (The author)

Another factor was parents' resentment at what they saw as interference in their right to dispose of their children's time and labour as they thought fit. At the Beneficial Girls' School in Portsmouth there were many skirmishes between parents and teacher over this. 'Worth absent again, sent for Mother, said she must keep her to mind the baby because it is so cross, and if she could not have her when she wanted her she should take her away & put her to another school', noted the head in February 1871, adding, 'Emma Scott brought the baby to school as her Mother was gone out – sent her home.'[64] Another girl, granted leave of absence during her mother's confinement, continued to stay away. When she was eventually sent for, word was returned that she could not come as she 'had to mind the shop'.

The fact that, except in cases of dire poverty, school fees had to be paid, added to parents' dissatisfaction. If children came to school without their pence they might be excluded by the teacher, thereby causing friction with their families and humiliation for the youngsters involved. 'I had to send seven children home to fetch their school fees', wrote the headmaster of Kent Street School, Portsmouth, in March 1874. This gave offence to several of the parents, and three weeks later he added: 'Mrs Smith threatened to keep her boy away because he was sent home for his school fee.'[65] On 6 December, 1872, his predecessor had underlined the dilemma faced by teachers, anxious for their pupils to attend and to benefit from the education provided, yet aware that if arrears mounted they would themselves be held responsible by the managers or the school board. Hence his comment: 'In order to prevent any further increase in the arrears of School Fees, it becomes necessary to admit no child on Monday mornings, who does not bring his Schooling money with him. All children sent home on Monday last who did not comply with the rule. Exception will be taken in case of absolute necessity only.'[66]

Where families were large or incomes low, or the principal breadwinner was sick or unemployed, parents found great difficulty in conforming. In cases of extreme poverty they could apply to the school board, or after 1876, to the Poor Law authorities to have fees remitted, so long as they could prove the validity of their claim. But often the complex procedures required for the remission or repayment of fees discouraged many from applying. In the early 1880s a superintendent of visitors (as school attendance officers were called in London) pointed out that most potential applicants in the capital did not even understand the meaning of the word 'remission'. He suggested the notice issued to parents be changed to read 'application for the school money to be paid'.[67]

The alternative to not paying fees was for children simply to stay away. This might be because there was no money available or because they were needed at home, or perhaps the amount they could earn at a temporary job exceeded any possible fine imposed for non-attendance. Some youngsters, of course, simply played truant. A Bristol girl and her brother used to 'mooch off' regularly, especially when they had been caned. They would hang about the market on market days.[68] In other cases, special events, such as a Band of Hope tea meeting or a Sunday school outing, would result in widespread truancy. At Kent Street School, Portsmouth, the small attendance on 15 June 1875 was attributed to 'the Circus and the Agricultural Show'.[69]

The London School Board even appointed special 'street' attendance officers whose task it was to round up youngsters found wandering on the streets or 'loitering' around railway stations, or carrying out odd jobs as errand boys, crossing sweepers and the like.[70]

Where children were persistent absentees, parents would be warned by the authorities and, if necessary, prosecuted. This stringent approach was increasingly applied from the 1880s. In London alone, the number of summonses issued for non-attendance jumped from 12,831 in 1889 to 28,836 in 1900. Likewise in the Kent Street, Swan Street and Green Row area of Portsmouth, the total of cases proposed for prosecution more than doubled in four years, from 133 in 1876 to 271 in 1879.[71] In the former year, when the occupations of about a hundred of the 133 parents were given, 30 per cent of the offenders were skilled workers, small businessmen, or tradesmen, who had perhaps fallen on hard times or who wanted their children's labour to help in the business. A further 30 per cent were the offspring of semi-skilled workers, and 40 per cent were the children of the unskilled, mainly labourers.[72] Of the total of 133, 17 per cent were women, some of them widows or deserted wives, or the wives of men who were away at sea and who may, as a result, have had difficulty in disciplining older boys. One persistent offender was Mrs Eliza Hudson, a mariner's wife. An entry in Kent Street log book for 14 March, 1878, is perhaps suggestive: 'William Hudson was brought to school by his mother who informed me that he had again played truant. I gave him six stripes with the birch rod.'[73]

Research shows that in poverty-stricken districts like the Jewellery quarter of Birmingham, sending children to school regularly could be a considerable financial burden. Not only were there school fees to pay, unless these were remitted, but the youngsters' potential earnings as workers had to be sacrificed. Clothing had to be found and especially boots, since children were normally not allowed to attend in bare feet. 'Boots, babies and illness', were the main reasons given by a *Birmingham Daily Mail* reporter for non-attendance in the city in November 1874. He regarded boots as 'the unsolvable equations of the domestic economy, hard to get, hard to keep and alternating between the pawnshops and the marine store dealer'.[74]

To cope with these difficulties, parents adopted various strategies. Clothing might be purchased through a clothing club, or from a dealer, or obtained second-hand from friends and neighbours. There were also charities, such as the Liverpool Children's Aid Society, which concentrated on supplying clothes and boots to enable pupils to attend school regularly. In this case parents were expected to pay for the clothes where possible, on an instalment plan, in order to boost their self-respect and independence.[75]

Sometimes mothers moved their children from one school to another, to keep ahead of the attendance officer, or they would send them to school when they could afford it, and bargain with attendance officers, teachers, managers and school board officials at other times over absences or the non-payment of fees. The abolition of the latter in most (though not all) schools as a result of a government fee grant in 1891 eased one problem, although absences from other causes continued, as the London figures quoted above bear out.

When parents were prosecuted, magistrates were often reluctant to impose penalties which would add to a family's hardship. Hence backsliders might escape even when regulations were blatantly flouted, or else fines were imposed which were too small to act as a deterrent. In 1900 the case was quoted of a Finsbury parent who had been summoned fifty-three times for his children's non-attendance, apparently without effect. As the chairman of the London School Board commented in 1882: 'To inflict a fine of 1*d*, without costs, on a parent who has been summoned sixteen times, is to encourage him and his neighbours in defiance of the law.'[76]

Such difficulties notwithstanding, large numbers of deprived children *were* brought into the elementary school system for the first time as a result of the legislation of the 1870s, and over the years attendance levels and academic attainments improved. Many school boards offered prizes or certificates and medals to regular attenders, and it became a matter of pride for some pupils to gain these. 'My love for schooling must have been intense when I recall that, for seven years, I was never late or absent once', wrote Walter Southgate of his years at Mowlem Street school in Bethnal Green during the 1890s and early 1900s:

> Every year I received a medal and the seventh was considered a 'gold' one. Between the various 'standards' there was a keen competition to maintain a high average attendance to gain the 'school banner', which was bound up with a government grant, I believe. I remember the time when, playing football in the street, . . . I . . . injured my knee cap severely. . . . A note was sent to school and the outcome – my classmates arranged a rota of boys for two weeks to carry me 'pick-a-back' to and from school rather than the attendance record should suffer.[77]

A charitable school dinner scheme in London, c. 1900. Bread and soup were on the menu. (The author)

There were annual prize-givings, too, when the teachers carefully coached the brightest boys to sing, recite, and put on a play for parents. Once the English teacher at Mowlem Street, 'an enthusiastic and devoted fanatic' of Shakespeare, took his pupils to see the *Merchant of Venice*, performed for their benefit at a local hall. Walter enjoyed it 'but I fear, at that stage of our mental development and half empty bellies, it was like introducing culture to children who cared more for Dick Turpin and Buffalo Bill than Shylock seeking revenge'.[78]

Furthermore, if the education legislation of the 1870s influenced the intellectual development of working-class children, it had important welfare implications as well. Foremost among these was an appreciation of the serious malnourishment among the nation's juveniles, and a realization that hungry pupils were unlikely to benefit from the schooling provided. Teachers like Mrs Burgwin, headmistress of Orange Street Girls' School in Southwark, London, began providing meals of bread, tea, coffee and warm milk for some needy pupils, and from these initiatives there developed various school breakfast and dinner societies to supply free or cheap meals. In London, six major organizations were in operation by the late 1880s, in addition to some minor ones. During the year ending March 1889, they supplied school board pupils alone with 7,943 free breakfasts, 26,585 free dinners, and a further 13,900 meals at costs ranging between a farthing and a penny apiece. But for the poorest, even those modest charges were too high. Only free meals would do. Sadly, too, despite this great effort it was estimated that under half of the 12.8 per cent of pupils in the capital's board schools who were habitually short of food were being fed by the voluntary schemes. In Manchester, Birmingham and Liverpool similar initiatives were taken but here, too, the scale of need outstripped the provision. The Schools Cheap Dinner Society formed in Birmingham in October 1884 soon discovered that many scholars 'could no more find a halfpenny for a dinner than they could find a half-sovereign'.[79]

One beneficiary of these arrangements was a Bristol girl, who had meals supplied by the Shaftesbury Crusade. 'We used to 'ave a great big basin of porridge and two great big pieces of bread an' treacle, an' a cup of cocoa [for breakfast]. Then on the dinner hour we used to go up and we used to have soup and we'd get potatoes an' meat.'[80]

A London headmaster, who was the honorary secretary of the Lambeth Teachers' Association Scholars' Free Meal Fund, favoured the provision of breakfasts rather than dinners, because they gave 'an excellent start for the day's work'. Meal tickets were not issued on Mondays because 'we consider the parents can, as a rule, help themselves on that day', by using left-overs from the Sunday dinner. Arrangements were made on four days a week, with each child receiving, on average, three meals weekly, from just before Christmas until early April. He regarded Thursdays and Fridays as the days of greatest need because then parents' income was at its lowest ebb. But on any day, half a dozen pupils would arrive in class without having eaten any breakfast: 'these cases proved not to be from any carelessness on the part of the parents, but from sheer distress'.[81]

Attendance at school also highlighted the serious incidence of dirt and disease among the most deprived youngsters. Epidemics were often mentioned in school log books for all classes of pupils, although the problem was most severe among slum dwellers. There was 'more than the usual amount of sickness', commented the managers' annual report for Nichol Street Boys' School, Bethnal Green, in January 1894. 'In this part there is the highest death-rate in London.'[82] At Orange Street Boys' School in 1877 an inspector even recommended the provision of a bath 'to wash the Boys' persons, and an oven to bake their clothes'. Twelve years later, despite improvements, some children were 'still sadly dirty. Years ago I recommended that means should be found for washing their persons and freeing their clothes from vermin. In a similar school the Birmingham School Board is setting up a bath – a most beneficial measure not yet tried in London.'[83] His suggestion was not adopted. Ringworm was another disease associated with poverty and dirt. Its victims were segregated from other pupils and had to lead a pariah-like existence for many months.

But often, as at Hulton Street Boys' School in Bolton, it was difficult to keep youngsters from homes with infectious diseases isolated from their fellow scholars. On 13 January 1872 the headmaster noted that one mother had declared 'that if her boy must not come while they had the smallpox in the house, he should not come any more'. A few weeks later he had to ask a second mother to keep her son away because there was smallpox in the family. Some critics argued, too, that the overcrowded, poorly ventilated schoolrooms proved ready breeding grounds for infections, unless stringent action was taken to isolate sufferers or, in extreme cases, to close the school altogether when an outbreak occurred.[84] Even in the 1880s there were cases of pupils encouraged to attend for the annual visit by HM Inspector when they were suffering from whooping-cough or similar diseases.[85]

Associated with these health issues were allegations in the early 1880s that children's welfare was being put at risk by the need to meet the requirements of the School Code, irrespective of the individual youngsters' innate abilities or state of health. In December 1883, *The Lancet* attacked attempts to teach pupils difficult subjects like physiology, when they were half-starved. 'We . . . have dared to educate a vast multitude with underfed and only half-developed brains, and a rare degree of immunity from penalty for our hardihood has been vouchsafed to us', it warned.[86] It was particularly critical of schools which gave pupils home lessons, arguing that 'unusual mental efforts in the evening' were likely to cause an 'unstable mental action, which is assuredly the precursor of more serious mischief'.[87]

Even *Punch* joined in the 'over-pressure' discussion in December 1883 with a poem entitled 'The School-Board Victim':

'Mother, how my head is aching,
In a strange and painful way.
See what sad mistakes I'm making
In my exercise today. . . .

I was cold and wet and weary,
Hungry too, at school today.
Why is learning all so dreary,
Is there never time to play?'

So the School-Board victim crying,
Bowed her little aching head,
And her Mother watched her, sighing
For to-morrow's daily bread.

Oh ye men of small discerning
On official red-tape nurst,
Though there's good no doubt in learning
We must feed the children first.[88]

Fuelling the debate both inside and outside Parliament was a report to the Education Department by Dr Crichton-Browne, one of the critics. He argued that 'liberal and regular feeding' was essential if a child were to profit by education. That comment, and a further suggestion that two pints of milk should be given daily to each pupil, found little favour in official circles, with their *laissez-faire* traditions. Eventually the Education Department published the report accompanied by a dissenting memorandum from J.G. Fitch, its Chief Inspector of Schools. In this he acidly pointed out that the object of schools was to teach and not to supply milk. Responsibility for the health and feeding of scholars rested with their parents and not the state. In this respect, he was echoing the views of the Charity Organisation Society that only aid which made a family self-dependent was acceptable. Palliatives like the giving of school meals or milk merely increased the culture of dependency.[89]

Ultimately 'over-pressure' became a subject of dispute between those who favoured the government's educational initiatives and those hostile to them, who saw the issue as a way of discrediting views they disliked.[90]

Children saving in a Post Office account at a London school. The Post Office encouraged youthful thrift by allowing schoolteachers to collect the pence either by the use of stamps or by setting up penny banks. (The author)

'Home lessons', however, were unpopular not just with Dr Crichton-Browne and his supporters but with pupils, too. Not only were they difficult to carry out in overcrowded, noisy homes, but youngsters often had household or money-making tasks to perform when they returned from school. Significantly when strikes broke out among schoolchildren in the autumn of 1889 in several major towns, the two main grievances voiced were home lessons and the excessive use of the cane. The strikes began in Scotland in late September and they ended about the middle of October, having affected schools in Hull, Liverpool, Bristol, Bolton, Cardiff, Swansea and London, as well as other major towns and cities. They occurred at a time of industrial unrest among unskilled adult workers, but were initiated entirely by children. They rarely lasted for more than a day in any single place, but, in all, several thousand youngsters were involved. Some of them, as at Cardiff, paraded along the streets, holding up makeshift banners and appealing to non-striking fellow pupils to join in.[91] They received widespread press coverage and a few newspapers shared the pessimistic conclusion of the *Western Daily Press* that when 'the very children rise against authority, society is in a bad state'.[92] More realistic, perhaps, was the comment by the *Western Mail* from Cardiff that the 'spirit of the strikers' was unlikely to survive 'the parental slipper'.[93]

A number recognized that the children had cause for complaint. In an editorial, the *Liverpool Echo* correctly predicted the movement would soon be stopped by teachers and parents, but expressed a hope that 'no savage reprisals will follow'. If the strikes need not be taken too seriously, nonetheless their 'purpose should not be altogether ignored': 'Too much book is as bad as too little, and home lessons constitute a very real grievance. The physical constitution of growing children is not sufficiently taken into account. Many scholars are burdened by a range of hours and an amount of work that their elders neither would nor could stand for a month.'[94] This sympathetic approach was in the minority, however, and the children's brief rebellion achieved little. Its importance lay in the way it revealed pupils' hatred of their 'strait-jacket curriculum' and the harsh discipline imposed upon them in most elementary schools.[95]

A more positive aspect of the education legislation of the 1870s was the boost it gave to the schooling of handicapped children. Under the 1870 Act all children had to be catered for, and although the handicapped were not specifically mentioned, neither were they excluded. Reactions varied, but in 1872 the London school board began discussions on the possible placement of blind and dead children. Two years later the first class for the deaf was opened and in 1875 provision was made for the blind also. Hitherto education of the handicapped had depended on voluntary effort and had been given largely in residential institutions. Although for some years the London scheme remained small, it paved the way for wider reforms. Sheffield opened a class for the deaf in 1879 and in the following decade, Leeds, Nottingham, Bradford, and a number of other towns followed suit. In Bradford action was taken after pressure from the local deaf and dumb institution in 1884, when it agreed to contribute towards the salary of the teacher. Nottingham took action a year earlier, with about thirty-five children receiving instruction in lip-reading language, spelling, reading, arithmetic and drawing. In 1890 geography, grammar, needlework, drill and woodwork were added to the list, while from 1888 an annual seaside trip, normally to Skegness, was paid for by well-wishers.[96]

Sunderland and Bradford school boards also arranged for blind children to be taught at special centres attached to certain ordinary elementary schools, thereby integrating the handicapped, in a minor way, into the wider educational system. By the late 1880s five school boards in England and Scotland were educating 194 blind children, of whom 133 attended one of the special London centres. A further ten school boards taught 577 deaf and dumb children, 313 of them at the London board's classes. For those with learning difficulties, special 'Standard O' classes were formed in some places, while in Nottingham in January 1893 two classes were set up for children who 'although not actually imbecile, require a special course of teaching based on kindergarten principles'. Six centres were eventually opened in the city, two for defective and four for dull children.[97] But many mentally handicapped youngsters continued to be excluded from mainstream elementary education. Not until the 1890s was any coherent strategy drawn up to cater for them.[98] Sometimes groups of retarded pupils could be found clogging up the lowest classes of ordinary schools, irrespective of their age.

Humanitarian motives alone did not account for this interest in the handicapped. Apart from the pressures exerted within the schools themselves by the presence of handicapped youngsters (and the small numbers of them admitted ensured that this remained low level), there were wider economic implications. In 1889 the Report of the Royal Commission on the Blind and Deaf, which also examined the position of physically and mentally handicapped children, suggested that their education was 'an economic expedient' rather than an 'ethical duty'. 'Indigence' was found among the vast majority of people afflicted, though not through any fault of their own. The report concluded:

> The blind, deaf and dumb, and the educable class of imbeciles form a distinct group, which, if left uneducated, become not only a burden to themselves, but a weighty burden to the State. It is the interest of the State to educate them, so as to dry up as far as possible the main streams which ultimately swell the great torrent of pauperism.[99]

After 1870, therefore, many aspects of working-class child life came under adult surveillance through the medium of the elementary school and the work of the teachers and inspectors associated with it. With the introduction of compulsory schooling, education marked a decisive point at which the child was separated and segregated from adult society. The school became the place where 'knowledge' was acquired, and where the cultural experience which the pupils had gained from their family background was treated as irrelevant, and even harmful when it encouraged precocious behaviour.

Girls learning to cook in a London school, c. 1900: part of the gender bias in late Victorian schooling. (The author)

Simultaneously there was a shift in the moral message which educationists sought to inculcate, from the early Victorian concern with religion, obedience to the law, and such virtues as cleanliness, punctuality and diligence, to a wider, more patriotic approach. This, in its turn, influenced the curriculum. For girls, it meant greater emphasis on the acquisition of domestic skills, to fit them to become good wives and mothers, capable of raising healthy sons and daughters to serve the nation and, ultimately, the British Empire. For boys, the emphasis was on manliness, hard work and physical fitness.

The preoccupation with female domestic skills was intensified at the end of the century following the outbreak of the Boer War in 1899, and its revelation of the poor health and physique of many would-be recruits from the larger towns. Other aspects of elementary education which were influenced by imperialistic fervour included history and geography. A Bristol girl who attended school in the 1890s remembered being taught to be proud to be British. 'We were the only ones on Earth.'[100] In Bethnal Green, Walter Southgate recalled the 'enthusiasm, rejoicings, flag waving, patriotic fervour and drunkenness' that swept through his street, and through the nation at large, when war was declared upon the Boers: 'We played games like "English versus Boers", wore celluloid buttons in our lapels portraying our favourite generals . . . It only required the relief of Ladysmith or Mafeking to set the whole populace dancing, singing, waving flags, . . . and finishing off the celebrations with bonfires and fireworks.'[101]

Even school magazines were affected:

Our soldiers have shown the courage and discipline experience has taught us to expect of them, and even when the fortune of war has gone against them their pluck and endurance have taken away the bitterness of defeat. . . . The present trouble has shown the world how the people of the British Empire can stand shoulder to shoulder, all party spirit . . . forgotten, united in a common cause – the upholding of the honour of the Empire,

declared *St Matthew's School Magazine*, Denmark Hill, in December 1899.[102] There was much more in a similar vein in later issues.

For the minority of children whose parents opposed the war the situation was difficult. Alice Foley's Irish father sided fiercely with the Transvaal cause and the family became keen pro-Boers. This brought conflicts with Alice's fellow pupils: 'I remember that we youngsters endured some good "hidings" when engaged in mock street battles . . . In school I was marked out as an odd creature when I could not share enthusiastically in victory rejoicings.'[103]

The preoccupation with physical exercise within the elementary curriculum at this time was also linked to the patriotic cause. As the London School Board put it in 1900, such activity was designed to achieve habits of 'discipline, obedience, quickness to hear and obey'.[104] Pupils learned to march to their places and to obey commands with smartness and alacrity. In 1896 the author of one teaching manual advised that a class at drill 'should be a mere machine, actuated only by the will, and at the word, of the teacher'.[105] Although the evidence of school log books, with their comments on truancy, unpunctuality and disobedience, shows that the

A makeshift regiment of would-be soldiers marching in London during the Boer War. (The author)

reality fell short of this ideal, it does indicate what the *object* of mass schooling was considered to be at the end of the Victorian era.

A report for 1897 by the Senior Chief Inspector of Schools underlined this. 'The formation of good moral habits', he declared,

> is the most important function of our schools . . . I fear that not much can be said on behalf of the truants . . . [But] on behalf of the large majority, . . . not one of them leaves school without an awakened sense of duty and moral responsibility . . . A boy who has been trained in true hero-worship and to admire acts of bravery will instinctively despise a drunkard who has destroyed the will and nerve required for a brave action . . . Our scholars should be taught before they leave school that good conduct alone can make a life admirable and beautiful.[106]

Yet despite officialdom's yearning for diligence and moral conduct on the part of the nation's elementary schoolchildren, there remained deep social and economic divisions. In the 1890s few working-class youngsters were able to gain scholarships to secondary education and those who did were, often enough, prevented by poverty from taking them up. Walter Southgate recalled how a friend won a scholarship to the Parminters Foundation School but because his elder sister 'had already won a scholarship the father said he could not afford to keep two children at school'. The boy went at fourteen into a printing firm.[107] Even the higher grade schools set up by a few boards, mainly in the industrial north of England, to provide quasi-secondary education, catered for a small number of better-off working-class children only, whose parents could afford the extra cost involved. As we saw in Chapter 2, such schools were likely to appeal to lower middle-class families, too.

A schoolgirl with her skipping rope. (The author)

Within the elementary sector itself there were differences based on variations in fees levied (especially up to the early 1890s) and on status and residence. 'Respectable' parents did not want their offspring to mix with 'street arabs', and in the late 1880s William Booth, founder of the Salvation Army, gave a pessimistic assessment of such contacts:

> The rakings of the human cesspool are brought into the school-room and mixed up with your children. Your little ones, who never heard a foul word and who are not only innocent, but ignorant, of the horrors of vice and sin, sit for hours side by side with little ones whose parents are habitually drunk, and play with others whose ideas of merriment are gained from the familiar spectacle of the nightly debauch by which their mothers earn the daily bread.[108]

It was to avoid such an eventuality that a hierarchy of elementary schools was developed, sensitive to the needs and changing status of a particular area. In this way the social decline of a district rapidly influenced the catchment area of an individual school. In the late 1880s, the Salisbury Road area of Bootle suffered from an extension of the docks to the north and the construction of large numbers of terraced houses. By 1887 the head of Salisbury Road school was lamenting the loss of better class parents from the district, and the 'increasing entry of "gutter-snipe" children' to his classes. One former pupil recalled her parents' relief when the opening of a new school in the neighbourhood enabled her to be transferred from Salisbury Road.[109]

It was a stark reminder of the limitations of the educational reform movement, and of the persistence of inequality in this, as in so many other aspects of life, in late Victorian England.

CHAPTER 5

At Work

In those days the younger ones had to take their elders' breakfasts and dinners. Breakfast was from 8 to 8.30 a.m. and the next on the list was initiated in the duties which began your workaday world when you were ten years old. Half-time at work and half-time at school alternately. . . . I remember getting up at 4.45 a.m. to have a drink of coffee and start on my walk to work at 6 a.m. I remember also the cold winter mornings, huddled under my elder sister's shawl. The duties of the little piecers were to oil the spindles, grease the cylinder, change the empty bobbins for full ones and learn how to piece up the broken ends, following the [spinning] mules backwards and forwards. We worked in a temperature of 80° humidity in our bare feet and a pair of drawers. At thirteen years old I had got the requisite school attendance to qualify for full time.

Reminiscences of James Holt (b. 1881), who worked as a piecer in a Lancashire cotton mill [1]

For much of the nineteenth century it was regarded as appropriate, and even desirable, that when circumstances demanded it, working-class children should obtain employment as soon as they were able, in order to contribute to household income. That did not mean a majority of them worked at any one time, but merely that where the need arose this was their duty. Many youngsters, for their part, were eager to take on a wage-earning role, seeing it as a rite of passage – a symbol of their entry into the adult world. Sometimes it might mean helping in a family business, or aiding relatives in a factory or workshop. In mid-nineteenth-century Preston, male spinners who had no children of the relevant age might employ other young relatives as their piecers. Where non-relatives were recruited the offspring of neighbours and lodgers were drawn upon, perhaps entering the spinner's household in a kind of 'quasi-familial relationship'.[2] Similarly at Burnley in the early 1890s, Elizabeth Hartley, the niece of a male weaver, worked as a tenter (or weaving assistant), probably for her uncle. She lived with the family and was the only working child in the home.[3]

Adult employees in textiles normally engaged their helpers on a sub-contract basis and this gave them a major say in the choice of assistants. The arrangement also freed masters from the responsibility of recruiting juvenile labour, with the problems that this could entail.

Although operatives welcomed the opportunity to select the children working with them, that did not always mean they took on their own offspring. In the pottery industry in the 1860s, it is clear widows' children and those of colliers were more likely to be engaged in the potworks than were the offspring of skilled potters, who could afford to keep their sons and daughters out of the labour market.[4] Likewise, a sample of 160 children aged from ten to thirteen years living in the Farnworth area of Bolton in 1891 reveals that of seventy-one of them with jobs, ten lived in households headed by a widow and fifteen were the offspring of coal miners. Other fathers included craftsmen like blacksmiths and stonemasons, as well as railway employees and general labourers. Fifty-five of the youngsters worked in cotton mills, but in only three cases (all involving mothers) did a parent work in cotton manufacture, too.[5]

In 1857 Prince Albert expressed a common early Victorian view when he argued that to the working man his children were 'part of his productive power'. If families were deprived of the help of their offspring this would 'almost paralyse [their] domestic existence'.[6] That applied not merely to the wage-earning activities they performed outside the home, but to the cleaning, childcare, and similar tasks carried out within it. Significantly, despite the proliferation of restrictive legislation during the nineteenth century, there was no attempt to outlaw juvenile labour. The aim was to regulate and control it, in order to prevent exploitation and ill-treatment.

During the course of the century these pro-labour attitudes were increasingly questioned by reformers, who argued that child employment was immoral and a society which allowed it to continue was to be condemned. Gradually stricter age limits were imposed on certain kinds of work, and some dangerous occupations and trades, such as those connected with the use of white lead and with dry grinding in the metal trades, were forbidden to the young, through factory legislation.[7] At the same time families who encouraged their children to work were, with few exceptions, looked down upon as ill-educated and of low status, or else they were condemned as avaricious and thoughtless. In 1899, Allen Clarke, a stern critic of child labour in the Lancashire cotton industry, savagely attacked the county's parents for treating their offspring 'as commercial speculations, to be turned into wage-earning machines as soon as the child's age and the law will permit. . . . No wild beast ever treats its young as too many of the fathers and mothers of Lancashire have treated and still treat theirs.'[8]

But the process of reform proved limited. Even in 1900 many youngsters, not merely in the textile districts but in the slums of large cities, continued to work, at least part-time. Official circles, too, were ambivalent in their reactions. All too often when there was money to be made or pleasure to be derived as a result of juvenile labour, principles were compromised and it was allowed to carry on. That applied as much to part-time assistants in shops or child entertainers on the stage and in the music hall, as to half-timers in the textile industries. Allied to this was a conviction that if youngsters were not fully occupied they would fall into evil ways. As the Interdepartmental Committee on the Employment of School Children declared in 1901, the poor boy who did not work in his spare time had, in most big towns, only the alternative of playing or loafing in the streets or of moping in dull rooms in a crowded tenement. We think that, quite irrespective of anything he may earn, it is better for him mentally, morally and physically to be engaged for a few hours a day in regulated labour rather than to spend his whole leisure in the public thoroughfares or in the penny music-hall . . . [A] small amount of regular employment is of itself a useful part of a boy's education. It would be well if a larger number of children could at an early age be introduced to some of the practical work of the carpenter, the shoemaker, or the blacksmith: but if this is impossible, even the running of errands, or the selling of newspapers helps to make them alert and industrious, and prepares them for the part they have to take in after life.[9]

In that sense child labour was seen as a sort of 'apprenticeship' to the adult world of work, and as a means of instilling the requisite disciplines associated with this. For the children, too, it offered a way of improving their status within the family. One Preston boy looked forward to becoming a half-timer at eleven, so as to equalize the relationship between himself and an elder brother, who was already a wage-earner.[10] A Port Talbot lad also relished the sense of importance earning money gave him as compared to his younger siblings. 'They . . . had nothing to say because they weren't bringing any cash in.'[11]

A boy helping to make windmills in one of the 'sweated' home trades. (The author)

Parents often took the initiative in finding a first job. A miner's son from Merthyr Tydfil recalled his mother arranging for him to work as an errand boy at a butcher's when he was nine years old, in 1893. This involved working on Friday evening and all day Saturday for 1s a week, plus two cooked meals, which he ate with his employer's family, and a pound of sausages, which he took home as a bonus. Immediately his standing rose, not only with his brothers and sister but with his mother, too: 'if I had got home from my work . . . before dad arrived . . . from the pub, where he spent a few hours every Saturday night, I was allowed to sit in his armchair while our mam was frying the sausage I had brought. "For you must be tired, my boy," said our mam.'[12] When he left school at the age of twelve, to work underground with his father in the pit, the brother next in age took over the job at the butcher's.

Juvenile employment had, of course, long preceded industrialization, with youngsters regularly occupied in helping around home, farm and workshop. Even in 1871, almost three times as many boys under fifteen worked in agriculture as in the cotton industry, and among girls, nearly twice as many were domestic servants as were cotton operatives.[13] Furthermore, the proportion of children at work varied not only between different age groups and between the sexes, with boys more likely to engage in paid employment than girls, but between and even within families. The household budget, the birth order, the availability of work in a given locality, and parental attitudes all played a part in deciding whether an individual child had a job, both in pre-industrial society and in the era of industrialization. Alice Foley, who was the youngest member of her family, never became a half-timer in a textile mill, unlike some of her school friends, because her father considered the system exploitative.[14]

According to the 1871 census of population, less than 1 per cent of children aged five to nine were in employment, while among those aged ten to fourteen, 32.1 per cent of the boys and 20.5 per cent of the girls were occupied. By 1901 those proportions had fallen to 21.9 and 12.0 per cent, respectively (see Appendix 1(b)). Although such figures almost certainly underestimate the true position, since many part-time, casual and seasonal child workers probably did not declare an occupation to the census enumerators, and in other cases parents may have exaggerated the age of youngsters who were in work, it is unlikely that this would materially alter the overall balance. Only in limited localities, such as the poorer areas of large cities, where children were widely engaged in casual labour, running errands, selling on the streets, and performing domestic work, might it be significant. In manufacturing districts tasks might include taking meals to relatives or neighbours working in the factories and, in the case of girls, acting as unpaid child minders for younger siblings or, for a small sum, to working mothers in the neighbourhood. Alice Foley had to hurry home from school at noon each day so that she could take a dinner to her elder sister, Cissy, who was a jack-frame tenter in a Bolton mill. The savoury 'hot-pot' was in a basin, with a towel tied round it to keep it warm, and there was tea in a 'billy can'. Thus equipped Alice ran off, to arrive at the mill at about 12.30. She went to her sister and then waited while Cissy ate the meal, before returning home.[15]

An older sister looking after her young siblings in Regent's Park, London, c. 1900. Girls were expected to take on a 'caring' role from an early age. (The author)

Alongside these continuing activities, however, technological change and the decline of certain traditional industries during the second half of the nineteenth century altered the nature of child employment. Apprenticeship, the traditional means of training youngsters in specialist crafts and trades, continued in printing, carpentry, plumbing, shipbuilding, and sections of the engineering and metalworking industries, although trainees now rarely lived in with employers, as had once been the case. But elsewhere the greater subdivision of processes and the use of new machinery led to youngsters concentrating on one part of the production process only. This was true of the boot and shoe industry, where the introduction of machines for closing and riveting led to an increased reliance on cheap boy labour. Clicking, or the cutting of the leather segments of footwear, remained skilled until the widespread recruitment of juveniles to cut the simpler patterns and leathers undermined apprenticeship here, too. When clicking machines were introduced in the 1880s, the trade's de-skilling was virtually complete. In the early 1890s a witness to the Royal Commission on Labour called semi-skilled boy labour 'the greatest evil we have in the trade' and claimed that 35 per cent of the clicking workforce was composed of juveniles.[16]

For girls, apprenticeship, usually to the dress trades, often became a euphemism for sweated labour. In the early 1840s young dressmakers were apprenticed in London at the age of twelve, although they only received payment when they reached fourteen. During the busy four months of the London Season their usual daily hours were about fifteen, but in an emergency could be eighteen or more. Similarly, an apprentice to a Bradford dressmaker earned just 1s a week, despite working very long hours. 'I suppose it was the accepted thing at the time . . . it was a matter of pocket money', she commented ruefully.[17] Small wonder that one medical man could claim that 'in no trade or manufactory whatsoever is the labour to be compared with that of the young dressmakers'.[18]

In other trades, including cottage lacemaking, mechanization and fashion changes undermined prosperity. Children were employed making lace in a number of market towns (as well as villages) in the south Midlands and Devon. Many began to learn the craft at about five or six years of age, since it was thought that only so could they acquire the dexterity needed to produce the best work in later life. Most attended one of the special lace schools which abounded in the lacemaking areas during the early Victorian period. These were unsatisfactory in almost every way. They were normally conducted in tiny cottage rooms by women whose prime recommendation was their lacemaking skill and perhaps their iron discipline in extracting the maximum output from their young charges. Although a few made ineffectual efforts to teach the children to read a verse or two of the Bible, education was virtually non-existent. The pressures under which youngsters worked were made clear by thirteen-year-old Caroline Chatwell, from Brackley, Northamptonshire. In the early 1840s she attended Mrs Buffin's lace school, where she had started at the age of ten. She began work each day at 8 a.m. and ceased at 5.30 in the evening:

> if I have not done my set work am kept till it's done; set nine hours and a half a-day; an hour at dinner, from 12 to 1. When it's very hot in summer we sit close against the door, and the windows open; feel very tired after a day's work, our arms ache so from working . . . ; very often about 10 o'clock feel faint, being so long without food; we breakfast before I go to work, about half-past six in the morning. About half a year ago was laid up seven weeks with water in the brain, the doctor said it was from sitting so many hours a-day; sat then about 11 hours . . . have better health now; have half a holiday on Saturday, have a day also at Christmas, Whitsuntide, and every fair day. When the missus gives us a slap with her hand, or a knock with a stick, it's not very big. A fire in the room in winter, but we don't sit near it, and feel our hands and feet very cold; work by candlelight in winter. We live very hard, have meat only once a-week; don't earn above 2d or 1½d a week.[19]

Not until 1867 was legislation introduced to regulate the hours and conditions of young workers in domestic trades like this, and even then enforcement remained difficult, given the scattered nature of the work units. But by then the craft was in decline, as a result of increasing competition from machine-made Nottingham lace and of falling demand from the dress trade. By the early 1890s its collapse was virtually complete.

But while jobs like these were disappearing, the expansion of the service sector, particularly retail distribution and transport, gave new opportunities for children to work as errand boys and girls, messengers, van boys, porters and the like. Errand boys might have to carry 'excessively heavy baskets' or be 'harnessed between the shafts of a ponderous and heavily laden handcart', while some youngsters were required to stand outside the shop, minding pavement displays or acting as door-boys for high-class stores. In 1901, 24.6 per cent of all the lads aged ten to fourteen who declared an occupation were employed in conveying 'men, goods, messages'. By contrast, textile production engaged less than half that proportion, at 11.8 per cent (see Appendix 1(c)). Walter Besant, in discussing life in late Victorian east London, concluded that in every trade an errand boy was considered essential: 'a greengrocer is lost without his errand boys; a suburban greengrocer in a flourishing way of business will have twenty boys in his employ; every small draper, every shopkeeper . . . small or great, must have his errand boy.'[20] Then there were van boys, whose duty it was to help load and unload boxes and parcels and to sit among them while they were being delivered, to make sure none fell off into the street or were stolen.

Other lads sought work in offices, where hours were long and pay often poor, but there was relative security and respectability. In 1853, one thirteen-year-old office boy recruited by a Liverpool dock company received a weekly wage of 4s for hours which extended from 8.30 a.m. to 7 p.m. each day.[21] Almost half a century later, a twelve-year-old Staffordshire lad went as a clerk in a shipping agent's office for 2s a week. There he copied letters, addressed envelopes, and delivered them to the post office. But his mother decided the paltry pay was not worth having, so after a fortnight he left. He returned to school for a year and then got another clerical post at a tile works. Although his headmaster gave him a good reference, he had to agree to be bound for seven years, in a kind of apprenticeship, in order to clinch the appointment. He began in the cashier's office, despatching the firm's catalogues to prospective customers. Later he moved to the general office, where he copied letters, and 'ran any errands that wanted doing'.[22] Nevertheless, the number of boys engaged in office work was always modest, with about 2 per cent of the juvenile labour force aged ten to fourteen so occupied in the early 1890s.

Throughout the period, only a minority of working children was employed in factories, responding to the relentless rhythm of power-driven machinery and summoned or dismissed to and from their labours by the ringing of the factory bell. Yet it was their plight, and that of youngsters in the mining industry, which concerned reformers and led to the passage of the first legislation designed to restrict hours and improve employment conditions.

By the 1830s change in certain preparatory processes had reduced the demand for children in sectors of the cotton industry, but this was counterbalanced by the need for more youngsters to work as piecers on the ever bigger spinning mules. J.R. Clynes, who was a piecer in an Oldham mill during the 1870s, remembered that although stricter limits were imposed on the age at which employment began and the length of the working day than had been the case early in Victoria's reign, the work was nonetheless exhausting. He started at the age of ten, rising each morning at about 4 a.m. in order to bolt a few mouthfuls of food before setting off

Boy selling matches in King William Walk, London, in 1884. (Greater London Record Office Photograph Collection)

to walk three miles through the pitch-black streets to the factory. Most families paid a 'knocker-up' to ensure that working members woke up in time to begin their labours at 6 a.m. A late arrival meant a fine and could lead to dismissal if it happened often. When Clynes first entered the mill he was deafened by the noise of the machinery, a feeling which most child workers shared:

> Clatter, rattle, bang, the swish of thrusting levers and the crowding of hundreds of men, women and children at their work. . . . Often the threads on the spindles broke as they were stretched and twisted and spun. These broken ends had to be instantly repaired. . . . That was my job. I performed it, unresting, in my bare feet, since leather on those oil-soaked floors would have been treacherous. Often I fell, rolling instinctively and in terror from beneath the gliding jennies, well aware that horrible mutilation or death would result if the advancing monsters overtook and gripped me. Sometimes splinters as keen as daggers drove through my naked feet, leaving aching wounds. . . . Running in and out, straining my eyes in the gas-lit gloom to watch for broken threads, my ten-year-old legs soon felt like lead, and my head spun faster than the pitiless machinery. But I had to keep on; the dinner-whistle would shrill some time soon; then I could rest my aches and regain my breath.[23]

Not all young workers were so fortunate in avoiding injury. Local hospitals reported cases of children badly mangled by the machines, like the twelve-year-old Rochdale boy who was caught by a strap and dragged into the engine. He sustained severe fractures of the legs and thigh which required immediate amputation at the hip. Sadly, he died within three hours.[24] Then there were three young girls working in Bolton mills in 1894. One had the greater part of her arm amputated in an accident; another had her eye so badly injured that it had to be removed; and the third lost most of her hand, except for the thumb.[25] Nor was this all. Youngsters in textile mills were prone to a range of illnesses, including skin diseases, poor eyesight, and asthma brought on by the dust and fluff. The heat in the weaving sheds caused a fever known as 'mill sickness', while the noise of the machinery affected their hearing.[26]

It was during the 1830s that the campaign against child employment in the textile industry first came to a head. Some reformers were inspired by humanitarian ideals, comparing the lot of mill workers with those of plantation slaves in the West Indies and the Americas. The Revd G.S. Bull was one of many who in 1832 condemned those 'who rave at the mention of Africa's wrongs' but could see 'a thousand redeeming qualities in white Infant Slavery, and its inexorable inflictors'.[27] The fact that in 1833 legislation was passed ending slavery within the British Empire added point to the debate. The mill operatives and their supporters also demanded change, one factory worker at Dewsbury telling an official committee in 1832 that 'English children were enslaved worse than the Africans'.[28] Others complained that the actions of some of the overlookers were like 'the doings of a West Indian slave-driver'. They were 'brutal beyond what would . . . be believed'.[29] The men set up short-time committees to demand a ten-hour working day and used the debate on juvenile labour not only to expose the hardships of the children but to press for a reduction in the working hours of adults. In the *laissez-faire* spirit of the times any direct attempt to achieve state regulation of the hours of men would have failed. But because juveniles aged ten to thirteen were a significant part of the factory labour force it was hoped that restrictions on their hours would improve the position of the rest. The adult operatives' main interest in legislation, it has been alleged, was not its direct influence on the child workers but its indirect effect on the wellbeing of adults. 'Measures aimed solely at children – such as educational, sanitary and health provisions – received little or no support', comments one critic; 'their specific recommendation for all abuses was always the Ten Hours Bill.'[30]

Many reformers also drew attention to the adverse effect the work had on the health and physique of the youngsters. They argued that this was undermining the future wellbeing of the nation's labour force. Even keen supporters of *laissez-faire* philosophy, like Thomas Babington Macaulay, called for state regulation on these broader grounds. If youngsters damaged their health by excessive work, that would reduce their productive capabilities later on. Overworked boys, declared Macaulay, would become 'a feeble and ignoble race of men, the parents of a more feeble and more ignoble progeny', and therefore a threat to their effectiveness as adult operatives. Even at the end of the century these arguments concerning the premature recruitment of youngsters were still heard. In 1901 the Interdepartmental Committee on the Employment of School Children maintained that:

> the too early employment of children may, like the premature work of horses, injure their future capacity, and . . . what is gained at the commencement of life is much more than lost at a later stage . . . Even on the lowest ground . . . of financial interest, it is not cheap to work a child so as to cause him to be prematurely worn out. It is more economical to start him in life after a healthy childhood with powers that will last longer, and keep him to a later age from being dependent on others for his support.[31]

That did not mean that it opposed all juvenile employment. Like many Victorian commentators on child labour, it favoured 'moderate work', which would not injure but would be 'in most cases . . . a benefit'. It left others to decide just what 'moderate' was in this context.

The debates which took place in the 1830s concerning youngsters employed in the textile industry led to the passage of the 1833 Factory Act. It covered all those working in textile mills except for silk mills. Under its terms, children under the age of nine were to be excluded from employment, while between nine and eleven (rising to nine and thirteen over an adjustment period of two-and-a-half years), they were limited to eight hours a day (or forty-eight hours a week). Between thirteen and eighteen years the working day of 'young persons' was restricted to twelve hours. In addition, those between nine and thirteen had to attend school for two hours daily, and to produce a voucher showing this had been done, before they could continue working. Thus was inaugurated the 'half-time' system combining work and schooling. It lasted in the textile industry, albeit on a declining scale, until after the First World War.

Card room workers at a cotton mill in Mossley, near Manchester. Some are half-timers.; all are wearing clogs. The small boy seated in the front row on the far left has his lunch box. (Tameside Local Studies Library, Stalybridge)

The exclusion aspects of the legislation had a minimal impact, since just 0.03 per cent of the cotton labour force was under nine even in 1833, before the legislation was introduced. In wool it was just over 1 per cent. Only in silk, at 2.77 per cent of the labour force, was it in any way significant, and silk was excluded from the 1833 Act.[32] The cynical might argue that the very youngest operatives were only forbidden to work when parents and employers had already decided their services were not required. More importantly, four inspectors were appointed to ensure the Act's provisions were observed. Although their policing role was at first resented by both manufacturers and parents, it soon became an integral part of the whole process.

Nevertheless, some mill owners, angry they had been singled out for regulation and unwilling to undertake the administrative duties involved in checking up on the conditions and schooling of young workers, dismissed all those under thirteen – thereby reinforcing the downward pressure on the recruitment of children. By 1839, only 48 per cent of Lancashire mills still employed half-timers.[33] Even 'benevolent' producers like Ashworths of Bolton, who already provided schooling for their workers, resented this selective display of the state's coercive powers. A few reacted by recruiting cheap and inefficient teachers to obey the letter if not the spirit of the law. There is, significantly, no evidence of an above-average surge in literacy rates in the textile areas after 1835, when the legislation began to be applied.

Parents, too, created difficulties. Some wanted their children to work in order to boost household income, even though the youngsters had not attained the legal minimum age. Deceit was encouraged by the fact that ages were difficult to establish at a time when there was no compulsory registration of births. Registration itself came only in 1837, and *compulsory* registration was delayed to the 1870s. Compliant medical men were found who would testify that an under-age child had the 'ordinary strength and appearance' of a nine or thirteen-year-old, this latter being the minimum for youngsters to work longer hours as 'young persons'. Even in the 1850s there were advertisements calling for 'boys, not younger than will pass for thirteen years of age' – the word 'pass' giving the game away.[34]

The children, for their part, were anxious to get through the medical examination so they could begin work. For, according to one contemporary, parents were furious if the factory doctor refused to pass a sickly or small child for half-time, and 'the child itself was considered disgraced, and snubbed at home'.[35] Ben Turner, who began in a Yorkshire woollen mill in 1873 when he was ten, remembered being anxious when he and other potential half-timers went to be examined. He need not have worried: 'We had to roll up our sleeves and show our [smallpox] vaccination marks. Then he just glanced at our teeth. I remember him saying to me, "Ah lad, but you're a little 'un," to which I responded – not wanting to be turned down – "Yus, but ah'm a good 'un".'[36] He was duly passed.

In other cases, parents produced forged birth records or borrowed the documents of older children in order to get younger ones accepted. In June 1874, Thomas Convine, a Bacup stone mason, was fined £2 and had to pay £1 5s costs for allowing two daughters to be employed as full-timers, although neither was thirteen years of age. It was noted that the defendant had 'uttered forged certified copies of birth'.[37] Occasionally the birth certificate of an older sibling who had died was produced. When questioned the children were well enough drilled to respond promptly with their 'factory age'.[38]

In the larger towns, too, youngsters changed jobs so frequently that the inspectors could not keep up with them. This affected school attendance also since many employers, for administrative reasons, insisted that all their half-timers attend a specific school. Hence the complaint of the headmaster of St James's National School, Bolton, on 12 May 1872, that the opening of a new board school had affected his numbers. 'Barlow and Jones' half-timers, about one hundred and fifty . . . , have been sent there from this school.' A week later, 'The children from Taylor's mill have not been this week, and I am informed that Slater and Beddows' have to be sent elsewhere on Monday morning next.'[39] In a town like Bolton, where so many older children were half-timers, such mass migrations hampered the running of a school, and by late June 1872 the St James's head was clearly growing anxious. 'The tide of scholars leaving school has been going on since May 12th,' he noted,

> & I find it the greatest difficulty to hit on the best mode of treating the children without their taking umbrage & leaving school. One girl in the 1st class H. Framley, whom I had threatened to punish if she did not leave off asking so frequently to go out, went to the mill & asked the Manager's permission to change school, which was granted – another girl in the same class asked for her copybook to-day, as her mother said that if H. Framley left she had to leave too.

In a Birmingham Soldering Shop.

Boys working at a Birmingham soldering shop. (From: Robert H. Sherard, The Child-Slaves of Britain *(1905))*

Although matters then settled down somewhat, as late as August 1873 the headmaster felt the need to go to Barlow and Jones's factory to question the manager and a clerk about their refusal to allow the firm's half-timers to attend St James's. It was to no avail.[40] A later head of St James's, Richard Waddington, was to be in the forefront of campaigns by the National Union of Teachers in the 1880s and 1890s to bring the half-time system to an end.[41]

The passage of a fresh Factory Act in 1844 reduced the minimum working age of children in mills to eight, but limited the working day of those between eight and thirteen to six-and-a-half or seven hours, while the half-day school session was now extended to three hours. Leonard Horner, one of the first factory inspectors, argued that with these shorter hours a child of eight would not be harmed by work in the mills. In practice, as we have seen, even before the passage of the legislation few youngsters of that age were being recruited.[42] In 1844, for the first time child workers in silk mills under the age of eleven were also covered by the Factory Acts.

After 1850, with the growing use of power looms in factories, large numbers of children were employed as 'tenters' by weavers (many of them women), since adults with child assistants could boost their output and income by looking after more looms. At the end of the century three-quarters of all the half-timers in Lancashire were in weaving sheds, rather than engaged in the spinning processes.

As tenters, they refilled the shuttles and fetched supplies of weft as and when needed. At the end of the week looms had to be swept and the alleys between the machines cleaned. Despite the fact that the 1844 Factory Act prohibited young workers from cleaning moving machinery, there continued to be serious accidents from this cause. Adults engaged on a piecework basis were reluctant to stop machines to allow for cleaning, since this reduced output and thus earnings. In 1899, it was declared that 'rarely, if ever, are tenters . . . permitted to stop their frames during mill hours to clean their card'. If an inspector arrived, warning signals were passed on: 'significant taps are made on the machinery and cleaning cloths and brushes drop on the floor as if by magic'.[43]

Sometimes children were employed in the morning from 6 a.m. until breakfast time. They would then go to school, before returning in the afternoon to work in the mills. Although such overtime was illegal, it was difficult to check. In the major weaving town of Blackburn the arrival of an inspector at one mill was quickly noised all over the town.[44]

In the later years of the century conditions in the weaving sheds and the card-rooms worsened. The introduction of new processes in card-rooms increased the amount of dust and floating cotton fibre, thereby causing more chest problems, while in a number of weaving mills, especially in Blackburn, 'steaming' was used to create artificial humidity. This allowed cheaper quality cotton to be used but made the atmosphere unhealthy for the workers.[45] The enervating mixture of heat and humidity, coupled with the unpleasant smell of cotton oil, left them drained of energy by the afternoon, and caused half-timers to be lethargic and inattentive when they were in school.

Harry Pollitt began as a 'tenter' when he was twelve, helping his mother, a weaver in a local mill. From the 1870s youngsters were allowed to work only if they could pass an examination in the three R's, signifying they had achieved a certain standard. One wet Saturday morning Harry and a small crowd of other boys and girls walked to the nearby town of Ashton-under-Lyne to take their 'labour' examination.

> All our conversation on the way was on what kind of sums they would give us. Would there be very hard words in the dictation? Would there be composition? We need not have worried. The mill-owners who controlled the educational bodies took precious good care that the biggest dunce in the school could pass it. . . . They wanted cheap labour, and intended to see that they got it. Within a very few days the certificate came saying that Harry Pollitt had passed and could now work half-time.[46]

Harry was delighted, but his mother was not. Although she needed his aid, since this saved her from paying another assistant to help with her four looms, she regretted the loss of his education. The first morning he set off proudly, but soon the long hours and the pressure of the job led to disillusion. Nevertheless, there was a brighter side. He was the only boy in that particular weaving shed, the other half-timers being girls. The usual pranks which adult operatives played on their juniors were played on him, although the weavers 'being a cut above the cardroom

. . . (as they thought) played only polite, ladylike tricks on me. It was left to the buxom girls and women in the cardroom to break me in by taking my trousers down and daubing my unmentionable parts with oil and packing me up with cotton waste.'[47] Even for children there could be companionship and fun at work, as well as drudgery.

Meanwhile public opinion in the textile towns continued to support half-time working, despite the growing criticisms from outsiders who saw it as a device for perpetuating juvenile labour rather than safeguarding the youngsters' health and welfare, as had been the original intention. The children, for their part, were also keen to work. A Bolton girl, who took her labour examination when she was eleven, in about 1898, entered for it without telling her parents. 'I wanted to go aworking . . . I wanted to be earning a bit of something, and . . . I passed, so I went and got a job on me own.' She became a tenter at 2s a week.[48] Similarly a Salford girl found herself a place as a hank winder. At thirteen she was earning 7s a week and out of this she paid for her mother's washerwoman. The mother had badly injured her ankle falling down some cellar steps and was a cripple.[49]

Adults, who had themselves begun working at an early age, were anxious for the system to continue, since they attached small value to a lengthy education. Many viewed it as 'a kind of *idleness*, incongruous with the organizing principle of family life in the nineteenth century'. They not only welcomed the children's earnings but regarded half-time employment as a good preparation for their future working life. As a correspondent to the *Cotton Factory Times*, the official organ of the cotton unions, put it in 1899, the half-timer was 'better clothed and fed' than 'thousands of the poor children' living in large cities, because of his earnings.[50] Even attempts to raise the minimum recruitment age were resisted. Nevertheless, this became ten in 1874 in textile mills, and in 1891 and 1901 was raised further.

Initially manufacturers of textiles had resented being selected for special legislative regulation, and had pointed to harsh working conditions in other industries. Claims were made that children too young to work in mills had gone to other, unregulated occupations which were still more unpleasant and dangerous. That included mining, until the 1842 Mines Act prohibited boys under ten from going underground, and women and girls from working below ground at any age. In 1872 the minimum employment age for boy miners was raised to twelve, but youngsters of that age could work full-time, whereas in the mills they were only half-timers. This caused ill-feeling among mill owners where the two industries competed for juvenile labour. The comment of one mother, upbraided by the factory inspector for allowing her boy to work full-time while he was under thirteen was indicative of general attitudes. 'Aw didn't know aw was duin' wrang', she declared defiantly, 'th' lad's a good scholar, aw suppose aw mun send him t'pit if you wunnot leet him work abuv ground.'[51]

In 1875 there were reports from factory inspectors in the textile districts that when legislation raised the minimum employment age from eight to nine, and then to ten, there was a great upsurge of applications from employers and parents for surgeons' certificates, covering 'all children of the neighbourhood who were then 8 years of age. By this means they are allowed to work . . . although under 9.'[52] Partly because of this the proportion of half-timers in textile mills reached a temporary peak of 12.5 per cent of the total labour force in 1874, compared to 8.9 per cent in 1871 and 11.3 per cent in 1878.[53]

Textile manufacturers still felt bitter at the way other mass-production industries remained outside the legislative net until the 1860s and 1870s. In the potteries, children were allowed to work from an early age when this was prohibited in textiles. Even in the early 1860s a minority of children began at five or six years, and in 1864 a factory inspector commented sourly on the way in which manufacturers placed the blame for this on their adult operatives, since these recruited and paid their own assistants; as a result, 'they, the masters, [had] no control over them':

> thus they attempt to get rid of the responsibility of this infantile employment. But the fact is, that, as they can and do discharge these children on the instant, and have discharged numbers who would have had to be sent to school had they been retained [under the 1864 Factory Act], so they might have discharged all the children at five years old that used to work before the Act was passed, had the moral question of their employment been impressed upon them.[54]

Charles Shaw of Tunstall began working in a pottery in 1839, when he was seven. He became a 'mould-runner' for a neighbour's son, who made plates. When a plate had been produced on the plaster mould which gave it the requisite shape, the boy helper had to carry it quickly into a hot stove nearby.

An emotive picture of children employed in a brickyard in 1870. The nine-year-old girl carrying the lump of wet clay had to walk about 12½ miles a day, from the clay heap to the brickmaker's table and back. The lump of clay weighed about 43 lb. (From: George Smith, The Cry of the Children from the Brickyards of England *(1879 edn))*

This stove was a room four to five yards square, shelved all round at regular intervals, on which the plaster moulds were placed . . . so that the soft clay plate just made could be dried to a certain extent . . . To enable the boy to reach the higher shelves in this stove-room, a small pair of wooden steps was used. Up these he had to run for all the higher shelves, say one-fifth of the whole number. He had to run to his 'master' with an empty mould, and return with a full one to the stove-room. . . . A boy would be kept going for twenty minutes or half-an-hour at a time, the perspiration coursing down his face and back. . . . Coarse oaths, and threats, and brutal blows in many cases following any failure to be at the bench at the required moment. . . . My wage was to be a shilling per week. For this large sum I had to work from between five and six o'clock in the morning, and work on till six, seven, or eight o'clock at night. . . The earlier hour only applied to Monday night, as the potters had a devout regard for Saint Monday. . . . On the other nights of the week work was rarely ever given up till eight o'clock.[55]

Another task was to get a fire lighted in the stove in the morning, so that work could begin at 6 a.m. Employers provided no kindling and boys had to prowl about the 'pot-works', picking up 'what they could of fire or wood'. If they failed to get the stove well heated in time, 'words and blows fell thick and fast'.

Concern at the poor education and long working hours of the children led to the passage of the 1864 Factory Act, covering pottery manufacture, and various other smaller unregulated trades, such as lucifer match making, percussion-cap and cartridge making, where there was a special danger of explosion, paper-staining, and fustian cutting, at which children were sometimes kept working as many as eighteen or twenty hours a day.[56] (See also Appendix 3.)

Three years later provisions were extended to various metal-working trades, while lace factories had been regulated by a special Act of 1861. The 1867 measure particularly affected the Birmingham area, the Black Country to the west of Birmingham, and the Sheffield cutlery trades. In addition, in a significant extension of control, regulation was applied through another 1867 measure, the Workshops Act, to small units employing fewer than fifty people. That included youngsters engaged in domestic industries like cottage lacemaking. These small workplaces were difficult to police and initially the task of regulation was given to local sanitary authorities rather than the factory inspectors. Only when this failed did the factory inspectorate take responsibility, in 1871. Even then the task of locating, let alone inspecting, countless backstreet workshops was virtually impossible, and the 1867 Workshops Act remained largely a dead letter. Ironically, too, even where the law was observed, easier conditions were imposed on workshops than on factories. Thus children in workshops did not have to be certified fit by a doctor, while provisions covering the fencing of machinery, ventilation, and the restriction of dangerous trades were less rigorous. In the early 1890s a representative of the Sheffield Federated Trades Council pointed out that youngsters who had been refused certificates to work in factories on grounds of poor health were able to gain employment in workshops, where the labour was more strenuous than in a factory.[57]

Some metal-working firms responded to the 1867 Act by dispensing with child labour altogether, rather than taking on the administrative responsibilities associated with it. The fact that night work was prohibited affected the attitude of the ironmasters, and according to one factory inspector, as a result of the new restrictions boys were 'practically expelled from the forges'. Certainly the number of lads under thirteen engaged in ironmaking fell from 2,686 in 1867 to 62 in 1871, while in foundrywork the drop was from 1,014 to 137 over the same period. By contrast the number of youths employed between thirteen and eighteen rose sharply.[58] Some excluded children moved into industries which were still largely, or entirely, unregulated, such as agriculture, brickmaking (with small brickyards remaining unregulated until 1871, and very imperfectly controlled thereafter), domestic service and street trading. Where no alternative work was available they simply ran wild, unless they were forced into school. For this reason in 1875 George Blenkinsopp, the sub-inspector of factories for the Wolverhampton district, pleaded for the age of boys working full-time in iron mills to be reduced from thirteen to twelve, since if there were no other trades in the area, they were debarred from work until they were thirteen. He considered this highly injurious: 'What are boys to do if they are not at work? They steal coal and get imprisoned; they will not work at all when they reach the age of 13 . . . Boys who do not work in iron mills till they are 13 will never, if they can possibly help it, work there at all.'[59]

In some towns, like West Bromwich, children were employed illegally at night, despite the efforts of the school authorities to prevent this. On one occasion Blenkinsopp claimed to have waited outside a large West Bromwich iron mill and to have caught a boy of eleven coming out; he had been working night and day on shift work for six months. 'Half a dozen others coming out caught sight of me, and at once bolted across a field.'[60]

Other inspectors pointed out that under the 1872 Mines Act boys over twelve could work full-time underground in a pit, whereas in an adjoining iron mill they could not become full-timers until they were thirteen. Children rejected by the iron industry on account of age were at once sent by parents to far more unsuitable work underground.[61]

The scope and effectiveness of the factory and workshop legislation thus varied widely even in the 1870s and 1880s, when its main principles had been established. Some industries were regulated while others, including domestic service, were not. Different Acts imposed different conditions on employers and their child workers, thereby giving rise to confusion and discontent. Thus while half-timers in textile mills after 1844 normally had to attend school for three hours a day, those covered by the 1867 Workshops Act need go for only ten hours a week. Again, while children could begin working at eight in factories and workshops until the 1870s, ten was the minimum for boys employed underground in the mining industry under the 1842 Mines Act, and this was raised to twelve thirty years later. Not until 1874 did the minimum age for employment in textile mills become ten. Four more years elapsed before that minimum was applied to other factories and workshops.[62]

During the final quarter of the nineteenth century, the use of half-time child labour outside the textile areas declined sharply. Even within the textile districts numbers fell, as the introduction of more complex machinery encouraged adult operatives to recruit adolescents as assistants rather than children. Only in districts of industrial expansion, where labour supplies were short, as in the cotton weaving towns of Burnley and Blackburn and the worsted centre of Bradford, did half-time employment remain buoyant in the 1890s (see Appendix 1(d)). In the year ending 31 August 1892, 54.5 per cent of the nation's 172, 363 half-timers were in Lancashire, and a further 26 per cent in Yorkshire (mainly in the West Riding), while Cheshire came third with 5.6 per cent, and Staffordshire and Leicestershire joint fourth, with 2.6 per cent apiece.[63] According to the Royal Commission on Labour about two out of every three children over ten years of age in Lancashire and about one out of every four in Yorkshire, Cheshire and Leicestershire, was a half-timer in the early 1890s. In Staffordshire it was one out of every fourteen children in that age group and, in the rest of England and Wales, about one out of every thirty-one.[64]

By the 1890s, therefore, juvenile labour was coming under strong critical scrutiny. When, in 1891, Parliament amended the new Factory Act, so as to raise the minimum working age of all half-timers from ten to eleven, *against* the wishes of the government, the move was welcomed by sections of the press in terms which questioned the validity of *laissez-faire* ideology. The campaigning *Pall Mall Gazette* referred to the doctrine as 'losing support in all directions, but in none more completely than in the matter of little children',[65] while the *Standard* observed ironically that 'the most rigid stickler for *laissez-faire* would hesitate about maintaining that ten is the age of discretion'.

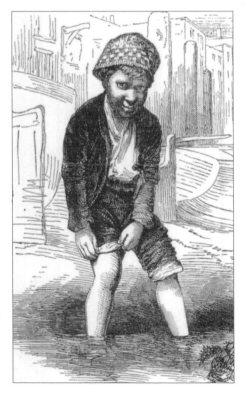

A London mudlark. Mudlarks worked at the edge of the River Thames, picking up coal, bits of old iron, rope, bones and copper nails dropped from ships. Copper nails were the most valuable of the items found. (From: Henry Mayhew, London Labour and the London Poor *(1861–2))*

Linked with this were international influences concerning juvenile employment. In 1890 a congress was held in Berlin, under German auspices, to consider the matter. At this Britain agreed to accept twelve as the minimum working age for factory children and fourteen for those going underground in the mines. Yet a year later, when the Home Secretary introduced a new Factory Bill the minimum working age was left at ten. He justified this by claiming that the Berlin Congress had been concerned with full-time employment and British half-timers were better off than their European counterparts, since only Denmark, of the countries represented at Berlin, had also adopted a half-time system. He added that if the minimum working age were raised even to eleven this would cripple the silk trade, which was already under pressure. In silk manufacturing towns like Macclesfield, Leek and Congleton about a fifth of the factory children were aged between ten and eleven. A.J. Mundella, a former vice-president of the Education Department, pointed out swiftly that the leading European silk producer was Switzerland, and the Swiss never allowed youngsters under fourteen in their factories.[66]

The *Child's Guardian*, journal of the National Society for the Prevention of Cruelty to Children, also listed the minimum ages at which children were allowed to take up factory work in other European countries. Whereas in England it was ten, in Switzerland it was fourteen, in Germany thirteen, in France, Austria, Belgium, the Netherlands, Portugal and Sweden, twelve, and in Hungary it was ten. Only Italy, with a minimum of nine, had a standard lower than that in Britain.[67] In a heated debate the Home Secretary's efforts to retain ten as the half-time minimum working age were defeated, and eleven was substituted. A further decade elapsed before new legislation fixed the minimum at twelve, as agreed in Berlin. In applauding the 1891 vote, *The Times* saw it not only as a benefit to children but as a 'matter of international good faith'. Although it was important for workpeople to be able to live in comfort, 'that they should be able to live in slightly more comfort is by no means indispensable when the improvement is obtained at the cost of their children's deterioration'.[68]

Others saw the issue as one of protecting children's rights as against those of parents. This was in marked contrast to the views put forward by Prince Albert and others in the 1850s, when the working man's child was described as part of his 'productive power'. Cardinal Manning, in supporting the Berlin proposal for twelve to be the minimum age for factory employment, stressed that children were 'not chattels . . . And if parents fail to protect . . . their children, the Commonwealth is bound to do so.'[69] Another commentator, Henry Dunckley, linked the issue to that of national efficiency. Although children 'belonged' to their parents they also belonged to the country:

In a few years they will enter into the material of which adult society is made, and we have to be on our guard against a damaged article. The nation has recognized its interest as well as its obligations by devoting millions of money every year to the instruction of the young, and it has a right to see that the utmost possible amount of benefit is derived from the outlay.[70]

Enlightened self-interest demanded that the state intervene if children's wellbeing were in jeopardy.

Yet, despite the growing numbers of young people protected against the most serious industrial excesses by the passage of labour legislation, there remained many working youngsters who were outside the legal safety net. That applied to those engaged in domestic service, which was a major employer of girls. Mrs Layton of Bethnal Green, for example, began to seek work as a 'step girl', cleaning people's doorsteps, when she was about nine. She was not very successful, and so at ten she went to mind the baby of a small general shopkeeper and to help in the shop. At thirteen she entered full-time service in Hampstead. Like many young maids in small households, she found the life very lonely, as she had no fellow servants to help with the laborious household tasks. There was plenty of food and her mistress was kind, but the basement kitchen where she slept swarmed with black beetles, and this kept her awake. She was only allowed out on Sundays to attend church, although sometimes, as a change, she took the three children of the household on to Hampstead Heath. Occasionally on a fine Sunday instead of going to church, she ran to see her married sister, who lived about a mile away. In order to avoid a scolding from her mistress, she lied about her failure to attend church, 'but there was always the risk of being asked what the text was'.[71] Later she went to a house in Kentish Town, where the mother died of puerperal fever after the birth of her fifth child, and the young maid had to look after five youngsters as well as carry out domestic chores. 'I had to work very hard, and very often was so tired with minding the children and doing housework that I have been found asleep on the stairs on my way to bed.' For this she received 3s a week, and used some of that to buy extra food for herself, 'as I always felt I could eat more than was given to me'.[72]

Also unregulated for most of the period were the countless youngsters who roamed the streets of major towns and cities, getting a living from whatever casual work was on offer. In London in the early 1860s it was said there was 'scarcely any age at which . . . money may not be earned'.[73] Interviews by Henry Mayhew about the middle of the century confirmed this. He estimated there were between ten and twenty thousand youngsters in the capital engaged as street sellers alone, offering anything from leather straps, matches, firewood, fly-papers, fruit and flowers to cheap jewellery, nutmeg-graters, shirt buttons, boot and stay laces and pins.

> Independently of the vending of these articles, there are many other ways of earning a penny among the street boys; among them are . . . tumblers, mud-larks, water-jacks, . . . ballad-singers, bagpipe boys, . . . porters, and shoeblacks. . . . A great many lads are employed also in giving away the cards and placards of advertising and puffing tradesmen, and around the theatres are children of both sexes . . . offering play-bills for sale.[74]

Others ran errands, carried parcels, and swept crossings. 'In the decade before the drive to force the nation's young into schools', comments James Walvin, 'there, was . . . an enormous pool of child labour surviving by its own wits and energies on the streets.'[75]

With the passage of education legislation in the 1870s efforts were made to restrict their activities, and by the end of the decade concern about the physical and moral effects of these street-trading ventures was growing in certain towns. In March 1878, Manchester Corporation approached the Home Secretary about 'the manifest evils resulting from the present practice of hawking newspapers, matches, and other articles by children of tender years at unseasonable hours.'[76] Two years later it pressed unsuccessfully for legislation to outlaw the practice. Finally, in 1882, when it promoted its own Corporation Bill, a clause was inserted to prohibit children under fourteen from selling on the streets after 9 p.m. from April to October inclusive, and after 7 p.m. for the rest of the year, unless they had attained a certain educational standard. In the following year slightly different street-trading clauses were included in the Sheffield and Birmingham Corporation Acts, and subsequently by Cardiff, Hastings, and a number of other towns. Elsewhere, as at Liverpool, Bristol and Newcastle upon Tyne, by-laws were drawn up to regulate street trading under the provisions of the 1882 Municipal Corporations Act. But they were difficult to enforce and in 1887 were invalidated when the High Court declared regulations drawn up by Newcastle upon Tyne Corporation were *ultra vires*.[77]

At this point the 'anti-cruelty' movement intervened. This had grown up in the 1880s, following the formation in Liverpool of the first English Society for the Prevention of Cruelty to Children in April 1883. It was based on a New York model and was followed in July 1884 by a similar body in London. Both organizations aimed primarily to protect children against physical ill-treatment by adults (including their parents), but their concern extended to those the London Society labelled 'child slaves' – youngsters sent out to beg or hawk on the streets until late at night. The Society appointed special officers to try to curb these activities, but the lack of an effective legal framework outlawing them made the effort unavailing. With the 1887 High Court decision rendering the Newcastle upon Tyne by-laws invalid, the London Society pressed for legislation to extend the protection already afforded young workers in factories, workshops and the mines to those earning a living on the streets.

Largely as a result of this lobbying, the Prevention of Cruelty to Children Act was passed in 1889. It laid down penalties for the mistreatment and neglect of children and prohibited boys under fourteen and girls under sixteen from singing, acting, performing for profit, or offering goods for sale on the streets or in licensed premises (other than those licensed for public amusement) between 10 p.m. and 5 a.m. Children under ten could not carry on these activities at any time, and fines or imprisonment could be imposed on those who caused children to break the regulations.

However, the debates surrounding the Act underlined the continuing ambivalence towards juvenile labour, particularly with regard to youngsters working in theatres and music halls. Originally it had been intended to include these in the prohibition on child employment under ten, but that evoked vociferous opposition not only from theatre managers and the general public but from parliamentarians, particularly in the House of Lords. As a result the Act was amended. Instead of child performers under ten being banned, those over seven

OFFICIAL CENSORSHIP OF PANTOMIME.

Policeman. "I WOULDN'T HAVE MINDED A QUIET PERFORMANCE; BUT TO BEGIN INSULTIN' THE LAWR UNDER MY WERY EYES!—(*Waxing wroth*)— MOVE ON! OR BLOW'D IF I DON'T RUN YER IN!"

Miscellaneous child workers, including a delivery boy, a newspaper seller and a shoeblack, forming part of the audience at a Punch and Judy show. (Punch, 1872)

could be licensed to appear by magistrates, providing that proper arrangements were made to secure their 'health and kind treatment', a conveniently vague phrase. Enforcement was put in the hands of the factory inspectors. It was a task they carried out with little enthusiasm.[78]

Benjamin Waugh of the NSPCC was scathing about the actions of those who had placed their own pleasures above the interests of the child performers. 'England has seldom shown herself to more disadvantage than she did in that pantomime fortnight', he wrote bitterly.[79] Not until 1903 did ten become the minimum licensing age for theatre children, at a time when the general minimum employment age was twelve (or eleven in some rural areas). Sir John Gorst, a former vice-president of the Education Department, condemned it as illustrating 'the immense influence which what is called "Society" . . . exercised over the British Government . . . Society, alarmed at the possibility of a curtailment of its pleasures' had pressed for theatre children to be exempted from stringent regulation, and that was what had happened.[80]

In 1894, a fresh anti-cruelty Act fixed eleven as the minimum employment age for children trading on the streets. In addition the hours during which they were forbidden to work were extended to between 9 p.m. and 6 a.m., instead of the previous 10 p.m. and 5 a.m. However, many towns were slow to enforce the provisions, partly due to fears of incurring expenditure by employing staff for the purpose. But the hostility of the employers of the child workers also played a role. They included newspaper proprietors and small tradespeople like barbers, milk dealers and shopkeepers, many of whom were well represented on local councils. They used their influence to discourage the adoption of measures likely to inconvenience their businesses.

Even cities like Liverpool and Manchester, which introduced a system of licensing child street traders following the 1894 Act, had little success. In Liverpool, where the licensing scheme came into operation on 31 March 1899, 1,146 children were given distinctive belts marking them out as licensed traders over the course of the next fifteen months. They sold newspapers, matches, hat guards, and similar small items.[81] But poverty in the city was so great that many unlicensed and illegal juveniles continued to work, and their activities were impossible to control. In 1904 the practice of arresting those found trading without a licence was virtually abandoned. On rare occasions only were parents prosecuted.[82]

Street selling was one way in which children could earn cash outside school hours, but there were many other 'moonlighting' activities they could take up. It was with these that reformers became concerned in the late nineteenth century. They included running errands, taking messages and, for the girls, domestic work. Their plight was highlighted by Mrs Edith Hogg in an article in the *Nineteenth Century* in 1897. She quoted evidence collected by the Women's Industrial Council upon fifty-four London schools, with 26,000 pupils from differing economic and social backgrounds. Of these, 729 boys and 523 girls were working for wages, or about 5 per cent of the total. That excluded the many youngsters working at home for parents or relatives without pay.

In a series of case studies, Mrs Hogg described the various tasks carried out and the paltry earnings. For delivering newspapers and milk the rate was about 1*d* or 1¼*d* an hour; shop work yielded a similar amount. For running errands it could be as little as ½*d* an hour. Of the 729 boys in the survey, 313 worked in shops and 102 sold newspapers, while of the 523 working girls, 135 were baby-minders and 115 were domestic cleaners. They included a boy of eight who delivered morning milk for 1*s* 6*d* a week, and another youngster who chopped lump-sugar 'for an uncertain number of hours' each evening for 2*d* a day. Then there were girls who worked 'at all hours' in such sweated trades as artificial flower-making, beadwork, fur work, box-making, paper-bag making and boot-sewing, usually alongside parents or siblings. But most hard pressed were the girls who carried out domestic chores for little or no pay:

It seems to the mothers only natural that a girl should help to clean, or baby-mind, and if there is no need of her services at home, then she can 'oblige' a neighbour. In the latter case she may get 6*d*, instead of 1*d* or 2*d* from her mother; but even if only 2*d* or 3*d* were offered, she would do the work all the same. . . . M.B., aged 10, minds a baby for six and a half hours daily and for thirteen hours on Saturday, for 6*d* and food. . . . C.D. turns a mangle for three and a half hours daily and for ten hours on Saturday for 2*d* and her food. Nor are the conclusions . . . more definite with regard to girls in home industries . . . Children of 7 to 10 years of age work five and six hours a day at artificial flower-making, getting for daisies ¾*d* a gross, for other flowers 1*d* to 7*d* per gross. . . . Furwork and jetwork brings them in about 6*d* to 1*s*, according to age; fancy box-making from 1*d* to 6*d* per gross; paper bags, 4*d* per 1,000.[83]

Mrs Hogg blamed large-scale casual child labour for the 'unpleasant fact' that of the boys leaving London's elementary schools in 1895, only 941 were traced to skilled employment, while 8,802 were known to have drifted into the ranks of the unskilled. 'The parents are too impatient for results to support their children through a long apprenticeship, the children too pleased and proud to be in a position of partial independence for any movement for the limitation of child labour to proceed to any appreciable extent from themselves.' Hence the need to extend the Factory Acts to cover these casual workers.

In November 1897 the Women's Industrial Council organized a conference on London home industries, which again provided examples of child overwork. Details were passed to the Home Office and the Education Department, and they prompted the latter to circularize the nation's schools, asking for information on pupils' out-of-school employment. The Home Office was less enthusiastic. In February 1898 the chief factory inspector argued that attempts to regulate children's work in the home would be little more than a 'pious opinion'. 'In a workshop or factory the mere presence of a child raises presumption of employment, but at home it suggests nothing. Home work could often be packed away out of sight at a moment's notice.'[84]

Shortly afterwards the Education Department's *Elementary Schools (Working for Wages) Return*, based on data sent in by the schools, revealed that of 147,349 working children identified, around a quarter were aged ten or less (with about 130 under seven). Approximately 28 per cent of the youngsters worked more than twenty hours a week, and 0.5 per cent fifty or more hours weekly. Many tasks were regular part-time commitments, like the boy who placed skittles for 34½ hours a week, from 6 p.m. to 11 p.m. daily, and who often fell asleep during afternoon lessons.[85]

In the light of this information and under pressure from the child protection lobby, in 1901 the Interdepartmental Committee on the Employment of School Children was appointed. Although it opposed a ban on child labour, it recognized the need for further regulation, at a time when an estimated 300,000 children were working for wages while attending school. These included 100,000 youngsters engaged in shop work and 50,000 (mostly girls) involved in domestic activities. Around 25,000 worked as street vendors, and the rest were in half-time employment in factories and workshops or in home industrial work, agriculture and miscellaneous occupations.[86] Not until 1903 did the Employment of Children Act seek to safeguard the health of these working children and to prevent their

Girls were frequently expected to collect water and to help with laundrywork either for their mother or for neighbours. (From: Mrs H.M. Stanley, London Street Arabs *(1890))*

employment interfering adversely with their education. Among its provisions was a confirmation of the hours during which boys under fourteen and girls under sixteen were forbidden to work, namely between 9 p.m. and 6 a.m. But local authorities could make these more stringent if they so desired. Unfortunately the Act's vagueness on certain points and its permissiveness on others reduced its value, and most local authorities were slow to draw up relevant by-laws.[87]

In many ways, therefore, despite the changes and the falling proportion of children under fifteen working full-time, youngsters continued to be 'used' by adults as economic assets to meet short-term financial needs or seasonal demand for labour. In seaside towns like Blackpool and Morecambe some spent the summer carrying bags for visitors, minding stalls, selling postcards and similar tasks. Most were influenced by parents in their choice of employment and, often enough, it was through family or older friends that they obtained their first position. A Lancashire boy who reluctantly took up mule spinning, recalled overhearing a fellow worker say to his father, 'I don't think your Bill likes spinning . . . !' To which the father replied bluntly, 'It's not what he likes, it's what he has to do!'[88]

Financial considerations also entered into it. A Bolton girl, who left school at thirteen, after working for a year as a half-timer in her mother's grocery shop, remembered she had 'always [been] more interested in confectionery, cake making and all that, but they couldn't afford to let me do it because you went for about two years for nothing', as an apprentice. She went instead to work full-time in a hosiery factory.[89] Similarly, a Blackburn boy, who became a tenter in a weaving shed at ten years of age, recalled bitterly that he had never been asked what he wanted to do for a living. 'I really wanted to be a Mechanic.'[90]

Although most children in the late 1890s did not work for wages, either full-time or part-time, a number slipped in and out of work on a short-term basis, particularly boys aged twelve or thirteen. But by then almost all parents recognized the benefits of education for their offspring and, except for the poorest, they accepted that childhood meant freedom from the responsibilities of paid work. There was, too, far less physical chastisement and thoughtless brutality towards the young than in earlier decades. Yet, when family circumstances demanded, child labour continued to be regarded as necessary and even laudable. Seebohm Rowntree, in his survey of York in 1899, repeatedly noted of the worst off households that 'as soon as the children [began] to earn money' they would be able to 'rise into a higher class'.[91]

There was a band of steel running through Victorian sentimentality towards children, which found expression in strict discipline and a feeling that they should 'compensate' parents for the 'kept' years of their early youth. Some claimed, too, that if youngsters began work as soon as possible they would become more skilful adult operatives than those whose entry was delayed. This ignored the fact that by the end of the century many boys, in particular, were entering unskilled jobs which they would have to leave when they became old enough to demand a man's wage. It was on these grounds that Jocelyn Dunlop, in 1912, referred bitterly to the sympathy accorded the 'paternalist', who urged the value of child labour in helping families combat 'temporary and accidental misfortune'. What was needed was not this parasitical dependence by parents on the earnings of their offspring, but a more generous provision of state aid in the form of sickness and unemployment benefit and the like, which would render it unnecessary. She condemned the 'unenviable legacy' bequeathed by the Victorians on the issue:

> The nineteenth century . . . raised juvenile labour to a fresh dignity, and regarded it as an independent factor in the labour market. As such, it stood in need of special regulations, and accordingly an impressive array of regulations were duly formed. . . . But the nineteenth century, content with its superficial diagnosis, made no attempt to prevent a child from spending years in work that made no call upon its intelligence, and from undertaking occupations that fitted it only for unemployment.[92]

Changes in production methods and the decline in apprenticeship reinforced these anxieties, with many young males entering 'blind alley' employment on leaving school.[93] Nevertheless, a minority of lads who entered a 'dead end' occupation were able to move to skilled work in their mid-teens. One London boy, for example, worked as a page, a shop boy, and a messenger before being apprenticed as a wood machinist, while a Staffordshire lad entered the carpentry trade after spending three years in the pottery industry. 'Among northern engineers', writes Michael Childs, 'it was common to begin as a half-timer, then become a full-timer in a textile mill before entering a fitting or turning shop.'[94] But these were the exceptions. A survey of London school leavers in the early twentieth century shows that most lads began work as errand boys, milk boys, or helpers to industrial labourers before moving on, by the age of sixteen, to become labourers in their own right, in industry or elsewhere. Out of a sample of one hundred and forty London school leavers, just twenty had become apprentices or learners at sixteen; seventy-nine were labourers, and fifteen were on vans.[95] Among the girls, domestic service was still the largest outlet, along with the dress and textile trades.

CHAPTER 6

Surviving

Consumption, rickets and malnutrition took their toll. The old cemeteries are filled with babies and young people. I remember at the age of 10 sitting in a carriage with the coffins of two little babies on our knees. Twin girls Doris and Lillian. In all, my mother lost ten babies. It was quite common to see funerals every day, mostly of young people.

Reminiscences of Mrs H. Jones of Orrell, Lancashire, b. c. 1887–8[1]

For all children the first years of life were the most hazardous, with about 25 per cent of deaths in England and Wales during the Victorian era accounted for by infants under the age of one. Youngsters under five contributed around 40 per cent of annual deaths over the same period, and one commentator claimed that to be an English baby at the beginning of the twentieth century was 'to occupy a position as perilous as that of a soldier about to go into action'.[2]

There were sharp differences between affluent and impoverished areas within every town, as we saw in Chapter 1. In London as late as 1901–3 well-to-do Hampstead had an infant mortality rate of 92 per 1,000 live births, whereas in deprived Southwark and Shoreditch the respective figures were 160 and 186.[3] Equally significant were the contrasts between towns. While 42.6 per cent of deaths in Portsmouth during 1880 were accounted for by children under five, in Liverpool that same year the figure was 49.6 per cent. In the Scotland division of the city alone it was a horrifying 62.1 per cent and in the Kirkdale district, 55.7 per cent.[4] Illegitimate babies were most at risk, with an estimated 35 per cent of such children born in manufacturing towns in the early 1870s dying before they reached the age of one. In London the proportion was nearer 75 per cent, with those babies put out to nurse with commercial minders particularly at risk.[5] Even at the end of the century the illegitimate infant death rate in the capital was about twice that for those born in wedlock.[6]

The high levels of juvenile mortality were largely due to deep-seated social problems, such as the overcrowded, insanitary condition of many homes, the effect of a poor diet, the lack of clean water, bad drainage, and inadequate personal hygiene. Few youngsters reached the age of ten without having personal experience of the death or serious illness of a sibling or other close relative. 'In the poorest areas of . . . cities, where could a child escape to when a relative was dying in its home?' asks James Walvin. 'Unless taken in by a neighbour –

themselves likely to be overcrowded – working-class children were obliged to witness the protracted and often painful process of death in their homes.'[7]

Symptomatic of this situation was J.R. Anderson's recollection that in his native Gateshead undertakers had special cabs for the funerals of babies. A glass-sided box was fitted under the driver's seat and the little coffin was pushed into the box from the side of the cab.[8] Walter Southgate, too, recalled that in Bethnal Green infants under one were buried in special white coffins. According to Walter, funerals were a major feature of East End existence, with three of his own parents' seven children dying young. They included his much-loved elder sister, Florrie, who died when she was nine and he was seven.

> I recall I crept up into mother's bedroom where Florrie lay crying and in pain. Her face was tear stained and its alabaster colour was heightened by her black raven locks. I climbed on to the bed to hug and comfort her until she fell asleep. The next thing I knew she was laying [sic] there in the coffin . . . with an angelic face and mother telling me, as a comforting thought, that her soul had gone to join the angels in heaven.[9]

Alice Foley, too, was deeply shocked when she returned home from school one day to find her sixteen-year-old brother in great pain from appendicitis. As a 'child of the streets' in Bolton she had encountered death, but only at a distance as 'something awful and mysterious' that 'would never happen to me and mine'. 'Occasionally a school play-mate fell sick and died. . . . The day before the funeral we trooped into the house of mourning to gaze our last on the dead face of our companion and, after the burial, we vulgarly pressed round the door in eager expectation of a piece of funeral currant-bread.'[10]

After the death of her brother, it was very different. The 'anguish and grief was too much for my overwrought sensitivity and for weeks I lay sick, striving only for mother's sake to return to normal life and activities'. Little wonder that a Somers Town headmaster, in London, remembered that pupils at his school were as likely to play at 'Funerals' as at 'Father and Mother'.[11]

Within the total of juvenile deaths, infant mortality was the largest single factor and it remained obstinately high throughout the century. In 1839–40, the national rate was 153 per 1,000 live births, and it stayed around that figure for the next forty years, before dipping a little to 144 per 1,000 births in 1876–80 and 139 per 1,000 in 1881–5. From then rates moved upwards once more to reach 163 per 1,000 births in 1899. This was the worst figure ever recorded.[12] The upsurge in the 1890s was largely due to a series of hot summers which, combined with the poor sanitation and hygiene of many working-class homes (including plagues of house-flies and vermin, as well as inadequate food storage space), led to outbreaks of diarrhoea. This could kill young babies in forty-eight hours. In the years 1898–1902 alone in a selection of urban counties (including Lancashire, the West Riding of Yorkshire and London), 21 per cent of all infant deaths were due to diarrhoea, enteritis and similar stomach disorders.[13] Even when babies survived these attacks many were seriously weakened and later succumbed to one of the epidemic children's diseases, such as measles, scarlet fever and whooping-cough, or to illnesses caused by damp and cold,

Middle-class motherhood used as an advertising device – in this case for Scott's Emulsion. 'For Coughs, Colds, Lung Troubles and building up after illness take Scott's Emulsion'! (The author)

like bronchitis and pneumonia. These latter accounted for 16.4 per cent of infant deaths in the urban counties between 1898 and 1902.

Babies fed artificially were especially at risk from intestinal infections, since most depended on contaminated cow's milk or nutritionally inferior tinned milk, or were given unsuitable substitutes like moistened bread and 'bits and sups' of whatever food was going.[14] At the end of the Victorian era the Finsbury Medical Officer of Health claimed that throughout London, milk had 'great bacterial contamination', with three-quarters of milk vendors in the Borough district alone failing to keep their supplies protected against dust and dirt.[15] A few years earlier his Bolton colleague recommended that all cow's milk for children should be boiled, as he considered it a prime cause of juvenile tuberculosis as well as a factor in stomach disorders.[16] Even the Manchester Children's Hospital was unable to procure milk guaranteed free from tuberculosis and by the 1890s was relying on sterilized supplies.[17]

Infants born to undernourished mothers were likely to be weak at birth and even if fed solely on breast milk would probably fall victim to disease. Some women would say of a sickly child, 'He hasn't come to stay; he's only lent to us for a little while.'[18] Premature birth, itself often the product of a mother's bad diet or too frequent pregnancies, also led to the death of many urban infants. At Middlesbrough Lady Bell described the disastrous toll exacted, with one wife giving birth to seventeen children, of whom twelve had died, and another to fourteen, of whom she lost eight. Out of 742 mothers whose husbands worked at the local steelworks, 275 had lost at least one child.[19]

Rickets, a common childhood complaint, was caused by environmental and dietary deficiencies arising from lack of sunlight and of vitamin D. In 1902 half the children in schools in the poorer areas of Leeds had had rickets although, interestingly, among Jewish children less than one in ten had been affected. This was because the Jewish diet was rich in vitamin D, including a high consumption of fish and fish products, as well as dairy produce. Eggs, fruit and vegetables were frequently eaten and 'Jewish women often combined together in the markets to buy large quantities of the cheaper fish. Herring, a fish rich in oil, figured widely in . . . diets.'[20] Jewish mothers breast-fed their children longer than their gentile counterparts and this, too, contributed to the relatively low level of mortality among their infants. For rickets not only led to malformation of the bones but it weakened the baby and increased his or her susceptibility to other diseases.

Croup, measles and whooping-cough were dangerous infant illnesses, too. In the mid-century years the latter killed more girls than boys, and in London it caused about one death in thirty, 'almost as many deaths as measles and smallpox combined'. It had no known cure, and parents resorted to folk remedies to relieve the sufferings of their children or else purchased patent medicines, like Hopper's Elixir, which pronounced itself 'The most Safe, Speedy and Efficacious Cure of Asthmatic and Hooping [sic] Coughs, Colds, Hoarseness, Difficulty in Breathing, Consumption, etc.'[21] Equally dubious was the claim by Roche's Herbal Embrocation for 'Hooping Cough, Croup' that it was the 'celebrated effectual cure without internal medicine'.

Croup, which especially affected small babies living in cold and damp conditions, normally disappeared when teething began. Unlike whooping-cough it was not a major killer. Nevertheless Elizabeth Gaskell was alarmed when her eldest daughter developed the disease in 1838. 'I heard a cough which though I had never heard croup I felt sure must be croup, & so thought Wm. [her husband].' He hurried to the Manchester Infirmary for medical aid and after a worrying night the treatment given 'got it under'. 'She has begun to come downstairs again muffled in a blanket, and is in capital spirits, though she still coughs at night & has got a bad tongue.'[22]

Less fortunate was the only child of Joseph Stamper's neighbours in St Helens. They were too poor to call in the so-called 'sixpenny doctor', who charged sixpence for each consultation. Although Joseph's mother arranged a collection among the other neighbours to finance the doctor's visit, it came too late, and the baby died.[23]

Traditional rearing practices might put the welfare of youngsters at risk, too. In urban Lancashire babies were rarely bathed in working-class homes and mothers of young children were horrified when the suggestion was made to them. Others refused to take their infants into the fresh air until they were several months old, thereby increasing their vulnerability to rickets.[24] In Sheffield a female sanitary inspector described one gloomy back-to-back home where a man, his wife and seven children lived with a paralysed grandmother. The eldest son, aged eighteen, was strong and fit, but the other children were all sickly. Four had had rickets, and the fifth, a baby, was 'getting rickety'. Some of the youngsters had been operated on to straighten their legs, but the real cause of the problem was that the grandmother sat by the fire, nursing each baby as it came along. As a result the infant rarely went out or used its limbs, 'and no breath of fresh air [was] allowed in the house'.[25] Only if this were changed would the situation improve.

Many mothers, unable to afford the services of a doctor or to join a medical club, supplied their own medication, preparing herbal remedies to cure fevers or to act as tonics. In other cases there were women like Mrs Stamper who, according to her son, acted as 'an embryo First Aid station' for the whole street:

> She had a little redwood box in the kitchen cupboard full of pennyworths of remedies. Flowers of sulphur, taken inwardly for pimples and blotches, mixed in oil to cure sores. Bicarbonate of soda, mixed into a paste for domestic scalds or burns. A penny packet of boracic crystals for bathing inflamed eyes; penny bottle of castor oil; senna pods; cream of tartar; Indian bark; a couple of homoeopathic remedies, aconitum and belladonna, for inward inflammation, these sixpence a bottle. And many others.
>
> For bandage Mother saved old white garments no longer wearable; cut into strips, boiled, dried, rolled, wrapped in clean paper, and stored in the 'red box'.[26]

Older children were encouraged to ignore relatively minor discomforts like itching, painful chilblains, running noses and sore spots. Or else, as in Walter Southgate's family, a mother would dose her offspring with 'horrible-tasting liquorice powder for constipation, brimstone and treacle for the blood, quinine, hot rum and boiled onions for a feverish cold, and hot salt laid on your stomach in a stocking for all stomach pains. Pepper, vinegar and mustard on brown paper were advised for toothache.'[27]

Because they failed to clean their teeth many youngsters suffered toothache. Even well-to-do children like Maria Cadbury complained of sleepless nights on that account, and of visits to the dentist, where fillings were inserted, only to be subsequently removed because they 'pressed against the gums'. Cotton wool, soaked with camphor, was then applied to the offending molars.[28] Among the poor, remedies could be still more heroic. A Bristol girl rubbed dry mustard on the gums to 'burn' out the pain. After a couple of applications she claimed it was successful.[29]

Some home remedies were more malign. The mustard-plaster prepared by a young London woman in the 1870s for her two-year old son's chest had caused a large open wound by the time it was seen by a district nurse.[30] Another youngster in Bristol became so addicted to brimstone and treacle that she almost poisoned herself. And in the mid-nineteenth century John Leigh, registrar for the Deansgate area of Manchester, claimed that a quarter of the infant deaths reported to him could be attributed to advice given by 'incompetent and unqualified practitioners'.[31]

The policy adopted by some working mothers of leaving fractious infants with child-minders, who then dosed them with opiates like Godfrey's Cordial, could be especially hazardous. In 1862 a Nottingham chemist, who was also a member of the town council, claimed to sell around 400 gallons of laudanum a year, half of which he believed was given to infants. And a Goole chemist, giving evidence in 1886 at the inquest of a baby that had died of laudanum poisoning, admitted selling 'plenty of it' every week.[32] Most infants escaped such overdosing but for a few unfortunates the practice, when combined with poor nutrition, proved fatal. Babies treated in this way became sunken-eyed and pinched of nose, and were 'so thin that you see nothing but bone'.[33] Some died of convulsions, while others went into a decline and succumbed to atrophy or wasting diseases. Even among survivors, a number ended up rickety and stunted, with crooked limbs, unsightly joints, and perhaps mental retardation as well.

As anxiety about the future health of the nation grew in the late nineteenth century, the importance of raising standards of maternal care was recognized as part of a broader drive for national efficiency. Much emphasis was placed on the value of breast feeding, while dirty homes were blamed for contaminated milk, rather than the farms and milk shops that supplied it. In a few towns these concerns led to the setting up of special depots to provide supplies of humanized milk under hygienic conditions. The first was opened in St Helens in 1899 and was based on a French model. Liverpool soon followed suit, with the milk supplied to mothers in batches of nine bottles, each containing a single feed.[34] Educational classes for mothers were also offered at the depots, but partly on grounds of cost and partly because medical men were reluctant to encourage any kind of artificial feeding, the schemes had limited success.[35]

The plans to provide maternal education won wider support. These ranged from the recruitment of health visitors, pioneered by the Manchester and Salford Sanitary Reform Association in 1862, to the teaching of infant care in elementary schools. In Stockport, the Sanitary Committee presented a prize to each school instructing the girls in elementary hygiene and infant welfare. Books on the feeding of babies were also distributed. Even some hospitals took up the instructional theme. By the end of the century the Hospital for Sick Children in Great Ormond Street, London, first opened in 1852, was teaching young and inexperienced mothers how to bring up their babies through a mixture of oral advice and the distribution of leaflets. Guidance was likewise offered to nursemaids employed by better-off families.[36]

The issue of maternal education was examined by the Interdepartmental Committee on Physical Deterioration, appointed in the wake of the Boer War disclosures about the poor physique of many would-be volunteers from large cities. The committee pressed for compulsory lessons in cookery, hygiene and domestic economy to be given to older girls in the schools. It commended the work of the Manchester and Salford Ladies' Public Health Society, formed in the late 1870s to bring 'within the knowledge of the mothers among the poor such information as will enable them to do their duty by their children'. The society's health visitors advised on sanitary matters as well as infant care.[37] Mothers learned how to prevent the spread of disease, 'and the laws generally which will enable them and their families to lead moral and healthy lives'. The linking of cleanliness and morality was a frequent constituent of the reform campaigns, and the didactic tone adopted angered more thoughtful working-class mothers, who were only too well aware of the environmental problems they faced. Not surprisingly, infant deaths were highest in families with the worst sanitation, the most contaminated milk supplies, and the poorest medical care.[38]

Critics also underestimated the nursing skills and the devotion of women seeking to do their best for their children, despite the odds. In the late 1880s, John Eldred contracted typhoid while living in a tenement off Walworth Road. He was about four at the time and Mrs Eldred nursed him with the help of a kindly doctor. 'She fought for me like a tiger', wrote John. 'I believe mother never took off her clothes during the entire term of my illness, but snatched what sleep she could in a bedside chair.' Through her single-minded care he recovered.[39]

Then there was the eleven-year-old son of a Bristol labourer, who caught typhoid in 1897 through drinking from a polluted stream near a tannery. His mother quickly realized that the illness was serious and without waiting for the doctor she took him to the Bristol Children's Hospital. This meant a long journey on foot, since they could not afford transport:

> I remember saying to my mother just before we got near the hospital . . . 'Well mother we got up here but I don't know how we are going to get back'. But I didn't get back and I was put into bed and it was the day before Queen Victoria's Diamond Jubilee, and there was tables all strewn with fruit and flowers and I thought to myself I'm in for a treat. But . . . I was unconscious and I remained unconscious for a month . . . at the end of the month I rallied round fit to go for convalescence and they sent me down to a little convalescent home they had in Clifton Road, Weston-super-Mare. . . . The nurses used to take us down on the sands twice a day. And . . . after three weeks I was as fit as a fiddle and came home.[40]

But it was his mother's prompt action in seeking treatment that saved his life.

Home conditions were of prime importance for child welfare, since even devoted parents were unable to prevent the spread of disease in overcrowded, insanitary dwellings. A survey of the larger towns of Lancashire in the mid-1840s revealed that of pupils attending St Matthias's Schools in Liverpool, 10 per cent of boys, 15.3 per cent of girls, and 24.5 per cent of infants coming from cellar dwellings regularly stayed away because of illness, whereas among those living in houses the respective proportions of absentees were 4.2 per cent, 5.9 per cent, and 2.3 per cent. Similarly a study of six Manchester schools showed a 40.8 per cent sickness rate among youngsters living in cellars and a 34.6 per cent rate among those living in courts, compared to just 11 per cent among those whose homes were in ordinary streets.[41] By the end of the century some of these differences had been eliminated through improvements in sanitation and in the water supply, but bad housing and overcrowding remained important factors in child ill-health throughout the Victorian period.

For older children epidemic diseases like scarlet fever, measles, diphtheria and smallpox were serious hazards. Scarlet fever increased in virulence from about 1840 until the 1870s, when its severity moderated. Although the death rate was highest among infant victims under twelve months, nearly half of whom died, the greatest incidence of the disease occurred among children aged four to eight. Often it came in localized epidemics, especially in late summer, and it was frequently associated with contaminated milk. It was worst in the towns of Lancashire, the West Riding of Yorkshire, the Black Country, Durham and South Wales, as well as London.

Children waiting for food in Cheapside, London, c. 1900. Charity was an important means of support for the poorest youngsters. (The author)

Unlike many children's diseases it also affected the well-to-do severely. Dr Tait, later Archbishop of Canterbury, lost five of his seven children from scarlet fever within a month in 1856.[42] Not until the mid-1880s did the link between contaminated milk and local outbreaks become firmly established, with dairymen found who were milking cows and selling milk while their own children were at home ill with the disease.[43] The fact that the better-off purchased more milk than the poor made them especially vulnerable to this particular means of transmission. In other cases, as with many of the infectious diseases, it was passed on through coughs, sneezes and personal contact. Infection was most acute when patients were at the peeling stage and the scaling skin showered everywhere. Contact with the clothes, dishes or even the bedroom dust of a victim could lead to the spread of the disease. The custom of visiting the dead and of holding large funerals was another way in which neighbouring children and relatives became infected. On occasion magistrates had to order that the body of a child who had died from scarlet fever be taken to a mortuary because of the number of visitors crowding into the home.[44]

In the last years of the century scarlet fever became less virulent, partly because the streptococcus was not so potent and partly through the introduction of a policy of notifying the disease to the authorities and isolating sufferers in newly constructed fever hospitals. Yet throughout the Victorian era scarlatina remained a major killer of children, with 95 per cent of all deaths from the disease involving youngsters aged ten or less.[45] Even survivors could suffer long-term effects. Investigations at Newcastle Institute for the Deaf and Dumb in 1894 revealed that 44 per cent of the 219 children in its care had become deaf mutes after scarlet fever. This compared to 33 per cent so afflicted through meningitis and 21 per cent who had had measles.

Measles, too, was highly contagious. It was spread through droplet infection or personal contact and was especially dangerous for the malnourished. In peak years like 1863 and 1874 it killed more children than scarlet fever.[46] Yet poor parents, whose offspring were most likely to be victims, were stoical about its effect, often failing to seek medical aid from a dispensary or outpatients' department at a hospital, even when it was free. In 1862 a St Pancras couple, who had lost two children aged four years and ten months, respectively, told the doctor they had considered measles too 'unimportant' to seek assistance.[47] Some mothers and fathers, on discovering that their child was seriously ill, concluded it had 'received the death stroke' and from that moment ceased to look for remedial measures 'beyond their own resources, quietly awaiting the child's death'.[48]

The failure to take effective action over childhood diseases angered the Portsmouth Medical Officer of Health. In 1891 he condemned the cavalier way even 'educated' people neglected to isolate measles cases:

some . . . go so far as to make their healthy children mix with their children who have measles with the idea that it is fated for everyone to have measles sooner or later, but there is no such fate and this carelessness or worse . . . leads to immense trouble and sorrow. In the ten years 1881–90 611 [Portsmouth] children died from the disease. How many suffered from this . . . and the many diseases which follow in its train is difficult to know. Whooping cough is another of these children's diseases which are considered by many to be trifling yet it results in many deaths, 509 in the ten years 1881–90. Greater care needs to be taken to isolate these diseases.[49]

Diphtheria, the third potentially fatal epidemic disease among children, emerged as a serious threat in the mid-1850s. It, too, was passed on through saliva and through touch, although outbreaks were also traced to contaminated milk. Among working-class children it spread through overcrowded homes and schools, proving especially lethal to those who were poorly fed. In London, where the publicly financed Metropolitan Asylums Board (MAB) began providing isolation hospitals for scarlet fever, typhoid, typhus and smallpox victims from the early 1870s, diphtheria cases were not admitted until the end of 1888.[50] Before that date isolation was difficult to achieve for many of the capital's sick children. The fact that the death rate was high made doctors fear that once the infection entered a hospital it would spread quickly. One estimate suggested that even in 1891 only 30 per cent of the diphtheria cases notified in London were admitted to the general and fever hospitals which catered for the disease. Not until the introduction of antitoxin serum in 1894 was there an effective treatment, and a sharp fall in mortality rates. However, the new treatment seems to have benefited the upper classes disproportionately because antitoxin was expensive, and was not distributed free to the needy. Birmingham, a notorious centre for diphtheria, did not supply free antitoxin serum until 1902.[51]

Overall from 1871 to 1899, 88.3 per cent of scarlet fever admissions to MAB fever hospitals and 87.4 per cent of diphtheria admissions were of children under fifteen, while the under-fifteens contributed 95.9 per cent and 97.6 per cent, respectively, of the deaths from the two diseases. These fever hospitals were thus primarily paediatric institutions and in that way they benefited both the families of the sufferers and the wider community, by isolating cases and thereby inhibiting the spread of disease; '. . . Parents in fever-stricken homes were relieved of the anxiety and fatigue inseparable from nursing sick children; . . . while the young patients were saved from the hazards of inadequate home-nursing and the after-effects, sometimes permanent, which deprivation of specialized care and convalescence entailed.'[52]

However, they had their darker side. In July 1875, three children named Bird were admitted to the Homerton fever hospital from St Marylebone parish suffering from scarlet fever. The next day Mrs Bird's six-month-old son was diagnosed as suffering from it, but on arrival at the hospital she found that one of the older children had already died. Despite this and the fact that the baby was already desperately ill, she was not allowed to remain to breast-feed him. It was said he was 'too weak to take lacteal nourishment from her'. Instead he would be placed in the hands of a skilled nurse. Two days later he died, without his mother being present. So incensed were the St Marylebone Poor Law guardians at this callous treatment that they contacted the Local Government Board, which had jurisdiction over MAB hospitals, to protest. But little was achieved, beyond a bland statement from Homerton that henceforth if the medical superintendent agreed, a mother would be allowed to remain with her child, should she so desire.[53]

There were also dangers from cross-infection. Two young children who were admitted to the MAB fever hospital at Stockwell in the early 1880s suffering from scarlet fever, subsequently developed smallpox. One of the unfortunates later contracted measles. Happily both of them recovered.[54]

Outside the capital, isolation wards and fever hospitals were slow to appear. In 1891 only about 400 of the 1,510 provincial sanitary authorities made arrangements to isolate infectious diseases. Some relied on workhouse facilities; in other cases, as at Manchester, sums were paid to a local infirmary for use of its isolation department. Preston, a notoriously unhealthy town with a population of over 107,000, had no fever hospital in the early 1890s.[55] Elsewhere, as at Windsor, fears among residents about the introduction of infectious diseases to their locality hampered developments. At Windsor, a temporary, corrugated-iron smallpox hospital was erected away from the town, alongside the sewage farm.[56] In 1896 fierce opposition emerged in the Surrey village of Carshalton when it was known that the MAB had purchased land on which to build a convalescent fever hospital for children from London. It was argued that ambulances carrying the convalescent patients might bring infection. Despite the protests construction went ahead, but over a decade elapsed before the hospital came into use.[57]

Portsmouth relied on accommodation in the workhouse infirmary until the 1880s, but most people were reluctant to allow their children to enter an institution which carried the stigma of pauperism. One mother 'indignantly denied the right of anyone to pauperise her husband' when it was suggested that her children, suffering from scarlet fever, should be removed to the infirmary.[58] Not until the passage of the 1885 Medical Relief (Disqualification Removal) Act did men cease to be classed as paupers merely because they, or members of their family, had made use of Poor Law medical treatment or hospital facilities.

There were also anxieties about the cost of running an isolation hospital and doubts whether the public would take advantage of it, even if it were provided. In January 1877, following a serious scarlet fever outbreak the previous year, a Portsmouth alderman asked whether fellow members of the local board of health would like a Medical Officer to 'drag' their own offspring to hospital if they caught the disease. 'His own wife, he knew, would make any sacrifice in order that her children might . . . remain under her own care. And he believed others would do the same.'[59] But the Medical Officer stoutly maintained that isolation alone would halt the course of an epidemic:

> What has occurred at Portsmouth . . . should be a lesson to sanitary authorities all over the kingdom. . . . [It] shows the inutility of . . . measures, such as the disinfection of houses, clothes, drains, &c. without a hospital in which infectious cases can be separated. During this outbreak 498 houses have been fumigated, together with clothes and bedding . . . 1,200 visits have taken place. Yet I believe . . . they have not influenced the course of the disease one iota; nothing but isolation in the early stages will ever succeed.[60]

Eventually a twelve-bed isolation hospital was opened in Portsmouth in 1883, but when a fresh scarlet fever epidemic broke out four years later, only 56 patients out of 647 people affected availed themselves of its facilities. Not until the early 1890s was this reluctance to use the hospital finally overcome, with 532 of the 1,023 scarlet fever cases in an epidemic during 1892 treated at the hospital. Soon plans were being made for its extension.[61]

The initial unwillingness of Portsmouth parents to use the isolation hospital for their children was symptomatic of wider suspicions about public intervention in the health field, beyond the sphere of sanitary improvement. That was particularly clear with regard to smallpox vaccination – the one area where there was an official programme to control an infectious disease. The serious smallpox epidemic of 1837–40 led to the passage of permissive legislation in 1840 authorizing vaccination at public expense, and placing on Poor Law authorities the duty of carrying it out. Thirteen years later came compulsory legislation, requiring parents to have their infants vaccinated within three months of birth. Although the new measure made the process more common, some parents still ignored it, either through indifference or on grounds of conscience. Finally, following a fresh smallpox outbreak between 1870 and 1873 (in which about 44,000 people died, nearly a quarter of them in London) a new Smallpox Act was passed in 1871. It imposed fines of up to 25s on those refusing to have their children vaccinated, and imprisonment for non-payment of the fine. Within two years around 85 per cent of infants were being vaccinated but there remained a hard core of parents who on religious or political grounds argued that individual rights must be defended 'against this new menace of a doctoring state'.[62] They included mothers like Ann Supple, who received twenty-five summonses for refusing 'to be party to the poisoning of her baby', as she put it. Parents such as she were prepared to go to gaol rather than submit to vaccination.[63]

Leicester, whose good smallpox record was due to a rigorous policy of isolating patients and their relatives, was a major centre of opposition to the new compulsory measure. The Leicester Anti-Vaccination League was formed in 1869 and over the next fifteen years there were sixty-one imprisonments in the town for non-compliance with the legislation. In 1885 it was the focus of a large demonstration attended by representatives of anti-vaccination groups from over fifty towns.[64]

Banbury in Oxfordshire was another centre of resistance, with an anti-vaccination post opened near the vaccination point, displaying such banners as 'Mothers Beware!' It also provided borax to wash the vaccine from the arms of children who had been compulsorily injected.[65] Although Banbury's Anti-Vaccination League had a middle-class leadership, most of its supporters were working men.[66]

Another determined opponent of compulsion was Ben Turner, a Huddersfield textile worker and trade union activist. He was repeatedly fined for failing to have his children vaccinated until he moved to Leeds, where despite his continued refusal to cooperate no action was taken against him.[67]

Eventually a drop in the incidence of smallpox (partly as a result of the reviled vaccination campaign and partly because of the disease's reduced virulence) persuaded the government to introduce a 'conscience clause' in 1898. This allowed parents to apply to the courts to avoid the compulsory vaccination of their offspring. 'The last time I appeared in court for one of my children', wrote Ben Turner, 'was to swear before the bench that I had a conscientious objection, and to pay 3s 6d for court costs in doing so.' Turner's opposition was based more on his dislike of compulsion than of vaccination itself, and when some of his offspring were treated during a later smallpox epidemic, he had himself revaccinated.[68]

The change led, however, to thousands of unvaccinated babies by the end of the century, so that from an estimated low of

> only 3.8 per cent of all registered births in England and Wales in 1875 and 5.7 per cent in London in 1881, the percentage of unvaccinated babies rose steadily to 22.3 per cent and 26.6 per cent respectively in 1898. The reduction in . . . vaccinations suggests not only the decrease in its urgency with the decline of the disease . . . but the degree of apathy, or ignorance toward preventive medicine which still prevailed and the strength of feeling about being bullied by a paternalistic state into good health.[69]

A similar anti-authoritarian mood may account for the readiness with which schools were blamed for the spread of epidemics among pupils, after the introduction of compulsory attendance between 1870 and 1880. Log books show some justification for the concern in that outbreaks of infectious diseases are reported with monotonous regularity. Diphtheria was passed on through slates and pencils, which became impregnated with children's saliva, and by class recitations where children breathed into each other's faces, or perhaps by the use of a communal iron cup attached to an outside tap or water container. At the

Beneficial Girls' School in Portsmouth, to quote but one example, a measles epidemic early in 1863, during which one child died, was followed a year later by an outbreak of smallpox. From 25 February to 22 June 1864, at least eleven girls were away with that disease, and again there was one fatality. The end of the year saw the return of measles, as well as whooping-cough among some pupils. Measles continued into 1865, with around a dozen pupils (or about one in ten of the scholars) suffering from the disease between 22 May and 3 June.[70]

If epidemics became widespread schools might be closed by Medical Officers of Health, but there were those who argued it was better for pupils from non-affected families to continue to attend so that their health could be monitored, rather than allowing them to stay at home, where they would probably mix with children already sick. This was the view of the Medical Officer of the London School Board in 1897 following a diphtheria outbreak in some of the capital's schools. 'My own strong opinion is that the closing of schools is a distinct danger in itself. It throws infected and susceptible children in unrestricted association', he declared. 'School discipline and organization, on the other hand, can be made a valuable help to the Sanitary Authority in checking the spread of disease', with daily examinations conducted in class. Significantly the epidemic began to decline once extra temporary isolation facilities had been supplied to accommodate the sick children away from home.[71]

Nor were elementary schools the only educational establishments affected by infectious diseases. In the middle-class sector an outbreak could threaten not only the pupils' health but the existence of the institution itself. In 1875, 'low fever', later identified as typhoid, broke out at Uppingham, the boy's public school, and the head feared this would mean the end of the prestigious establishment he had built up. It was decided to evacuate the school to North Wales and to stay there for a year until the drains had been attended to and the locality was declared safe.

The chairman of the governors of the Royal School, Lansdown, Bath, compared the effect of outbreaks of measles and scarlet fever to 'the devastation caused by the Jutes and Vikings'. In this case the school was closed for a term in 1897 while new drains were installed. Perhaps most feared was diphtheria and when a case appeared, pupils were sent away as speedily as possible. If this were impossible, as in the case of schools catering for missionaries' children whose parents were overseas, pupils went to friends or relations, if these were available, or stayed at the school under the care of the staff.[72] As Gillian Avery notes, before antibiotics, 'the shadow of epidemics hung over all schools . . . ; scarlet fever and diphtheria could kill a school as well as the pupils', as parents hastened to remove their children from 'suspect' institutions.[73]

Worst affected of all were establishments associated with the Poor Law, where overcrowding was endemic, especially during the early Victorian years, and the poor health of many youngsters on entry made them vulnerable to infections. At St Pancras workhouse in 1856, a doctor described the wards for children as so overcrowded and lacking in ventilation that the youngsters vomited each morning, apparently from lack of oxygen and from the stench.[74] In one room children slept four to a bed and in another eight; in the former room, fifteen sick youngsters were intermingled with the healthy, 'but the vitiated atmosphere and the undernourishment of the children' soon made them all ill. Nor were the specialist district and workhouse schools opened from the late 1840s much improvement.

In 1852 the Plashet school was set up in London and almost immediately there were reports of widespread scabies and ophthalmia, a highly infectious eye complaint. In April 1853 scarlet fever broke out. Throughout the 1850s and 1860s the medical officer examined the 250 to 300 child inmates each Saturday morning. A sixth of them were in hospital in 'normal' times but this often reached a half, with fevers never absent. By 1857 ophthalmia had become so widespread at Plashet that the guardians applied to the Poor Law Board for permission to pay ten guineas to the London Ophthalmic Hospital so that pupils could be treated. In 1858 an epidemic of whooping-cough was followed by mumps, and plans had to be made to extend the infirmary. The outbreaks of disease at Plashet continued until the school was closed in 1869.[75] But even when new or adapted schools were opened in the 1870s, disease plagued these pauper institutions. One Local Government Board inspector in 1873 found that half the children in London Poor Law schools were suffering from ophthalmia, and although eradication programmes were implemented, infection remained a constant danger in the large urban establishments all over the country to the end of the century.

Working children could also face hazards connected with their employment. In 1843 it was pointed out that the dry grinding process used in the manufacture of Sheffield cutlery caused serious respiratory and pulmonary diseases, including phthisis.[76] Twenty years later, the ill-health of boy file-cutters was commented on, including mention of 'their complexion with its dirty, sallow, yellow-white hue . . . [and] blue line around the gums'.[77] One boy, aged eleven, suffered from 'a fearful cough'. He had been a grinder since the age of eight and when he was examined by a doctor it was found that the upper portion of both lungs was extensively diseased. Among themselves the grinders recognized the danger they faced by the phrases they used. 'Fork grinders were said to "go off like dyke water, so quick",' if they started young, and a scissor grinder aged eighteen thought 'he should go off'.[78]

Other industries had their occupational diseases. In Macclesfield and the silk towns generally young piecers suffered from tuberculosis as a result of constant stooping, aggravated, presumably, by the atmosphere in which they worked.[79] In the textile industry generally and in the metalwork trades of Birmingham and the Black Country, fingers, hands and even arms were mangled in accidents at work. At the Queen's Hospital, Birmingham, a house surgeon claimed that half the outpatient accidents among child workers involved the loss or injury of fingers and thumbs from stamps and presses. One fourteen-year-old had recently lost an arm by being drawn in between the rollers in a rolling mill, as he stood 'on the putting-in side of the rollers'.[80] Yet more disturbing was the fate of an eleven-year-old London lad who had worked at sandpaper-making for just three weeks before suffering severe respiratory problems. Although taken to the Royal Infirmary for Diseases of the Chest, he died from exhaustion about a month from the time he began work. As a result of this case the doctor examined two of the boy's fellow workers, who were about the same age. They, too, suffered from the same complaint and also died. This fatal chest disease, caused by the inhalation of particles of sand and powdered glass during the manufacturing process, was said to be 'common' among children making sandpaper[81] (see also Appendix 3).

Initially few juveniles went into hospital. In January 1843 a survey of London hospitals revealed that of 2,363 patients, only 26 were children under ten suffering from diseases 'peculiar to their age', and about 136 children under ten were in hospital altogether. Medical knowledge of childhood diseases was very limited, not least because of the lack of opportunity to study them systematically. Only in the case of accidents, industrial diseases and cures for deformities were children normally admitted. This was partly because hospital authorities were wary of taking in youngsters who would require a good deal of nursing and were highly susceptible to infection. Parents, too, were reluctant to leave their offspring in the alien atmosphere of a hospital, and there is evidence that the children themselves shared those reservations. One youngster, rushed to hospital with a badly spiked arm and in danger of amputation, later remembered, 'They put fourteen stitches in the arm while I sat dumb with fear, not through my injury, but petrified by the bevy of white vestments around'.[82]

As a consequence, the dispensaries and out-patient departments of hospitals were particularly important in treating children. In the 1840s the Children's Dispensary in Manchester, first opened in 1829, was treating about two thousand patients annually. Its waiting room became so crowded that to avoid disagreements 'a system of numbered tickets was introduced'.[83] The Royal Universal Dispensary for Children in Waterloo Road, London, was also very

Visiting day at Great Ormond Street Children's Hospital, London, c. 1900. (The author)

popular and it was a leading physician there, Charles West, who determined to establish a specialist children's hospital to match provisions made in many other leading European cities, including Paris, Berlin, Frankfurt, Copenhagen, Vienna and Moscow. With the help of friends and a determined fund-raising campaign, the Hospital for Sick Children was opened at Great Ormond Street in February 1852.[84] It admitted as in-patients children aged between two and twelve years of age, infants under two usually not entering as in-patients because of the undesirability of separating them from their mothers. But very young children were treated in the out-patient department, and by the mid-1860s around 44.5 per cent of the total comprised children under two, with a further 14.2 per cent aged between two and three years.[85] Of 11,685 out-patients treated at Great Ormond Street in 1865, 1,528 were suffering from diseases of the skin, 1,011 from coughs, 978 from rickets, and 941 had diarrhoea. Among the 658 in-patients treated in the same year, diseases of the bones and joints, tubercular illnesses, inflammation of the lungs, and scarlet fever predominated. There were eighty-one deaths, including nine from 'congestion of the brain' and eight from inflammation of the lungs.[86]

Initially the hospital had only ten beds but by 1865 these had increased to seventy-five, and further expansion took place to the end of the century, with two hundred and forty beds in use by June 1893.[87] Well-to-do subscribers were encouraged by being allowed to nominate patients for treatment and by knowing that as the care and understanding of children's diseases improved, their own offspring would benefit. There were also regular fund-raising campaigns. In 1854, *Fraser's Magazine* praised the treatment given and the order and cleanliness of the wards. Among the convalescent children was a 'merry young gentleman . . . trundling a hoop under difficulties, running after it with the assistance of a crutch'. He had been treated for a severe disease of the hip. Then there were two or three girls, laughing as they played on a roundabout. They had recovered from 'some serious affection of the chest', but looked 'more healthy, and in better spirits, than half the children you meet in the fashionable squares'. In *Fraser's* view wealthy mothers who subscribed to the hospital were 'twice blessed: the poor will be benefited directly, the rich ultimately, by the skill and experience acquired here by those to whose care their own sick children may hereafter be entrusted'.[88]

In Manchester the efforts of a German-born refugee, Louis Borchardt, led to the provision of in-patient care at the Children's Dispensary. In 1855 this was renamed the General Hospital and Dispensary for Sick Children, and its objects were defined as 'The Medical and Surgical Treatment of Poor Children'. It, too, expanded rapidly and by 1868 was treating 7,000 patients a year, including 350 in-patients.[89] Unlike Great Ormond Street, it abolished the use of subscribers' recommendations for admission in 1860 because of the difficulty mothers had in getting the vital piece of paper. 'Many a poor woman had been seen drenched to the skin, cold and hungry and weary, who had been all day long rambling from point to point seeking a Recommendation for her sick child.' Sometimes it was obtained too late in the day for her to present the child for treatment and she had to wait overnight.[90]

The East London Hospital for Children was opened in 1867 by two sisters who had been shocked at the lack of provision for youngsters when they helped nurse cholera victims in the East End during the 1866 epidemic. The hospital treated women as well, and was the first in the country to admit infants under two on a regular basis. It made no charge to either in- or out-patients, and was described as a 'haven' for the children of the East End. It even allowed mothers to assist with the nursing of the youngest patients. By 1895 its hundred and two beds were 'always full' and it handled over thirty thousand out-patients a year.[91]

In 1869 Baron Ferdinand de Rothschild established the Evelina Hospital in Southwark in memory of his late wife. It had a separate ward for Jewish children, with a kitchen for kosher cooking, and a ward for whooping-cough patients. By its third year it claimed 21,492 attendances in the out-patients' department, despite the fact that it charged $1d$ for every bottle of medicine prescribed. Initially it had thirty cots for in-patients but these nearly doubled by 1874–5 to fifty-six, and at around that time it began sending children to convalescent homes in the country or at the seaside. Former patients were supplied with clothing, where necessary, when they left the hospital.

The Evelina's case register for in-patients reveals that in 1874, one hundred and fifty-three children were treated, of whom twenty-five died. By 1876, the number of in-patients had risen to three hundred and eighteen, of whom forty-three died. Meningitis and heart disease were among the causes of the fatalities. As at Great Ormond Street, many youngsters suffered with diseases of the joints, and in 1876 alone, there were twenty-three admissions for hip disease.[92] Eleven years later, out of four hundred and sixteen patients, twenty-three lived outside the capital, coming from Cornwall, Hampshire, Northamptonshire and Durham, among other counties, but the vast bulk remained Londoners, as they had always been.[93] In 1893 there were also more than twenty-six treatments of casualties, a reminder of the risks attending child life in the capital's crowded homes and busy streets, with their numerous horses, carts and carriages. One of Walter Southgate's friends suffered a serious accident while taking an illicit ride on a brewer's dray. A heavy ladder, used by the draymen for unloading beer barrels, fell off and the lad fell with it, crushing a leg. This had to be amputated.[94]

Other towns, including Norwich, Birmingham, Liverpool, Nottingham, Brighton and Bristol, soon had their own children's hospitals. The Bristol Royal Hospital for Sick Children, like its Great Ormond Street and Manchester predecessors, began as a dispensary before developing as a hospital in 1866. Women and children attending its out-patients' department were expected to make a small payment, with children charged $6d$ for a first visit and $1\frac{1}{2}d$ for subsequent ones. Medicine cost $6d$ a bottle. From the 1880s arrangements were made for convalescence, and meals were provided for some former in-patients after they returned home, to ensure they obtained an adequate diet, at least for a time. From the start notes were not required for in-patients. As the hospital's annual reports put it: 'Enough that a child be sick and poor, it will be admitted, provided there be a vacant bed, and that the Medical Officers consider the case a suitable one for the Hospital.'[95]

Elsewhere efforts to improve child health led to the establishment of day nurseries, where the infants of working mothers could be cared for. Manchester and Salford had three of them by 1870, run by volunteers and catering for babies as young as two weeks. The Salford Greengate Nursery was said to accomplish wonders by taking 'very puny children, and scabby and dirty, and in a month you would not know them, the change is so marvellous'.[96] One of the Manchester nurseries was opened in 1869 by a local hospital surgeon. On arrival the infants were stripped, washed, and had their hair combed with a fine-tooth comb, to get rid of the lice. But the next day they would return in much the same condition. The charge made was relatively low, at 4*d* a day, but the nursery did not prove popular. Its founder attributed this to the mothers' dislike of charity, but others have suggested it was more likely that they objected to 'interference "from above" and the imposition of standards which entailed an uncomfortable change of habits'.[97] Day nurseries thus had limited success in improving the health of working-class children.

For all Victorian parents, no matter what their station in life, the high levels of child mortality, especially in the first year or so of life, made the loss of a son or daughter an ever-present possibility. The speed with which this could take place was devastating. In 1851, Charles Dickens told a friend of the sudden death of his small daughter, Dora. 'I had just been playing with her, and went to preside at a Public Dinner to which I was pledged. Before it was over – she was dead. I had left her well and gay.'[98] Like many contemporaries in similar circumstances, Dickens gained consolation from the belief that she had entered a better and higher existence, declaring 'it is a part of the goodness and mercy of God that if we could call her back to life, now, with a wish, we would not do it'.

The Anglican cleric, Henry Alford, experienced similar emotions when his ten-year-old son died after five days, from peritonitis, while the family was on holiday at Babbacombe. The helplessness of parents in such circumstances is made painfully clear in diary entries, with Henry going to Torquay to get medicine, calling in a doctor and, when the child was dying, vainly trying to revive him by applying a mustard poultice and giving him a hot bath.[99] But, as he told a friend, his main comfort was the knowledge that the boy had been 'taken from the trials of a distracted and evil age, to be in full fruition of heavenly knowledge and light'.[100]

The view that child death could be construed almost as a blessing was expressed by some of the novelists of the day, including Dickens himself, even before his personal experience of tragedy. In *Oliver Twist*, the workhouse child, Dick, was anxious to send a message to Oliver to tell him that he was glad to die while still 'very young; for, perhaps, if I had lived to be a man, and had grown old, my little sister who is in Heaven, might forget me, or be unlike me; and it would be so much happier if we were both children there together'.[101]

In Silas K. Hocking's *Our Benny*, a best-selling story of Liverpool street life, Benny's young sister, Nelly, died from tuberculosis, aggravated by an accident. While the boy was at her bedside in hospital a nurse consoled him with the thought that it was better for his sister to die, so that she would no longer have to tramp the streets in the cold and wet; 'you must think that what is your loss will be her gain.'[102] For the good child, death could be presented as 'an entry to a better world as much as a departure from this'. Some mothers even had a conviction that if a child wanted to keep clean it was unlikely to survive. A bereaved Middlesbrough woman declared of her six-year-old daughter, 'I knew I should lose her: she was too clean to live.'[103]

Through moral tales and improving verse, death could also be used as a warning to youngsters of the fate that awaited them if they misbehaved in this life and were condemned to eternal damnation. Children were taught to accept the transience of human existence by repeating such lines as,

> There is an hour when I must die,
> Nor do I know how soon 'twill come;
> A thousand children, young as I
> Are call'd by death to hear their doom.
>
> Let me improve the hours I have,
> Before the day of grace is fled;
> There's no repentance in the grave,
> Nor pardons offered for the dead.[104]

Neither were youngsters shielded from the rituals of death, and that was a practice strongly approved of by Queen Victoria herself. 'I think it quite wrong that the nursery are not in mourning, at any rate I should make them wear grey or white or drab and baby wear white and lilac, not colours. That I think shocking', she declared firmly on one occasion.[105] In better-off circles children were expected to mourn for a year for the loss of a parent and for six months for a brother or sister.

Often, in poorer homes, a child's coffin had to be placed on the table of the living room for lack of space, until the funeral. Since Sunday was the day usually chosen for interment by working people, as any other would have involved a loss of pay, a corpse might remain in the living quarters for as long as a week. Walter Southgate remembered that when his sister Florrie died, a dark grey blanket was hung from a string across the room, and behind this, resting on trestles, was the small elm coffin in which she rested.

> Relatives and neighbours came and went to gaze upon her little body as she lay in white calico sheets. They had come to pay their respects and to weep. One had to pass and re-pass through that parlour from the kitchen to the street so the presence of death in the semi-gloom was inescapable. There was the smell of flowers laying [sic] at the head of the coffin, the chrysanthemums especially, and that smell for years always reminded me of my childhood playmate.[106]

Still more distressing was the experience of a Dewsbury child, whose five-year-old sister died when she herself was three. The two girls had been very close and while the sister lay dying of tuberculosis the younger child was allowed to sit on her bed and play with her – a striking instance of the Victorian disregard for the dangers of cross-infection even at the end of the century:

. . . then she died and she was so tiny . . . and altogether she shrank, and she was laid out on the big couch in the sitting room and in those days . . . the curtains were kept drawn from the moment of death until after the funeral. And . . . my mother was ill. She collapsed after Eva's death and was in bed and I used to tip-toe into her room and say, mother, can I . . . go and – talk to Eva. . . . I used to go and sit on a little stool by the side of the couch and I was allowed to take the handkerchief off her face and I talked to her. . . . What I am amazed at is that my father took me to the funeral, that was a cruel wicked thing to do. And I was dressed in black . . . Three years old . . . And – I stood by the open grave, . . . and saw the little coffin go down and screamed. And my father had my hand, held me, he was very upset of course – he said, ssh, you mustn't . . . I said Eva's calling, she doesn't like being in that box and – she mustn't be put in that hole. . . . And my mother said when I got home I went in to her and threw myself on the bed and sobbed. They put Eva in a hole . . . and she didn't want to go and she cried out. Funerals were wicked things . . . those days . . . I can see the horses with their big plumes on, you know, most of the coaches had a pair of horses and their big plumes on.[107]

Even badly off parents wanted to avoid the humiliation of a pauper burial for their offspring. Sometimes this led the poorest or the most desperate to abandon dead infants in ditches or on rubbish heaps rather than having a proper funeral.[108] In other cases, efforts were made to raise funds to pay for a burial by selling or pawning possessions. Lady Bell described a Middlesbrough couple who met the cost of the interment of their small child by pawning a hanging clock, 'which was about the only thing available left in their bare little house'. And she added sadly, 'There is absolutely no credit given for a funeral; for that purpose ready-money must somehow be found'.[109] Occasionally parents entered into informal arrangements with an undertaker for their baby to be buried in someone else's grave. For a tip of a few shillings the man would take away the small wooden box with the dead infant inside, and when the coffin of a better-off person had been lowered into the ground and the mourners had gone away, the grave-digger would be given sixpence to dig away some soil at the side of it and slip in the small box with the dead baby, before filling it in.[110]

To avoid such difficulties many parents entered their children into burial clubs soon after their birth, so that funds would be available should the need arise. Edith Lewis, whose baby brother died when she was two, recalled that her mother had a struggle to find cash for the funeral, as her father was away at sea. 'After this harrowing experience she immediately joined a burial club on my behalf, in case the same thing happened again.'[111]

But there could be a dark side to this where parents joined more than one club for an infant or where the funds received exceeded the funeral costs incurred. Under the 1855 Friendly Societies Act, the maximum sum payable for a child up to five years was £6, while for one aged five to ten it was £10. Claimants had to present a doctor's certificate to the local registrar of births and deaths and he then issued an 'insurance' certificate for a shilling fee. Unfortunately the Act only applied to registered societies. This encouraged parents with questionable motives to join unregistered clubs. The arrival of industrial assurance in the

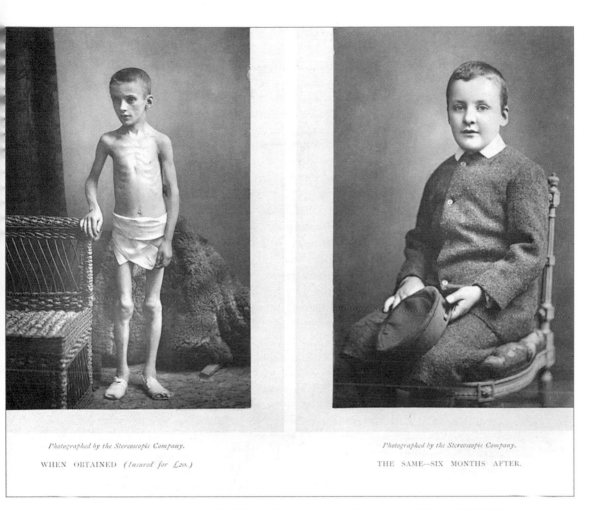

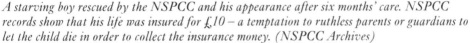

A starving boy rescued by the NSPCC and his appearance after six months' care. NSPCC records show that his life was insured for £10 – a temptation to ruthless parents or guardians to let the child die in order to collect the insurance money. (NSPCC Archives)

1860s offered a still safer method of investing outside the scope of the Act.[112] The Prudential, in particular, came to dominate the field of child life insurance. Often the only limit was the amount of money parents could afford to spend each week. In 1875 a new Friendly Societies Act widened the controls over burial societies but problems continued, with cases quoted of parents who killed or fatally neglected their young children in order to gain the insurance money.[113] Critics even claimed it was fear of an inquest in the event of a child's death rather than confidence in a doctor's skills that encouraged some mothers to call in a physician. As the Kensington Medical Officer of Health commented drily in 1875, the calls came largely because of parents' 'desire to avoid a fuss about a certificate of the cause of death'.[114]

In the 1890s the National Society for the Prevention of Cruelty to Children mounted a vigorous campaign to outlaw child life assurance. The columns of its journal, the *Child's Guardian*, included numerous instances of neglect, cruelty and death, with the rider added, where appropriate, 'The child was insured'.[115] But efforts to outlaw the practice foundered on the opposition of the insurance companies and of working-class families who wanted to join burial societies for the legitimate purpose of giving their children a 'proper' funeral. One estimate suggested that in the early 1900s four-fifths of England's poor infants were insured.[116] Nonetheless, there were mothers of large families who spoke almost flippantly of the death of their children, declaring, 'It is better they died, for I had them all insured.' Lady Bell reported how one woman responded to condolences on the recent death of a baby by lamenting 'it would not have mattered so much in another week, as by then the Insurance would have come in'.[117]

Particularly at risk were those infants, often illegitimate, who were left with commercial baby farmers while their mothers worked. In 1870 the Infant Life Protection Association was formed to press for regulation of the baby-farming business, in response to trials like that of Charlotte Winsor in 1865. Winsor made a business of 'putting away' unwanted infants in exchange for payments of £3 to £5. She simply smothered the baby while the mother waited in the next room. To many the case was clear evidence of the existence of professional infanticide.

In 1872 the Infant Life Protection Act required all those receiving for payment more than one baby under the age of one for longer than twenty-four hours to register with their local authority. Unfortunately people looking after one infant at a time were exempt, as were those receiving children over the age of one. Even in London, where the Metropolitan Board of Works, the predecessor of the London County Council, took the matter seriously, few people were registered.[118] The board repeatedly pressed the Home Secretary to extend the legislation to include 'one-child' cases up to five years of age and to outlaw 'lump sum' adoptions, for where such payments were made it was in the child minder's interest to allow her small charge to die quickly. This was particularly true in London, and there were instances like that of Joseph and Annie Roadhouse where considerable sums were obtained in this way. In the late 1880s the Roadhouses secured at least thirty-five infants by means of advertisements, and then disposed of them to other baby farmers. Ten subsequently died. The cash received totalled £219 and there were, in addition, clothes and jewellery to the value of £35.[119]

Criminal baby farmers were also linked to the life assurance business. In 1884 Mrs Flannigan and Mrs Higgins of Liverpool collected insurance on at least eleven babies who had died in their care. 'The going rate was between £3 [and] £10 per child.'[120] Four years later it was found that George and Mary Heys of Swindon had 'adopted' seven children, whom they crammed in a room twelve feet square, in conditions of appalling squalor. The couple were convicted of neglecting two of the youngsters, a boy who had been found tied to a chair and a baby girl too weak to walk. Mrs Heys was sentenced to two years' imprisonment and her husband to nine months. The children had been insured for ½d a week with the Victoria Legal Friendly Society and the judge, in sentencing them, called such burial clubs 'those pests of society which insured the lives of children but which seemed to be instituted for their . . . destruction'.[121] He called for their suppression and that was a sentiment with which, as we have seen, the NSPCC heartily agreed.

In 1897 a new Infant Life Protection Act raised the age of protected children from one to five and required commercial child minders who kept more than one youngster up to that age to 'notify' their local authority. The authorities could appoint inspectors to check that the premises and conditions of care met the standards laid down in the Act but, as before, carers with only one child of the appropriate age were exempt from its provisions. The weakness of this was underlined by Miss Zanetti, an infant protection visitor working in Manchester. She revealed that of 809 children she had seen between 1898 and 1901 in a check on baby farms, nearly 80 per cent were in single-child establishments and thus outside the Act's protection.[122] Baby farming affected only a small number of children but it remained open to abuse until the end of the century, even if some of its most blatant excesses had been curbed.

One area of 'violent death' involving young children did increase in the late Victorian period. This was infant suffocation which almost always occurred when parents crushed their baby by 'overlying' it as it shared their bed. The danger was particularly acute at weekends, giving rise to suspicions that offending couples smothered the infants accidentally while in a drunken stupor after a Saturday night spree. During the 1890s the issue became bound up with the temperance cause, with the NSPCC labelling alcoholism 'the single most important root-cause of parental wickedness'.[123]

Pupils travelling by ambulance to a 'cripple school' run by the London school board, c. 1900. (The author)

More optimistically, by the end of the nineteenth century the death rate among all children *except* for infants under one year had fallen, as a result of improved sanitation, better housing (with cellar dwellings virtually eliminated in most cities), and the tackling of epidemic diseases. The growing use of isolation hospitals led to the quarantining of smallpox, scarlet fever and diphtheria, and in the case of smallpox there was also vaccination. The anti-toxin serum was likewise available for diphtheria. So while the male death rate among children aged five to nine inclusive had been 9.7 per 1,000 living in 1838–40, this had fallen to 6.7 per 1,000 in 1871–80 and to 3.8 per 1,000 in 1899. Among girls the decline was from 9.4 per 1,000 living in 1838–40 to 6.3 in 1871–80 and 3.9 in 1899.[124]

Yet there remained concern about the poor physique of many working-class youngsters from the larger cities. This intensified in the aftermath of the Boer War when it emerged, for example, that boys from a Salford slum were, on average, four inches shorter and sixteen pounds lighter at the age of thirteen than their counterparts from a better-off working-class neighbourhood.[125] As the Medical Officer of Health for Manchester pointed out, the root of the problem was malnutrition: 'to get good soldiers you must rear good children, you must see that children are adequately fed'.[126] Recent research has cast some doubt on just

A neglected and malnourished baby brought to an NSPCC shelter. Many children were rescued from the edge of starvation by the Society. (NSPCC Archives)

how far town children had become shorter and weaker over the century as a result of industrialization and the effects of urban life.[127] But to imperialists the overriding concern was whether the male inhabitants of the poorer quarters of large towns with their 'white, pinched faces, . . . ill-developed bodies, . . . all-too-prevalent and apparent signs of disease in skin and eye' could sustain the expanding British empire.[128] Many shared Charles Booth's fear that even if the puny children of the slums survived, they would as adults swell the numbers of needy and enfeebled people 'whose burden of helplessness' the rest of the community had to bear.[129]

Meanwhile there was growing awareness that some of Britain's continental rivals were taking action in the welfare field where she was failing. During the 1880s research into the health of schoolchildren was conducted in the newly annexed German territory of Alsace-Lorraine, and in 1883 the first school doctor was appointed at Frankfurt-am-Main. Two years later Lausanne, Switzerland, made a similar appointment, and in the 1880s medical inspection became widespread in French schools. By contrast the first English school medical officer was only recruited in 1890, when the London School Board made a part-time appointment. Bradford followed suit in 1893.[130] Both appointees were responsible for the broader aspects of child health and hygiene, rather than an individual examination and observation of pupils.

Yet already the child study movement had begun to focus research on the mental characteristics of young children. In 1884, Francis Galton opened an 'Anthropometric Laboratory', where parents could have their children's 'powers' measured.[131] Four years later the annual meeting of the British Medical Association appointed a committee to 'investigate the state of development and brain power of school children', and, with the support of the Charity Organisation Society, to publicize the results. Dr Francis Warner, a consultant paediatrician at the East London Children's Hospital and a pioneer of anthropometric methods, was given prime responsibility for coordinating the work. He stressed his belief in the close links between physical and mental development and called on teachers and others to observe pupils in order to assess their capabilities. He considered that knowledge of the physical condition of children was essential 'to distinguish those slightly defective, from those merely stupid and lazy, who ought to be made to work and not exempted or spared from punishment'.[132] The BMA initiative eventually led to 100,000 children being surveyed, from 168 different London schools, of whom perhaps 1 per cent were judged by Dr Warner to be suffering from a physical or nervous defect which required special education in separate schools.[133] But this broad-brush approach, concentrating on the connection between physical disability and mental handicap, had the disadvantage of causing the more subtle aspects of child development to be ignored or underestimated.

It was in this atmosphere of growing interest in child welfare that the chairman of the School Management Committee of the London School Board issued a memorandum in 1900 pointing out that the capital was 'almost alone' among the great cities of the world in not providing regular medical inspection in its schools. In Berlin and other large German towns, as well as Paris, Antwerp, Brussels and the major Swiss cities, visits were paid weekly or fortnightly. This led to a growing awareness of the causes of infectious illnesses and the way they were spread.[134]

As part of the new London programme children were to be weighed and measured and arrangements made to prevent the spread of diseases such as ringworm and ophthalmia. These initiatives, the memorandum declared, 'must be judged neither by our convenience, nor by our prejudices, but solely by their success in saving children from disease and its consequences'.[135] It marked a new approach to the care of the young and was to lead, in the early twentieth century, to the introduction of national legislation for school medical examinations and rate-aided school meals, as well as municipally funded infant welfare centres. Yet, as recruitment for the First World War was to show, weaknesses in the health and physique of youngsters from the poorest areas of major cities were neither easily nor rapidly rectified.[136]

CHAPTER 7

At Leisure

Our street games were simple and traditional, but we found them wholly captivating. They came round with the seasons, . . . shuttle-cock and paddle; skipping rope; hoop-bowls; hop-flag and marbles. We smaller children loved the singing games, the quaint rhymes married to old ballad tunes and handed down from generation to generation . . . In blossom-time we organised May Queen processions; a tiny girl was chosen as queen to be adorned in odd finery, with a tinsel crown and a long curtain carried by her train-bearers, followed by a straggling section of grubby children. . . . Most of the older boys played football in the front street and were often chased by the local bobby; at weekends they hung around the back streets or at gable-ends playing pitch-and-toss.

Alice Foley, *A Bolton Childhood* (1990 edn), pp. 17–18. Alice was born in 1891

The way children spent their leisure hours and the amount of free time they had depended not only on their age and gender but on their social class as well. Working-class youngsters fared better at the end of the nineteenth century than in earlier decades, as labour legislation restricted their working hours and school attendance provided a firmer pattern to their daily lives. But the material factors which determined 'the nature – or non-existence – of adult recreations, namely free time and the economic ability to enjoy it, applied equally to the young'.[1] There were still some who argued that it was better for urban youngsters to have a job than to spend their leisure 'gambling for buttons on the kerb-stone', or whiling away the hours in a penny music-hall.[2]

Even at the start of Queen Victoria's reign most children were able to snatch precious moments of play away from their other tasks, and those under the normal minimum employment age of eight or nine were likely to have still more time to themselves. Working children, too, were free to pursue pastimes when their daily labours had ended. According to James Essex, a Pontypool surgeon, in the early 1840s young people of all ages employed in the local iron industry could be seen 'in great numbers eagerly engaged in amusements and games requiring considerable exertion and activity, quite incompatible with previous exhaustion'.[3] Similarly an eight-year-old watercress seller encountered by Henry Mayhew in mid-century London confirmed that drudging toil did not preclude all pleasures. Although she had never visited a public park, she did have occasional games of 'honeypots' with other girls in the court where she lived. 'We plays, too, at kiss-

THE SHUTTLE-COCK NUISANCE.

Little Girl. "OH, I BEG YOUR PARDON, SIR!—IT WAS THE WIND AS DONE IT!"

*Children's street games could annoy adult passers-by. (*Punch, *1857)*

in-the-ring.' She had a few toys which had been given to her by Jewish people for whom she worked on Fridays and Saturdays, carrying out the minor domestic chores which their religion precluded them from performing on the Sabbath.[4] Other working youngsters, like a thirteen-year-old boy employed in the pottery industry, enjoyed 'play days at Easter and Whitsun, and Christmas, and at wakes and races', while many, in the early Victorian years, had a day off each week on 'St Monday', even if this meant working long hours at the end of the week.[5]

Parents residing in overcrowded tenements lost no chance of sending their offspring into the street to amuse themselves. Once there, the games they played and the activities in which they engaged could easily annoy passers-by as well as local residents. In 1853, *Punch* complained that pavements in London were made impassable by children playing shuttlecock and tipcat, while a few years earlier a Portsmouth solicitor found his business interrupted by boys and girls playing noisy games and using foul language in the square outside his office.[6] On one occasion the Portsmouth police had to be called in to break up a fight involving between two and three hundred lads who were pelting each other with stones.[7]

Even snowballing might lead to a court appearance, as when a seven-year-old Grimsby boy was charged with 'wilfully damaging a window' while throwing snowballs at other children. One of the missiles went through the complainant's window, but because she admitted it had been an accident, the case was dismissed.[8]

Children's leisure pursuits fell into three broad categories, namely those undertaken in and around the home; those involving events away from home, such as visits to a circus, fair, holiday resort, music-hall and theatre (including the penny theatre or 'penny gaff'); and those concerned with formal organizations such as Sunday schools, the Band of Hope, and, at the end of the century, the uniformed youth movements, such as the Boys' Brigade, the Church Lads' Brigade, and the like. In the world of the theatre and the circus, youngsters participated both as members of the audience and as entertainers, especially after legislation in 1843 opened up the licensing of theatres and created greater opportunities for juvenile performers. Youngsters costumed as elves, sprites and woodland animals in pantomimes could, by their skills in singing, dancing and marching, make a major contribution to the success of an entire production.[9] Kate Terry, whose parents were both on the stage, began her theatrical career at the age of three, 'dancing a hornpipe in a sailor's jumper, a rakish little hat, and a diminutive pair of white ducks'. When she was eight she played her first Shakespearean role in London and four years later, in 1856, was joined by her sister, Ellen, who was three years her junior. Admiring Ellen on her debut were Prince Albert and Queen Victoria, while Lewis Carroll described her in his diary as 'a beautiful little creature who played with remarkable ease and spirit'.[10] Soon Kate and Ellen were earning enough to make a major contribution to the support of the Terry household.

Middle-class youngsters had a far wider range of pastimes than their working-class counterparts. The younger members of better-off families often had a nursery, complete with a presiding nanny, where they could play with their toys. The fact that most of them also enjoyed a prolonged adolescence, compared with youngsters from humbler homes, added to their opportunities for pleasure.

Such families normally refused to allow their children to play on the street, since this was considered vulgar and likely to lead to undesirable friendships. For the same reason prohibitions were laid on those with whom they might associate. One girl, the daughter of a Tunbridge Wells grocer, was forbidden to play hopscotch on the pavement. Although playmates could be invited into the garden, there was not much enthusiasm for it: 'perhaps my mother turned a blind eye . . . particularly my brother used to bring in some of his friends'.[11]

These children were likely to be taken on 'improving visits' to museums, art galleries and the Crystal Palace, and to be encouraged to take up hobbies. They would probably have holidays away from home at the seaside or in the country, perhaps visiting relatives or staying in rented rooms. The diary of a fourteen-year-old clergyman's son, Hastings Rashdall, early in 1873 records visits to Westminster Abbey, the National Gallery, and 'an entertainment at the Polytechnic' during a trip to London. On 18 January he accompanied his uncle to the Crystal Palace where he enjoyed a wonderful Acrobatic Entertainment. Then a very amusing *true* Pantomime i.e. the Characters not speaking. . . . I don't know how it is I did not appreciate the Palace fully, when I was here before. The Courts, exact models of various buildings or parts of buildings, illustrating various styles of Architecture, are beautiful . . . and the whole place is full of plaster models of all the finest statues in Europe; they look much better by gas light. The Aquarium is very interesting. It is very curious to see the fish . . . wrigling [*sic*] about in the water; they seem quite accustomed to strangers . . . .[12]

In the evening he accompanied his mother to a performance of songs, readings and recitations put on at a local church. 'A Gent. read or rather acted a piece from "David Copperfield" wonderfully well – almost too pathetic.'

During his Easter vacation from Harrow, Hastings stayed with farming relatives in Herefordshire, where he went riding and learned to shoot with a double-barrelled muzzle-loader, although without much success. 'I prowled in vain, seeing but few rabbits, & getting a shot at none, then discharged vainly at small birds', reads one diary entry. In the summer there was a visit to Dawlish, where his late father had been vicar, and a holiday in Dorset, where he spent much time by the sea at Studland, hunting for fossils.[13]

Youngsters playing in Farnworth Park, Bolton, c. 1900. (Farnworth Library, Bolton)

Diary entries by John Neville Keynes, another comfortably off schoolboy, reveal visits during the 1860s to London to admire the acrobat Blondin at the Agricultural Hall in Islington and to attend penny readings by Charles Dickens. He also went to see Wombwell's Menagerie at the Crystal Palace and Franconi's 'cirque imperial' at the Royal Alhambra Palace. There were summer picnics in the New Forest, and games of croquet, blind man's buff, bagatelle and chess played with friends or members of his Salisbury family.[14]

Margaret Fletcher, whose father was an Oxford don, received expensive toys, including exquisite wax dolls purchased in Paris which she was only allowed to play with on Sundays and great occasions. There was also a clockwork toy called 'Velocipede man', which her father had bought in France. 'When wound up, he dashed round in a circle like a bandmaster, and sitting on a machine not unlike the modern bicycle.' From her nursery window Margaret observed the visits of itinerant entertainers to the crescent where she lived. There were dancing bears with their keepers, performing dogs, Punch and Judy, acrobats, 'gaudily-dressed children dancing on stilts and endless Italian organ-grinders, each with their attendant monkeys cap in paw held out for pennies'. There were few public entertainments deemed suitable for Margaret and her friends to attend, so every family regarded it as a social duty to give a Christmas party:

> Great pains were taken in preparing these parties and in devising surprises. At first they did not go beyond traditional games and romps. Christmas trees . . . were lit with wax candles, precariously wired to branches already laden with cotton-wool snow and toys. Luckily amateur firemen were always present armed with rods tipped with wet sponges. I can remember no precautions against the dangers of the game of snapdragon, for which raisins piled on dishes were steeped in spirits and set alight, when the children were encouraged to snatch them out while still burning.[15]

In another professional family, whose cash resources were tighter, home entertainments were popular. Children acted plays, arranged black minstrel shows, and performed on the piano, clarinet, mandolin, and banjo: 'we all played something'. There were occasional visits to the theatre and on Saturday afternoons they played tennis or went cycling with their father. There were always plenty of books to read in the house.[16]

The pleasures such children enjoyed (even when hedged about with parental restrictions on the friends they might make and the places they could visit) were out of the reach of virtually all working-class youngsters. But even among these poorer children, there were sharp differences between the recreations available in market towns and other non-industrial centres and those in manufacturing districts. In the former, many leisure pursuits resembled those enjoyed by country children, as with an Oxford boy who fished in the river with jam jars, attended the traditional St Giles's fair, and played in the yard of a public house where the bargees' horses from the canal were stabled. Similarly a Cornish lad, born at Camborne in 1888, remembered that although there was no recreation ground in the town he and his friends collected money to buy a football. 'And then we'd go down to a farmer's field and play, until the farmer came. And then we was ordered out.'[17] On other occasions he and his friends played in the streets or in the back yards and the gardens of one another's houses. They were pursued by the policeman when they played pranks on neighbours, 'tic-tac we used to call it, tapping the windows and tying the doors and – putting [a] bag over chimneys . . . 'cos we had . . . nowhere else to go, we had to make our own fun.'

Later he joined the Church Lads' Brigade in a nearby village. This had a bugle band and members 'went away to Lyme Regis to camp'. The family always kept a couple of pigs and some poultry, which had to be looked after. When the pigs were slaughtered some of the meat was sold to a local butcher or a nearby bacon factory to cover the rearing costs. The rest was salted down by his mother for family consumption.

Even youngsters living in large towns might walk miles in search of the countryside. A Bristol girl remembered that she and her friends played truant in order to visit a place called Snuff Mills. It meant a walk of about six or seven miles but once there they took off their shoes and stockings and paddled in the stream, or caught 'tiddlers in jam jars'. Before leaving they picked flowers and leaves to take home with them.[18] Walter Southgate, too, in the late 1890s walked from Bethnal Green to the banks of the River Lea near Springhill, Clapton, and to the Hackney Marshes, before he was nine years old:

> It could only be attempted during our school holidays with other adventurous boys. This meant going without a dinner at home and we dare not ask for sandwiches. We had a weary trudge homewards footsore and terribly hungry searching the gutters for apple cores and the like.
>
> The fascination about these back-rivers was that we could fish and bathe in the water without disturbance . . . Our parents forbade us to go near the place . . . because of the danger to non-swimmers and the evil reputation it had. Those back rivers on Sundays were the haunt of gamblers, card players, and others playing pitch and toss free from the attention of police. We caught very few tiddlers and bathing in the doubtful purity of the waters we were not encumbered with bathing trunks, had no towels to dry ourselves so we ran about and let nature do the job. Of course, we arrived home tired and hungry and had to face up to a caning and were sent to bed. It made no difference. As each summer holiday came round . . . we went back to nature regardless of the consequences.[19]

Most youngsters played games which did not require expensive equipment. Leapfrog, tag, blind man's buff, hare and hounds, and hopscotch were just a few of them. One early Victorian visitor to London espied a boy playing, amid countless others, on a piece of waste ground. First he hung by his legs to a piece of temporary railing, with his hair sweeping the ground. Then he went to a secluded corner and did handstands, whistled a tune, clapped his shoeless soles together and went through 'certain telegraphic evolutions with his legs', before resuming his normal position.[20]

Playing on the streets. (The author)

Youngsters in Newcastle would hang over the dockside in an effort to spike apples with a table fork attached to a piece of string, as the apples floated in the filthy water between the quay and the boats. Many children made skipping ropes from lengths of old rope or twine, constructed carts and toboggans from soap-boxes and the wheels of disused perambulators, and rigged up kites from a piece of cane and a page from a copy-book. Rag dolls and paper balls could be just as entertaining as the more elaborate toys of richer children, and with a little imagination a piece of cord fastened to the back of a chair might become a pony and trap.[21] Boys bowling metal hoops pretended they were steam engines or stage coaches. 'Many children, boys and girls', remembered one man, 'bowled their hoops at speed and then, running very fast beside them, got through them as they rushed along – without knocking them down.' He also recalled the seasonality of games, with hoops belonging to the autumn and marbles played in the spring.[22]

As school log books confirm, children stayed away to watch parades or to attend fairs, outings and tea parties. 'Numbers short on account of the town Regatta and Sanger's circus', reads an entry at All Saints Boys' School, Portsmouth, on 18 August 1871.[23] About three years later the head of Kent Street School in the same town reported children staying away 'to see the troops from the Gold Coast disembark', and to attend 'a Band of Hope Demonstration'. Soon after, a 'great many boys' were away 'owing to Orange St Sunday School Treat'.[24] Other illicit pleasures included London pupils taking annual trips to Epsom for

Derby day, while national celebrations usually led to holidays and entertainments. In March 1863, the headmistress of the Beneficial Girls' School, Portsmouth, took 104 pupils to Southsea Common to celebrate the Prince of Wales's Wedding Day. When they returned they were each given 'a threepenny cake & four new pennies'. At least one child seems to have come to school expressly for the treat. A nine-year-old had made her first attendance on the day before the wedding. She joined in the festivities the following day, but 'never came again; sent several times after her – various excuses made – the last – gone to work', was the mistress's resigned comment.[25]

At the hop-picking and fruit-gathering season youngsters went away with their families from schools in south London and the East End, and from Birmingham and the Black Country, combining business with pleasure on an unofficial harvest holiday. A survey of sixty board schools and fifteen voluntary schools in London in 1900 showed that 4,169 pupils were absent for an average of four weeks each in order to pick fruit and hops.[26]

Poorer children, like Walter Southgate, would use ingenuity to provide equipment for their games. That could mean

> coats down in the road for goal posts; the lamp post for a cricket stump; a rough piece of wood shaped for a cricket bat; . . . balls of pressed paper and string and glass marbles . . . four a penny . . . There were . . . spinning tops; iron hoops for boys and wooden ones for girls; cherry stones for 'bobs'; 'conkers' on string (proud was the boy who had a 'twentier' from his 'kills'); five stones and hop scotch chalked on the pavement for girls. . . . Children also took rides on the back of the horse-drawn water cart sprinkler . . . Should, however, the driver of this sprinkler cart catch a child taking a free ride, then beware of a sudden shower.[27]

Walter and his friends ingratiated themselves with the night watchman so that they could bake potatoes on his brazier fire and imagine themselves characters in 'redskin stories from the pages of Fenimore Cooper'. Cigarette cards were then becoming popular and the children pestered passers-by for them. They also played cards in the gutter, which meant that the cards became coated with dirt, soot, horse dung and other filth, making them a health hazard.

At the end of the century youngsters joined enthusiastically in the excitement which swept the country when the South African war broke out. Walter, like other boys, played at 'English versus Boers'. The relief of Ladysmith or Mafeking led to great rejoicing in the neighbourhood, with dancing, singing, the waving of flags, and celebrations with bonfires and fireworks. 'We children enjoyed it immensely especially as the fire brigade was called out to save the cottages from going up in flames too.'[28] The spirit of imperialism which inspired these displays was encouraged by some of the late Victorian uniformed youth movements, with their emphasis on patriotism and duty to Queen and Country.

Older children engaged in gambling games like pitch and toss, betting with halfpennies and farthings, or buttons and nuts if they had no cash. If caught they could be fined, or even imprisoned for non-payment of the fine. Alice Foley in Bolton remembered it as one of the tasks of the younger children to give the alarm should a policeman approach, so that the lads could scatter quickly. Occasionally one was caught and was fined five shillings by the magistrates. A street collection was then organized to pay this, the money being handed over in pennies and half-pennies.[29] Many boys, especially in the rougher districts, joined street gangs and had scuffles with their rivals. An Oxford lad, who lived in St Thomas's parish, remembered being 'at daggers drawn' with youngsters from Osney. 'They used to call us the St Thomas's Bulldogs and we used to call them the Osney Arabs and throw stones at one another up the lane.'[30] Another boy, the son of a Bristol docker, became 'king of one gang', and fought the lad who was 'king' of another from the next street. When he beat the latter, 'all his mob came over on my side'. There were about six or eight boys in the gang, and apart from skirmishes with other youngsters they would play cards, 'what they call 'alfpenny banker'.[31]

In better-off homes, where there was sufficient space, children played parlour games like ludo, dominoes, draughts, and happy families, as well as snakes and ladders, which was introduced in 1892–3. Card playing was forbidden in many households because of its association with gambling. Middle-class families also purchased 'improving' games likely to increase the knowledge and skills of the children, such as nursery lotto. This was sold in the 1890s with the recommendation that it would 'afford the young people an immense amount of amusement, and at the same time will greatly . . . assist them in their mental arithmetic'.[32]

There were opportunities to read, and to pursue hobbies like coin and stamp collecting, or fretwork for boys and painting and needlework for girls. Magic lantern shows were held in some homes, and an Edmonton boy, given a magic lantern for Christmas, remembered it had other uses. When he and his brother were sent to bed early they would light the lantern, making sure it did not show outside the door, and then play a game of nap under the bedclothes, using a pack of cards smuggled in by his brother. 'If we did not make a noise so that my father came up to see that we were all right we didn't need to go to sleep as quick as we were supposed to.'[33]

For children from overcrowded tenements, lack of space meant that almost the only communal amusement the family could enjoy indoors was a 'sing song' on Saturday or Sunday evenings. A few friends would meet in the home of one of them, bringing such musical instruments as they could muster. Popular music-hall tunes were played, 'all lustily shouting the choruses and busily drumming with their heels on the floor', to the annoyance of neighbours who were not sharing in the fun. Among some Irish families, the art of story telling still survived and old folk would recount to the young 'ancient legends and fairy stories'.[34] Joseph Stamper's mother, too, told her children stories as they sat in the dark on winter evenings, by the fireside. She was of Welsh extraction, and although Joseph liked the fairy tales she related, it was the supernatural ones from her Celtic background he relished the most. 'Kids enjoy being scared stiff', he declared.[35]

The array of toys available grew enormously during the Victorian years. Even in the middle of the century a London toymaker told Henry Mayhew of the cheap wooden carts, horses, omnibuses, and other playthings he made for poorer children. But when trade was bad, as it was at the time of the interview, and there was much unemployment, his business suffered. Parents could not afford toys for the children.[36] In other cases cheap wooden dolls and simple hobby horses were sold at

Children dancing to the music of a street organ. (The author)

fairs, while street pedlars retailed dolls costing between 1*d* and 6*d* each: 'as long as ever there are children from two years old to ten, there will always be purchasers of dolls', one vendor told Mayhew, adding that spoiled children were the best customers.[37] The heads of the dolls were imported from Germany and that country was a major supplier of many toys purchased by Victorian youngsters.[38]

For the well-to-do, toy emporia such as the Lowther Arcade, the Soho Bazaar and Cremer's of Regent Street offered a range of enticing wares. One angry pedestrian complained that shopkeepers were blocking the passageways of the Lowther Arcade near Charing Cross with 'drums, children's tea things, Birmingham and Wedgwood trumperies, rocking horses and lambswool poodles. Besides these there were model theatres . . . , magic lanterns, dolls of all kinds, clockwork trains, musical automata, doll's houses complete with every imaginable piece of furniture, three-wheeled prams, balancing figures, model shops, building bricks and castellated forts.'[39]

At the end of the century elaborate metal toys were produced, including ships, trains and filigree doll's house furniture. Plasticine made its appearance in 1897, carrying with it the encouraging recommendation from the maker: 'Rest for the Nurse – Pleasure for the Children.'[40] But for most youngsters such items were too expensive. Indeed, there were probably many like Mrs Elizabeth Layton, who carefully made doll's clothes from a piece of material given to her by a dressmaker in hopeful anticipation of getting her own doll. Eventually someone gave her a cheap wooden Dutch plaything, of which she was not particularly fond, 'but I was able to fit on the clothes that I made'.[41]

For the poorest, charity and, at the end of the century, free gifts supplied by manufacturers in exchange for wrappers from their wares, were two other means of obtaining toys. In the 1880s, cheap wax dolls were offered in return for tea coupons, but it was the soap makers who were most active in this form of sales promotion. In 1896, Sunlight Soap advertised paper dolls, dolls' furniture, a village fair and a Punch and Judy show to purchasers who sent a certain number of wrappers from the Sunlight or Lifebuoy brands, while Pear's Soap gave away colour reproductions of famous pictures with their shilling Christmas annuals. A third company, Lovelace's Soap, offered a small paper screen with scenes from fairy stories for use in a doll's house.[42]

Improved printing techniques, largely pioneered in Germany, made available books with brightly coloured pop-up scenes, rather like miniature theatres, and there were nursery books about animals which contained a bellows mechanism capable of emitting appropriate animal noises when strings were pulled.[43]

Toys for sick and needy children were purchased with the proceeds of bazaars or of appeals made to the general public, and were widely distributed at Christmas. *Truth* magazine asked readers to provide toys for a major toy show and offered a prize for the best home-made entry. Afterwards 'the thousands of toys submitted were taken to the young patients in London's hospitals and workhouses'. So popular did this annual event become that it had to be held in the Albert Hall.[44] Then there were organizations like the Liverpool Children's Aid Society, whose main aim was to provide clothing for needy children and day nurseries for the infants of working mothers, but which gave away playthings donated by well-wishers as part of its Christmas treat.[45] The Happy Evenings Association was a further variation on the theme. It offered out-of-school activities, including drawing and painting, cutting out paper figures to make into toys, various handicrafts, and playing with dolls, to some of London's poorest children. 'The little people with the dolls are all seated at desks, each with a doll, whose dress so gloriously outshines her own', commented a visitor to one 'Happy Evening'. 'Some are dressing or undressing them; others are merely sitting perfectly still, nursing the waxen lady; rapt, sober, wholly content.'[46] After two hours the toys had to be handed in, and the children went home.

The growing list of books and magazines published especially for children was an important development in the Victorian period. In many ways the Sunday school movement had pioneered the upsurge in children's periodical literature, with such publications as the Sunday School Union's *Youth Magazine and Evangelical Miscellany*, and the *Primitive Methodist Children's Magazine*. Tracts, books, testaments and Bibles were distributed in tens of millions to Sunday scholars.[47] However, by the 1830s and 1840s other influences were at work. For middle-class children, there were fairy stories, including the works of the Brothers Grimm and Hans Andersen, which became available in translation. Edward Lear's *Book of Nonsense*, which appeared in 1846, offered 'unselfconscious irresponsible gaiety' to young readers. In the 1850s and 1860s new kinds of adventure stories for boys were published. 'The writers who now gave boys excitement or romance instead of moral prattle . . . wrote for that very purpose', comments Harvey Darton:

William Henry Giles Kingston's *Peter the Whaler* was published in 1851; . . .
Robert Michael Ballantyne, drawing upon first-hand experience more directly
than some later rivals, produced *The Young Fur Traders* in 1856. They opened
between them, the door of contemporary romance . . . The true novelty in
these books was the absence, in the majority of them, of any appeal to dogmatic
religious belief, or any *open* theory of conduct or education.[48]

In the mid–1880s Robert Louis Stevenson, himself the author of juvenile classics
like *Treasure Island*, *Kidnapped* and the *Black Arrow*, noted the appeal of these
romances to their young readers' imagination: 'There never was a child . . . but
has hunted gold, and been a pirate, and a military commander, and a bandit of the
mountains; but has fought, and suffered shipwreck, and prison, and imbrued its
little hands in gore, and gallantly retrieved the lost battle, and triumphantly
protected innocence and beauty.'[49] In his case, the 'highwayman was my favourite
dish'.[50]

Thomas Hughes's *Tom Brown's Schooldays* (1856), based on the author's
experiences at Rugby School, popularized the school story with its account of the
exploits of the spirited young hero. It gave rise to numerous imitations of varying
merit, while Lewis Carroll's *Alice's Adventures in Wonderland* (1865), with its
portrayal of a little girl travelling through a mysterious imaginary world, gave
fantasy a major place in the literature of childhood.[51] Later in the century the
growth of imperialism added to the popularity of authors like G.A. Henty, whose
adventure stories were set in the farthest outposts of the British Empire. Such
tales accustomed young readers to the 'professional military image, and the use of
military technology, ranks and titles', which were to form part of late Victorian
youth organizations.[52]

Among girls, the scope for vigorous or stirring fiction was limited, since their
own lives were hedged around by the demands of duty and domesticity. However,
books like Louisa May Alcott's *Little Women* showed that even unpromising
home-based themes could be of interest. 'The fate of a plum pudding boiled by
the untrained hands of a girl of fourteen becomes under Miss Alcott's pen an
affair of nearly as great moment as some of the wildest of situations under other
pens', was one contemporary tribute.[53] By the end of the century school stories,
too, were appearing, to correspond to those already available for boys, and there
were biographies of famous women, like Elizabeth Fry and Florence Nightingale,
to serve as models of desirable conduct.[54]

Alongside these, 'moral' stories for children still survived, as with Hesba
Stretton's best-selling *Jessica's First Prayer* (1867). This recounted the doings of a
forlorn street child and the way she effected the religious conversion of a
caretaker/coffee-stall owner who befriended her. Stretton followed it with other
books in a similar vein, and she inspired a number of imitators. In the highly
popular *Froggy's Little Brother* by 'Brenda' (1875), the 'good slum child' again
featured prominently.[55] These accounts of virtuous young slum dwellers making
the best of their miserable lot remained an aspect of juvenile literature which the
Sunday school movement, in particular, did much to promote. But most
contemporaries accepted the need for children's writers to transmit a suitable

moral message. Even those like Edward G. Salmon, who approved of the new adventure stories for boys, argued that the authors had a mission to accomplish: 'By a mission I would imply that a writer should never lose the consciousness that the sentiments he expresses and the end he proposes will assist in the mental development . . . of the sons and daughters of England.'[56]

But many working-class youngsters, especially those verging on adolescence, were satisfied neither with milk-and-water tales of virtue rewarded, nor with the mainstream children's books, which they may, in any case, have had difficulty in obtaining. As literacy improved, the numbers of such youngsters increased, so that by the end of the century about 97 per cent of males and females marrying could sign the register (the only crude measurement of literacy rates available). This compared with 69 per cent of males and 55 per cent of females able to sign half a century earlier. Publishers responded to the growing market for cheap juvenile fiction by producing sensational 'penny dreadfuls' issued in weekly parts. Those most condemned by middle-class moralists enjoyed the largest circulation among young people, with tales investing 'with knightly qualities . . . highwaymen, jail-breakers, house-breakers', proving particularly popular.[57] At a time when concern was growing over the apparent rise in juvenile delinquency, these periodicals were accused of encouraging lawlessness among the working-class young. Particularly criticized were stories of street urchins like *The Wild Boys of London* (1864–6). These lads hatched their plots 'round the fire in their haunt beneath the sewers of London', and during their violent adventures they fought off 'ruffians, salvaged corpses and trafficked in stolen goods'. Their opponents included thieves, murderers, kidnappers, grave robbers and bumbling policemen. 'From piracy to lynching, *The Wild Boys of London* ran the gamut of crime', wrote one commentator.[58]

It was the publication in 1866 of a periodical entitled *The Boys of England* that proved most significant in the battle for purchasers of juvenile magazines. It ran until 1899 and claimed to 'enthral' its readers by 'wild and wonderful but healthy fiction'. Circulation soon soared to 150,000 copies a week, and middle-class parents forbade their sons to read it. Many, however, followed the example of Edgar Jepson and obtained copies surreptitiously. In Jepson's case this meant hiding them in the hay-loft and then recovering them to read in secret.[59] Working-class boys, especially those who were earning, had no such inhibitions and they read avidly stories of heroes like Jack Harkaway, who began his fictional career as a schoolboy defying authority and ended up adventuring all over the world. By the early 1870s *The Boys of England* was selling around 250,000 copies a week, and its successful mixture of patriotism, violence, adventure, and upwardly mobile heroes soon brought competitors into the field, including Charles Fox's *Boys' Standard*, which ran for twenty years.[60]

To counter this upsurge of 'penny dreadfuls', in 1879 the Religious Tract Society launched its journal, the *Boy's Own Paper*. It, too, relied on adventure stories to capture readers, and many of them contained a good deal of violence. But it avoided the glorification of child criminals which had offended middle-class critics of the 'dreadfuls'. Salmon, in a survey of boys' magazines, considered it the 'only real antidote' to the pernicious influence of these journals.[61] Quite quickly more than

The patriotic image. Boys' and Girls' Magazine *(n.d., early 1900s)*

half a million copies of the *Boy's Own Paper* were being printed weekly, with some copies distributed free of charge to pupils in the London board schools, in an effort to widen circulation and wean youngsters from undesirable competitors. Typical of the opponents of sensational literature was the Revd Freeman Wills. In 1886 he argued that while the Education Act had been proposed as a means of abolishing ignorance, it was lamentably failing in that aim. 'The education it has enforced is worthless . . . a mere capacity to read which leaves its possessor brutal and uncultured.' The printed material favoured by the youngsters depraved their minds and caused them 'to long for "highly-spiced criminal excitements"'.[62] A year earlier the Recorder of the City of London even claimed there was 'not a boy or young lad tried at our Courts of Justice whose position there is not more or less due to the effects of unwholesome literature upon his mind'.[63]

In the 1890s the 'penny dreadfuls' came under pressure from another source, when Alfred Harmsworth began his publishing career in children's periodicals by producing *Comic Cuts* at a halfpenny to compete with the leading penny comic of the day, *Ally Sloper's Half-Holiday*. Its success led to other Harmsworth publications, like *Illustrated Chips* (1890), the *Halfpenny Wonder* (1892) and the *Halfpenny Marvel* (1893). In publishing the latter Harmsworth made clear his determination to wage war on the 'dreadfuls'. The 'healthy stories of mystery, adventure etc.' offered in the *Marvel* would overwhelm them. Soon came *Union Jack* and *Pluck* (both in 1894) and the *Boy's Friend* (1895), which contained a still stronger denunciation of the 'penny dreadfuls' and served as a vehicle for the imperialistic mood of the day. Although Harmsworth included tales of violence, most of his publications were not especially sensational. Hence A.A. Milne was scarcely fair when he claimed that 'Harmsworth killed the "penny dreadful" by the simple process of producing the ha'penny dreadfuller.'[64] More to the point, as Patrick Dunae points out, was the fact that by the 1890s the cheap press was no longer the object of suspicion it had been a quarter of a century earlier. Popular education had ceased to be controversial and, as a result, 'the juvenile periodical press, which developed largely because of the Board Schools', was also accepted.[65]

Girls were not entirely left out of this publishing revolution. Their 'penny novelettes', with stories of improbable romance and murder, were castigated by the critics as just as pernicious as the 'dreadfuls'. Edward Salmon argued that the 'high-flown conceits and pretensions of the poorer girls of the period, their dislike of manual work and love of freedom' could be traced to the noxious ideas 'imbibed in the course of a perusal of their penny fiction'. In his view there was 'hardly a magazine read by them which it would not be a moral benefit to have swept off the face of the earth'.[66] To counter these 'undesirables', the Religious Tract Society issued the *Girl's Own Paper* in 1880. But an examination of its pages reveals that it was directed at middle and lower middle-class adolescents rather than younger children or those lower down the social scale. Some of its features could, indeed, have offended working-class readers, as on 2 December 1882, when it declared loftily in an article on 'Cookery for the Poor': 'There is no class of the community which needs to be instructed in cookery so much as the very poor.' Among the recipes were those for ox-cheek stew, cow-heel with parsley sauce, and pig's fry, or 'poor man's goose'.[67]

Other issues of the *Girl's Own Paper* ran along similar lines, as well as including serials, poems and instructions for knitting, embroidery and dressmaking. In 1886 Edward Salmon praised the magazine's moral influence and its prize competitions, which were 'the medium of much charity. For instance, in 1885, 700 mufflers and 1,224 pairs of cuffs sent in competition were presented to occupants of London workhouses, after the prizes had been awarded.'[68] In the early 1880s the *Girl's Own Paper* had a circulation of about two hundred thousand weekly. A new magazine, the *Girl's Realm*, which appeared in 1898, was directed at much the same market.[69]

But whatever the merits of the literature on offer, there is no doubt that publishing for children had been transformed when compared with the situation at the beginning of Queen Victoria's reign. Then the market had been dominated by the books and journals issued by the Sunday school movement, plus some nursery stories, a sprinkling of 'moral' tales, and a few lurid 'penny dreadfuls'. By 1900 works catering for all tastes were available and most of the doubts about the adverse influence of cheap literature had faded away.

Similar debates to those conducted over the 'dreadfuls' took place from the 1830s over the role of penny theatres, or 'penny gaffs'. These were unlicensed temporary theatres, frequently set up in converted shops or warehouses and offering a programme of dancing, singing and sensational drama. Their mixture of violence and *double entendre* was believed to have a damaging effect on the morals of working-class youngsters, who comprised most of their clientele. By 1838 there were perhaps eighty to one hundred gaffs in London, many of them in the East End, and Henry Mayhew, who visited some of them in the 1840s and 1850s, condemned their crudity:

> Here the stage, instead of being the means for illustrating a moral precept, is turned into a platform to teach the cruelest [*sic*] debauchery. The audience is usually composed of children so young, that these dens become the school-rooms where the guiding morals of a life are picked up; and so precocious are the little things, that the girl of nine will, from constant attendance at such places, have learnt to understand the filthiest sayings, and laugh at them as loudly as the grown-up lads around her.[70]

The cheap theatre was felt to threaten not merely sexual purity but attitudes towards the law as well. In 1839, the Metropolitan Police Act empowered the police to close down unlicensed 'gaffs' and the prosecutions that followed were linked to the general belief that the plays they staged, glorifying the exploits of highwaymen and house-breakers, were contributing to the rise in juvenile crime. In 1841 the Inspector of Prisons for the North-East District of England claimed that an examination of almost a hundred boys held in Liverpool prison had revealed 'the mischievous tendency of such productions' in encouraging criminality.[71] There were allegations that young patrons were prepared to steal in order to obtain their entrance money. Yet it was not the enforcement of theatrical licensing laws which spelled the end of the penny theatres but the rise of cheap music-halls from the 1860s. Unlike the 'gaffs', which were mostly supported by working-class youngsters, music-halls became prototypes 'of the modern mass communications industry, appealing across both age and class barriers' to secure their audiences.[72] Already by the end of the 1860s there were thirty-nine music-halls in London and a further three hundred over the rest of the country.[73]

Children in the provinces might also be enthusiastic theatregoers. In Leamington Spa, the young George Hewins was so impressed by a black minstrel show that appeared at the Theatre Royal that he and his friends set up The Bakehouse Minstrel Troupe, with an entrance fee of a halfpenny, and for a time they were moderately successful. 'I liked everything about it', recalled George, 'dressing-up, singing, folks clapping and cheering.'[74]

At Merthyr Tydfil, Jack Jones, the son of a Welsh miner, remembered weekly theatre trips with his mother and her large brood of children, the smallest of whom was carried there in the mother's arms. Until 1894 Merthyr Tydfil had no purpose-built theatre and Jack's family patronized the two wooden playhouses the town boasted. Shows were put on by travelling companies and to obtain admission Mrs Jones and the children were prepared to go without food. The weekly shilling earned by Jack as a butcher's errand boy was 'theatre' money, and when there was not enough cash to pay for the whole family to attend their twice-weekly treat, his mother devised various stratagems to meet the deficit. These included lending items of furniture for stage sets or supplying 'whichever baby happened to be new at the time to add to the realism of plays of the class then called "domestic drama".' In return, free passes were given to the children:

> Whenever a circus came to town we children distributed handbills in return for free passes. . . . 'Maria Marten or the Murder in the Red Barn' was a great favourite of our mam's, but we children preferred the plays with sword-fighting in them, such plays as 'The Corsican Brothers' and 'The Duke's Motto.' And we fought off oncoming sleep to stay awake for the farces which followed the plays, the nightcap of laughter which those little theatres so generously gave their audiences.[75]

Two or three years after the town's permanent Theatre Royal opened, when Jack was about twelve or thirteen, he got a job selling refreshments to the gallery audience. The seven shillings a week he earned solved the family's theatre entrance problems, and although the more sober citizenry of Merthyr Tydfil might deplore the devotion of hard-earned funds to such a frivolous end, Jack himself had no regrets; it was regarded as 'heaven upon earth' by 'mam and us kids'.

Middle-class children went to the theatre, too, particularly the Christmas pantomime, in which large numbers of working-class children would take part as members of the chorus or of specialist dancing troupes. Gordon Roe, the son of a well-to-do late Victorian London family, regarded the theatre as 'the gateway to a world of make-believe more vivid than reality'.[76] After their return home, such children might stage their own 'theatrical' performances for the benefit of the family, or they would play with model theatres, many of them manufactured in Germany. Quite small children could manipulate these by turning a handle at the side of the stage, thereby winding a new printed scene into view.[77]

Throughout the period adults had a firm belief that if youngsters were left to their own devices, they would get into mischief. Regulation of their leisure hours was, therefore, a continuing concern. It even found expression in bizarre demands for the control of sweet shops, since these were felt to encourage the undesirable habit of smoking among boy patrons by their sales of tobacco, and of gambling by their provision of penny-in-the-slot machines, whereby youngsters could insert a penny in the hope of getting threepence worth of sweets. Shopkeepers claimed that this was a game of skill not of chance, since if the player were clumsy he or she lost the penny, but critics were unconvinced. They demanded that 'a rigid system of licensing and State supervision' be extended to such shops.[78]

It was, however, the Sunday school movement which was the main weapon in the battle to encourage respectability and good order among the urban young in the nineteenth century. That applied not merely to the religious instruction given and the books issued, but to the movement's wider social role. For many children, Sunday school outings and the Sunday school anniversary were major events in their year. In the north of England Whit Walks were of particular importance, with youngsters parading the streets in new clothes, with a band at their head and, often enough, carrying the banner of the Sunday school they attended. A Cheshire woman remembered the 'Whit Friday Walk' as a highlight in her town's annual calendar:

Whit Walks in King Street, Dukinfield, Cheshire, c. 1900. All the participants were clearly dressed in their best clothes. (Tameside Local Studies Library, Stalybridge)

all the churches and chapels, led by their bands, paraded around their parishes carrying banners and the children carrying baskets of flowers delighting in showing off their new clothes. New clothes were very important . . . and the children might not have got any new clothes if it hadn't been for Whit Friday. . . . And . . . children not only went round with the procession, but they used to come knocking at your door showing their new clothes, wanting some money to be put in their pockets . . . It was a form of begging really. . . . Following the walks there were refreshments at the schools. In the afternoon they all enjoyed joining in the sports on their chosen fields which were hired from the local farmers.[79]

In Manchester, the Whit Walks became an expression of sectarian loyalty, with the Catholics parading on Whit Friday and the Anglicans on Whit Monday. Afterwards clothes were pledged in pawn shops by some of the poorest families, and there was a great effort, if it were a wet day, to make sure they were not damaged and their value depreciated.[80]

Another landmark in the Sunday school year was the anniversary when even 'the poorest houses turned out little girls in white frocks, . . . with hair generously combed and oiled'. Poems were recited, choruses sung, and one school in the Midlands even performed a medieval miracle play as part of its celebrations.[81]

But for many youngsters it was the annual outing which was most looked forward to, since this might provide their only opportunity to visit places away from their immediate home area. Before the coming of the railways, children from London's East End went by wagon to Richmond Park, and Manchester children travelled by canal boats on their Whitsun outings.[82] With the railways more elaborate expeditions were possible and they enabled children to be removed from undesirable 'counter-attractions'. In 1844, the Wigan Sunday School Union announced a rail outing to Bootle, near Liverpool, for about 4,000 children and teachers in order to withdraw them from the 'demoralizing fascination of the racecourse'.[83] But even routine visits were welcomed by children who rarely had a holiday. A North London woman remembered

those wonderful days of 1893–5 when children and teachers from our Sunday Schools in Islington clambered up into horsedrawn brakes. . . . Soon the streets were left behind. Country roads, hedges and trees and fields took their place until we arrived at Epping Forest where we could walk or run on the grass, play games and run races. . . . In 1896 we went from a London station by steam train to Southend. What an adventure that was! My first sight of the sea![84]

From 1847 the Band of Hope united the values of the Sunday school with those of the temperance cause. Although the Band was itself non-denominational, close ties were formed with churches and chapels of all persuasions, and meetings were held which combined temperance ideals and entertainment so as to effect the 'cultural reconstruction' of the working classes, and turn them from the 'demon drink'. From the early 1850s, local associations were formed, especially in the industrial north. Through these equipment was supplied, including lantern slides, and speakers were sent to individual societies. Alongside the signing of an anti-drink (and sometimes also an anti-smoking) pledge, youngsters learned to enjoy music through the temperance songs and religious hymns sung at rallies. Simple orchestras were formed and members were given free lessons on their selected instrument. Large concerts were held in London for massed choirs of Band of Hope members, the first being given by a choir of one thousand singers in 1862. These became annual events, with that for 1886 having three choirs with a total of fifteen thousand singers performing at the Crystal Palace.[85]

The Band of Hope proved most attractive to the children of skilled artisans. Less interest was displayed by the poorest children, whose parents often had little sympathy with its anti-alcohol message or with the idea of devoting meagre resources to such a cause. By the end of the century doubts were being expressed about the effectiveness of the movement in spreading the temperance message. Although national membership at that date was around three million, it was clear that many youngsters forgot their temperance pledges when they grew up.[86] Some were perhaps like the Bristol girl who joined her local Band of Hope 'because the kids from the street used to go, on a Tuesday night'. But she did not take its message very seriously. 'I used to go straight home an' fetch my mother's penneth of beer for her supper, and have a drink out of the jug.' What she most enjoyed was the annual outing: 'They used to have furniture vans. We used to pay a penny. Put all the chairs in the furniture van and get in. Go up on the Downs and have a sing-song.'[87]

By the end of the century membership of the broader Sunday school movement was beginning to stagnate. Numbers had jumped from 2.6 million in 1851 to 5.7 million in 1881, but then climbed slowly to reach 5.9 million in 1901. As a percentage of the British population, this latter represented a small downturn compared to 1881, from 19 per cent of total population enrolled at that date to 16 per cent in 1901.[88] Changes in population structure and the rise of secularism, plus the establishment of alternative forms of youth organization, all contributed to this process.[89]

Meanwhile in certain areas charities were set up to provide poor children with holidays. In London the Children's Country Holiday Fund was founded in 1884 under the auspices of the Charity Organisation Society to 'provide fresh air' for deserving children. By 1889 it was sending about 20,000 youngsters to the country each year at a cost of more than £13,000, to which parents contributed just over a third.[90] The fund enabled Walter Southgate and his sister to spend a fortnight 'in the real country to us, at Stock in Essex'. Walter was nine years old and it was the first time he had seen fields of grass, wild flowers and corn, or cattle and sheep grazing.[91] In Manchester and Salford a similar organization was formed in the 1880s and within nineteen years had sent nearly fifteen thousand poor children to the country for a three-week holiday.[92]

Even employers might give their workers annual outings. In Birmingham during the 1860s so-called 'gipsy parties' were sent to Malvern and other places of interest. They were so much enjoyed that according to one commentator, some younger operatives fixed 'the date of their coming to work from a "gipsy party" a year or two back'.[93] Charles Iles, a hook and eye manufacturer, was one employer who gave such

"THOSE YELLOW SANDS!"

THE BROWNS DEPART FOR THE SEA-SIDE, TO THE WISTFUL ADMIRATION OF THEIR LESS FORTUNATE NEIGHBOURS.

Fortunate children off to the seaside, watched by envious young neighbours. (Punch, 1886)

excursions to his workers, and he claimed it had broad social benefits. 'It induces the people to keep themselves tidy to be fit for it, and it enlarges their ideas by showing them things which they do not see at other times.'[94]

In the textile areas at the end of the century some mill workers saved up to have a few days away (without pay) during wakes week. It was this which contributed to the sharp increase in visitors to Blackpool during the last two decades of the nineteenth century, while other resorts like Morecambe and Llandudno expanded, too. One lad who began work as a weaver in about 1894, when he was thirteen, remembered that when trade was good he and his family saved enough to take a modest holiday at Blackpool or Morecambe. 'You did not board, but took your food with you. It meant a busy week beforehand for Mother, baking all the bread and fancy cakes needed for seven people for a week. You could get good beds for half-a-crown a night! We had a much battered oblong tin box in which we packed all the provisions, and any surplus luggage was shared by the family.'[95]

These brief breaks were very different from the lengthy annual visits to the seaside or the country enjoyed by middle-class town children. Some, like Molly Hughes, went to relatives. In her case this meant staying with her mother's family on their farm near the Cornish coast. There were picnics, bathing in the sea and hunts for anemones, shells and seaweed. Afterwards Molly and some of her cousins painted while the rest watched the sea for distant steamers. There were games on the farm itself and charades in the evening. 'When all else failed we fell back on drawing and painting in the front kitchen. I can remember no dull hour at Reskadinnick.'[96]

'Muscular Christianity'. Abingdon School Four rowing on the River Thames near Abingdon in 1897. (Abingdon School)

Certain urban families, like the Gaskells, took their children away not merely for health and enjoyment but to give them country interests. As Mrs Gaskell told a friend when they were lodging in a farmhouse, it was important that the children should 'learn country . . . ways of living and thinking', since these were very different from Manchester, where so much of their time was spent.[97]

Moral values and recreational pursuits were also brought to bear through the influence of the school. For upper middle-class youngsters, particularly boys, the great emphasis on sports at the public schools during the era of 'muscular Christianity' in the second half of the nineteenth century affected out-of-school interests. The Royal Commission on the Public Schools underlined this in 1864, when it claimed that games were not only valuable for promoting pupils' health and physical activity but for their leisure hours as well:

> they implant the habit, which does not cease with boyhood, of seeking recreation in hardy and vigorous exercise. The cricket and football fields . . . are not merely places of exercise and amusement; they help to form some of the most valuable social qualities and manly virtues, and they hold . . . a distinct and important place in public-school education. . . . The importance which the boys themselves attach to games is somewhat greater, perhaps, than might reasonably be desired, but . . . it is . . . the best corrective of the temptation to over-study which acts upon a clever and ambitious boy, and of the temptation to saunter away time which besets an indolent one.[98]

Other middle-class schools shared this enthusiasm. The magazine of Christ's College, Blackheath, in the mid-1890s devoted more space to an account of sporting contests in which the boys had been involved than to anything else. It even added *Football Weekly* to its meagre library, and when discussing the setting up of a games room it was careful to warn that this should not 'keep boys indoors when they might be gaining health and strength by outdoor exercise'.[99]

Belief in the reformist role of sports was extended to the schooling of older girls, for whom games like tennis, rounders and hockey were increasingly accepted, and to youngsters lower down the social scale. It was from the 1870s that elementary schools in many towns began to encourage physical exercise, ranging from military drill in the playground to cricket, football and swimming, where appropriate facilities were available. Boys played football in back streets and school playgrounds, or wherever else they could, and in the larger towns they accompanied fathers on Saturday afternoons to watch professional matches. By 1895–6 the senior HMI for London reported that there were few schools in the capital without a football club and a cricket club. Some years later Dr Niven, Medical Officer of Health for Manchester, declared that every field that could possibly be obtained had been 'snapped up all round the city for football clubs and cricket or one game or another. There is a very great eagerness on the part of Manchester children to get spaces for games.' Swimming was particularly popular, with almost 340,000 visits to the baths made by scholars during the year ending 7 November 1901. Just over 177,000 of these were made free of charge. Dr Niven added that there were twelve gymnasia in the city, many of them used by poor children. 'I certainly do think that physical exercise is pursued to the limit of practicability in Manchester.'[100]

Something of the enthusiasm engendered among pupils by school sports can be discerned in the log book of Malmesbury Road Boys' School in London. Not only did the headmaster record meticulously the results of inter-school football matches, but in November 1888 the pupils presented him with an illuminated address, which they had all signed, thanking him for the interest he had taken 'not only in our studies, but . . . in forming successful Cricket, Football and Swimming Clubs'.[101]

This broadening of the curriculum was extended to other areas, with schools establishing libraries, forming school museums and arranging excursions. At Malmesbury Road the headmaster took older boys to the Royal Academy in July 1888 and followed this up three months later with a trip to an Italian exhibition, to look at sculptures and paintings. After that came visits to a marionette show and the theatre. Later the father of one of the boys wrote to thank the head for arranging a much-appreciated outing for his son.[102]

For school-leavers, education authorities provided evening classes. In London they covered subjects such as cookery, wood-carving and music as well as the basics: reading, writing and arithmetic. By the early 1890s, 24,000 students were receiving technical instruction in the capital's evening classes, compared to around fourteen thousand in Manchester at that date. Birmingham in September 1895 had twenty-seven evening classes open with an enrolment of 6,037.[103] Only a small minority of young people took advantage of these opportunities for self-improvement, but they added to the variety of leisure pursuits at the end of the century.

In the last two decades of the Victorian period the uniformed youth movements likewise began to play a part, building on the desire to promote imperialism, physical fitness and morality, as well as on the failure of Sunday schools to retain boys once they had reached the age of twelve or thirteen. Even if such lads did attend, they were often indisciplined. It was to counter this that William Smith set up the Boys' Brigade in Glasgow in 1883, drawing on his experience as an officer in the Volunteers, a part-time military force. In applying military methods to the sphere of religion and moral conduct he was, to some degree, following the Salvation Army (from 1878) and the Church Army (from 1882) in demonstrating that 'religion in uniform' was acceptable.[104] Smith wished to create a sense of solidarity in the Boys' Brigade which would make members proud of their own company and would extend the public schools' *esprit de corps* to those from humbler backgrounds. 'It . . . seemed to us that by associating Christianity with all that was most noble and manly in a boy's sight', he declared in 1888, 'we would be going a long way to disabuse his mind of the idea that there is anything effeminate or weak about Christianity; an idea that is far too widespread among Boys.'[105] Parade-ground drill and strict discipline were used to reinforce the Gospel. To establish a sense of identity, recruits were fitted out with a simple uniform of pillbox cap, leather belt, and white haversack, worn with their ordinary clothes.[106]

The Brigade catered for boys between the ages of twelve and seventeen and by November 1885 it had spread to England, with companies formed in London, Manchester and Penzance, among other centres; Liverpool, Nottingham, Newcastle, Bristol and Sheffield soon joined in. In Nottingham companies were formed jointly with boys' clubs and although most recruits came from the better-off working classes, in Sheffield and Liverpool poorer boys also joined. In the latter city the clergy considered that the Brigade had recruited 'a class of lads our Sunday School and other organizations have failed to reach and not only humanizes but Christianizes them too, in the truest and highest sense'.[107]

Walter Southgate, who was attracted by recruitment drives in the East End of London, had less lofty views. He regarded the Boys' Brigade as 'nothing more than dressing up boys in army-type uniforms, drilling, marching and carrying wooden rifles, blowing bugles, banging drums or organising drum and fife bands'. At first he and his friends 'flocked to join', but disillusion soon set in:

On the opening night, the local mission hall was crowded with boys . . . , all eager to put on a pill-box hat and a canvas belt with brass buckles, ready and prepared to shoulder a wooden rifle. Unfortunately, there was not enough equipment to go round, which caused a great deal of dissatisfaction. A boy without a pill-box hat and other accessories felt naked and ashamed to go marching and drilling. . . . The upshot of that opening night was that every boy disregarded orders and words of command. They formed themselves into groups and marched round the hall singing all the popular music hall ditties with appropriate cockney wording and ribald phrasing unbecoming for a church hall.[108]

Other boys, however, found the experience rewarding. Along with Bible class, the most regular meeting held by each company was the weekly 'parade night', which initially concentrated on military drill. William Sharpe, who joined a London company in the 1890s, enjoyed drilling: 'I took to it and my shoulders are still square . . . I honestly think it was that which taught me to walk upright.'[109]

Bands were formed from the 1880s and in addition to playing on parade nights and at Sunday services, they were soon in demand in the wider community, performing at concerts, flower shows, and similar events. Proficiency badges and company prizes were awarded, and for many working-class boys they offered a chance to learn to play a musical instrument and to join in an 'otherwise adult or middle-class activity'.[110]

Perhaps most innovatory was the Brigade's introduction of camping holidays. Initially these were held with the boys sleeping in a building, but by the 1890s many companies were using bell tents. Camping not only improved the boys' physical health but was credited with moral and social benefits as well: 'No better method could be devised for teaching the boys the duty of sinking the wishes of the individual in the commonweal, for inculcating the true spirit of comradeship, and for putting into practice these principles of manly Christianity for the advancement of which the Brigade exists.'[111]

Children spending precious pennies on ice cream at the foot of Stockwell Street, London, in 1884. (Greater London Record Office Photograph Collection)

By 1899 the Boys' Brigade claimed a membership in England and Wales of 19,715, divided into 470 companies, and its successful combination of recreation, religion and military training led others to follow its example. The Church Lads' Brigade was formed in Fulham in 1891 by Walter Mallock Gee. Like William Smith of the Boys' Brigade, he had been a member of the Volunteers, as well as secretary of the junior branch of the Church of England Temperance Society. He was anxious to promote the temperance ideal while teaching 'the lads of the Church on distinctly Church lines'.[112] His methods followed those pioneered by Smith and within six years every diocese in England and Wales was represented in his organization. In addition, a London Diocesan Church Lads' Brigade was set up in the early 1890s to promote total abstinence, but in other respects following the principles of its larger predecessors.[113]

In the Jewish community a proposal to create a youth group along Brigade lines had been made as early as 1891 in a letter to the *Jewish Chronicle*,[114] but nothing came of it and it was left to an army officer, Lionel Goldsmid, to form the Jewish Lads' Brigade in 1895. The aim was to instil 'habits of orderliness, cleanliness, and honour', so that members in learning to respect themselves, would 'do credit to their community and country'.[115] But an important underlying aim was to help 'Anglicize' and assimilate into English society the large numbers of young Jewish immigrants who had recently come from eastern Europe and were settled in the ghettos of the East End of London. That involved what was called 'ironing out the Ghetto bend', so that they would learn to 'walk straight' and take an active part in sport.[116] By the early twentieth century the Jewish Lads' Brigade claimed membership of a thousand, and, like its Christian forerunners, it not only took part in parades and communal events but organized annual camps. The first of these was held at Deal in 1896, when about twenty lads followed a Boys' Brigade company to a site on a local farm.[117] Discipline began even before they reached Deal, with orders issued that they were to form up at Cannon Street station with a kitbag containing two towels, a brush and comb, and extra clothing. Cap, belt, badge of rank and uniform swagger stick served as their uniform, and each boy was issued with a dummy rifle.[118]

A Catholic Boys' Brigade was created, too, in 1896, based on a boys' club in Bermondsey, and with the ulterior motive of stemming the outflow of youngsters from the church. Members were largely the sons of unskilled or semi-skilled Irish Catholic dock workers and at first they drilled with sticks or broom handles, before graduating to rifles. Like the other Brigades, this, too, concentrated on a mixture of 'military drill and religion, physical exercises and ambulance classes, sports and camping'.[119] It was soon taken up in other parts of the country, including Ireland, and by 1906 claimed a national membership of around 8,000.

Finally for those opposed to the militarism of the existing movements, the Boys' Life Brigade was set up in Nottingham in 1899 by a Congregational minister. It was part of the Nonconformist National Sunday School Union and its emphasis was on life-saving (from fire and water) as a substitute for drill. The Boys' Life Brigade embraced all the qualities its founder admired in the older Brigades without displaying 'the least tincture of militarism'.[120]

All these organizations had characteristics in common. They sought to instil the principles of conformity, respectability, cleanliness and discipline into members and to inculcate appropriate religious beliefs and practices. With few exceptions they appealed to the sons of skilled working-class and lower middle-class families, while leaving out the children of the slums who shared neither their interests nor the financial means to support membership. Indeed, as at Enfield in London, persecution by local hooligans was a common experience for early Brigade members. It was 'a long time before Drill and other gatherings could be held without the risk of interruption from rowdies outside', recalled an early activist.[121] Even adult officers in uniform were pelted with bottles and other missiles as they went to drill and the boys often had to defend their uniform with their fists, which was scarcely what the movement's founders had envisaged.

In some larger towns boys' clubs were formed in the 1870s and '80s to provide leisure pursuits, mainly for unskilled working lads. Many in London were promoted by leading public schools, imbued with a spirit of social and religious conscience and anxious to bridge the gap between rich and poor in the interests of community cohesion.[122] They included the Mallard Street Club, run from 1880 by Eton College for so-called 'rough' boys in its Hackney Wick 'mission district'. Marlborough College set up a club in Tottenham in 1882 and Harrow formed its Notting Dale mission a year later. A carpenter's son remembered 'practically living' at the Eton Manor Boys' Club, formed by Eton College Mission, when he was in his mid-teens. The club had extensive playing fields, a library and a games room: 'There'd be three or four hundred children there you know, and I daresay on average . . . there'd be a hundred . . . every night . . . you met better class boys [and played games] such as draughts and chess – in the library, reading . . . mixing with 'em and that . . . you try to get to 'em . . . you go a little bit cleaner, a little bit smarter.'[123]

But not all clubs ran smoothly. At Portsmouth where a Mission was supported by Winchester College and run by a tough Irish-born clergyman, the Revd Robert Radclyffe Dolling, the gymnasium he opened in the 1880s was the scene of much violence in the early days. Hooligans strummed on the piano with their feet, broke chairs, and damaged bagatelle tables and climbing apparatus. But Dolling soon established order. On one memorable occasion he personally threw out each member of a disruptive gang and, when they returned, threw them out again. Finally they admitted defeat and from then on gave him, and the gymnasium, a wide berth.[124]

By 1900, therefore, it was widely accepted that every child ought to have at least some leisure free from the responsibilities of work and domestic duties. The commercial entertainment on offer had greatly expanded, and the desire of adults to curb juvenile high spirits and reduce the threat to public order of lads idling on the streets had led to the formation of boys' clubs and the uniformed youth movements. Yet many children in the 1890s, as in the 1830s, found outlets for their energies in playing traditional games and improvising their own fun from things they found around them in their daily lives. A few of the poorest were still burdened with family cares and had no chance to pursue their own pastimes. 'Never no time to play', one of them wistfully told Charles Booth in the 1890s.[125] But by then such luckless youngsters were very much a minority of the juvenile population.

CHAPTER 8

Rescue and Reform

> Among the social questions with which the nation has to deal, there is none
> . . . so important as the question of the children. The wise treatment of this
> question . . . must affect the eventual solution of all other social problems . . . .
> They have a special claim on us in their powerlessness to right themselves.
>
> Gertrude M. Tuckwell, *The State and its Children* (1894), p. v.

The ambivalence of society towards children and their welfare was nowhere more
apparent than in its approach to those on its fringes – the destitute, the orphaned,
and the juvenile delinquent. On the one hand there were those who emphasized
the need to preserve childhood 'innocence', and who saw the child's mind,
'providing the passions are properly guided', as 'a fountain of all that is
beautiful'.[1] But others stressed the innate tendency of most youngsters for
wrongdoing and the need to curb and discipline them. The Bristol penal
reformer, Mary Carpenter, was not alone in lamenting the 'innumerable
multitudes' of neglected, destitute and criminal children 'swarming in our large
cities and haunting all its by-ways', who were growing up 'in utter ignorance of
everything that might profit their immortal souls'.[2] To remedy this she
underlined the importance of recognizing the special qualities of childhood. 'We
hold that children should not be dealt with as men, but as children', was one of
her recurrent cries.[3]

Such ambiguities characterized some of the charities formed to help vagrant
youngsters, like the Society for the Reformation of Juvenile Offenders, whose
purpose was to supervise convicted lads if they were given a conditional pardon,
and the Children's Friend Society. This had begun life in 1830 as the Society for
the Suppression of Juvenile Vagrancy and had been formed, according to its
founder, to clear the streets of unemployed children, 'who swell the daily
catalogue of juvenile offenders'.[4] Many of those involved in helping needy
youngsters combined a desire to rescue and reform with a wish to eliminate the
threat posed by the destitute and the delinquent to the smooth running of a law-
abiding society.

These concerns applied with particular force to girls, who were felt to be
sexually endangered unless they were protected by their family or some external
organization. In much of the literature of the day the innocent female child was
portrayed as an instrument for redemption in a sinful world, as with Little Nell in

Charles Dickens's *Old Curiosity Shop*, or Sissy Jupe, the former circus child, in the same author's *Hard Times*.[5] But also significant in Victorian ideology was the perception of the girl as a temptress, who could lead men astray. It was symptomatic of the attitude of a patriarchal society that the precocious sexuality of the child was blamed rather than the actions of the males who utilized her services. Hence in the mid-1880s there were complaints of 'shoeless, impudent, little girls' pushing 'vile pictures in the faces of passers-by' in London, and cautionary tales were told of small female beggars pursuing male pedestrians, plucking at their elbows and trying to excite their interest by lewd remarks.[6] These issues were examined in the debate which surrounded the raising of the age of consent from twelve to thirteen in 1875, and, after a long and controversial campaign, to sixteen a decade later. In 1881 the police told a government inquiry that procurers could obtain girls 'without any difficulty whatever above the age of 13'. Many of these children lived at home and plied their trade 'with the knowledge and active connivance of the mother and to the profit of the household'.[7] In 1882 the Select Committee on the Law Relating to the Protection of Young Girls claimed that juvenile prostitution 'from an almost incredibly early age' was 'increasing to an appalling extent in England, and especially in London'. Medical journals discussed the incidence of venereal diseases among some of these girls and it was to check the scandal caused by young prostitutes that the age of consent was raised in 1885. The potentially 'contaminating' influence of the sexually aware child also led many homes for female orphans in the mid-Victorian years to include a proviso that those admitted must be 'innocent'. Both to penal reformers and to society at large, 'a delinquent girl was far more offensive than a miscreant lad'.[8]

Alongside these two major strands of the argument, depicting the deprived child either as innocent victim or malign wrongdoer, there were others, like the painter, Dorothy Stanley, who stressed the street child's resilience and self-reliance. Mrs Stanley criticized the tendency to show such youngsters as 'pale whining children with sunken eyes, holding up bunches of violets to heedless passers-by; dying match girls, sorrowful water-cress girls'.[9] These were not the 'merry, reckless, happy-go-lucky' urchins she met in her walks through the city. But while many of the needy were able to overcome their difficulties in the way she described, her remarks were concerned with the superficial trappings of their daily existence only – the jaunty face they showed to the outside world. She did not consider the precarious nature of their daily existence, with its ever-present danger of mistreatment, disease and hunger. It was left to the 'child savers', particularly the National Society for the Prevention of Cruelty to Children, to focus on these deeper problems in the final years of the century.

At the beginning of Victoria's reign the number of youngsters who through poverty, family hardship, or criminality found themselves on the edges of respectability, was growing rapidly. It was the unfortunate by-product of an expanding and fragmented industrialized and urbanized society. Political unrest, associated with demands for parliamentary reform and universal male suffrage in the 1840s, fuelled middle-class fears about the consequences of allowing large numbers of juveniles to grow up without education or moral influence. In 1848

The girl as temptress. Juvenile prostitution was a regrettable fact of life in parts of London (and other large cities) in the 1880s. (The author)

Lord Ashley referred to more than thirty thousand 'naked, filthy, roaming, lawless, and deserted children, in and about the metropolis', who earned a living as crossing sweepers, costermongers, errand boys and girls, and in other casual occupations.[10] These were shelterless children and did not include the many child beggars living in common lodging-houses or slum tenements. Almost thirty years later Dr Thomas Barnardo could still put the number of destitute and homeless juveniles under sixteen in London at around thirty thousand.[11] Prominent among them were 'Irish cockneys', the second-generation offspring of Irish immigrants, who congregated in the poorest districts, like the St Giles rookery, and were disproportionately involved in juvenile crime. Charles Dickens compared these gangs of ragged and defiant youngsters, many of whom slept under archways or beneath the stalls in public markets, to 'wild birds, pilfering the crumbs which fall from the table of the country's wealth'.[12] Even on the 'very lowest ground' of cost, it was expensive to allow 'swarms of young children to grow up yearly into a mass of wild brutes, preying on society'.[13]

Outside the capital, the larger towns and cities had their own retinues of neglected and homeless youngsters, living and working on the streets and seeking shelter in sheds and cellars or lodging-houses, when they could find sufficient pence to pay for a bed for the night. In Manchester in 1840, the police found 3,650 children sleeping rough, while in Sheffield, too, large numbers of vagrant children were 'prowling' about.[14] In supporting themselves they displayed much the same resourcefulness as their London counterparts. In addition to those who begged or sold goods on the streets, there were many who financed themselves by stealing anything they could lay their hands on, be it hens on roosts and pigeons in lofts or washing from clothes-lines. Joseph Stamper recalled how in the 1890s the poorest children in St Helens would steal food from one another in the streets, cramming it into their mouth as they ran off. 'Sometimes little starvelings would knock at the door and when Mother went: "Can you spare a bit of bread, missus?" Mother would . . . cut a butty, [and] take it to the child. The child would eat [it] there and then, to make sure nobody stole it.'[15]

Theft from the docks was widespread in ports like Liverpool or Bristol. In the latter city police reported little boys of six and seven taking bits of old iron, copper, brass, and ropes left on the quays, while in Liverpool youngsters swarmed and scavenged among the bales and then escaped by hanging on to the bottom of the loaded waggons as they passed through the gates. So successful were they that a number conducted their own market in the cellars of empty houses, where they 'sold their swag to scrap-merchants and ran off for more. Others robbed drunken people who fell unconscious in the streets, or stole lead and gas-pipes from housing sites.'[16] Ill-gotten gains could be passed on to dealers or taken to lodging-house keepers, some of whom only admitted youngsters on the understanding that they disposed of all their booty to the master. Any attempt to leave or to sell property elsewhere led to the receiver threatening to have them arrested. Second-hand clothes shops and marine stores were other ready recipients of stolen goods, and there were real-life villains like Charles Dickens's fictional Fagin, who trained youngsters to pick pockets.[17]

The work of the newly established statistical societies from the 1830s had underlined the growth in juvenile lawlessness and the links between delinquency and overcrowded slums. The pejorative language used to describe these youngsters revealed the deep unease they caused. In 1851 the first Recorder of Birmingham, Matthew Davenport Hill, noted the dangers that would arise if reforms were not instituted to rescue them from the temptations of city life:

> by some they are called the Arabs of the streets; by others the outcasts of society; by others again, human vermin. . . . It . . . becomes of the very deepest importance, not only with regard to the temporal and eternal happiness of that particular class, but for the safety of all, old and young, high and low, rich and poor, that the state of neglect and mistaken treatment in which these miserable beings are found, should cease to exist.[18]

Self-interest was thus a major factor behind the rising concern for destitute children in mid-Victorian England. As Elaine Hadley has drily commented, it was not 'the rags and hungry eyes' of neglected youngsters that stimulated philanthropic initiatives but a vision of the 'jaunty clothing and chop-house feast' they had gained through delinquent behaviour.[19] These fears also encouraged the better-off to treat as criminal acts, conduct which, in calmer times, might have been dismissed as youthful high spirits. In 1862 Henry Mayhew was shocked to find 'little creatures of six years of age branded with a felon's badge' in the House of Correction, Tothill Fields. Their crime had been 'the heinous offence of throwing stones, or obstructing highways, or unlawfully knocking at doors – crimes which the very magistrates themselves, who committed the youths, must have assuredly perpetrated in their boyhood'.[20] In this way the belief that there was an upsurge of juvenile crime became, to some extent, a self-fulfilling prophecy.

There was a class-related element to the question, too. Mary Carpenter and Henry Mayhew both criticized the practice of imposing different penalties on offenders according to their social standing. To rob an orchard might be regarded as a clever feat for a 'gentleman's son at a public school', commented Carpenter sourly, whereas a boy who stole lead from a roof would be threatened with the severest penalties.[21]

Parents whose drunken and feckless ways were blamed for their offspring's lawless conduct were fiercely condemned. In 1851, Charles Dickens suggested they should be deprived permanently of the custody of their children, while compelled 'if they have any means of existence' to contribute something towards the youngsters' support.[22] Mary Carpenter, too, claimed that after fifteen years of visiting the poor in Bristol, she could confidently assert that in ninety-nine cases out of a hundred a family's distress was due directly or indirectly to habits of 'intoxication or other vice'.[23] Such arguments ignored the harsh reality faced by many working-class families, for whom seasonal unemployment, or the death or serious illness of the major breadwinner could bring dire distress, without any accompanying moral weakness. Thus of 189,279 children receiving poor relief outside a workhouse in 1898, no less then 103,284 were the offspring of widows and a further 10,274 were orphans or deserted children.[24] These unavoidable causes of hardship were confirmed at around the same time by the findings of Charles Booth in London and Seebohm Rowntree in York concerning the nature of contemporary poverty.

It was, then, amid rising anxiety over juvenile wrongdoing that the state and the voluntary agencies began to take increasing responsibility for needy youngsters, despite the official commitment to a policy of *laissez-faire*, or non-interventionism. The mid-century growth of the Ragged Schools, with their emphasis on a religious-based education and the promotion of associated savings clubs, temperance societies and similar schemes, was one aspect of this desire to rehabilitate the young. The schools' promoters regarded them more as mission stations than as purely educational institutions, and they also offered practical experience in dealing with poor and neglected children to social reformers who subsequently developed other interests. Mary Carpenter gained valuable insights into childhood deprivation through her work at the Bristol Ragged School and was to turn it to good effect in her penal reform activities. Similarly Dr Thomas Barnardo's encounters with homeless boys at the Stepney Ragged School where he taught encouraged him to set up his first refuge.

Portsmouth gaol in 1900. Two brothers named Pickett, aged 11 and 13, were sentenced by the city's magistrates to fourteen days' hard labour for throwing stones at a door. (Warwickshire Record Office)

Other pioneers, like Benjamin Waugh of the London Society for the Prevention of Cruelty to Children, stressed the need to give children rights (including rights against mistreatment and exploitation by their parents), not merely for their benefit but for that of society at large. In the first issue of the Society's journal, the *Child's Guardian*, in January 1887, he reminded readers that children were 'not only born into homes, they are also born into a country . . . they are under the guardianship of the Crown'.[25] A year later Mary Tabor echoed these sentiments when she attributed the mass of 'chronic poverty, of pauperism, disease, and crime which at this moment . . . forms one of the most insoluble problems of modern life' to 'the refusal or neglect of the natural claims of children'. She argued that every youngster had 'as its birthright a claim to the minimum of clothing, shelter, food, and training needed to fit it for becoming in due time a self-supporting member of the community'.[26] Failure to supply these essentials menaced the peace and security of the nation itself. Hence the rights of children were 'identical with the interests of the State'.

Of the thousands of youngsters needing aid from official sources or from charity, the largest single group were those under the Poor Law. They formed a substantial constituent of the total number on poor relief, comprising about a third of the pauper population throughout the period.[27] Most were on out-relief, and were classed as the 'dependants' of parents or grandparents, to whom were given the scanty doles provided for their subsistence. Many were the offspring of widows, and their total seldom fell below 200,000 a year throughout the period from 1834 to the end of the century. However, their maintenance allowance usually amounted to a paltry 1s or 1s 6d a week, plus, in some cases, a loaf of bread. Very few Poor Law unions followed the example of Bradford and allowed 'deserving' widows with dependent children a comparatively generous 4s a week for the first child, 3s for the second, and 2s for each additional youngster, plus 5s for the mother herself.[28] Anxiety to ensure that such children were not put at an advantage compared with the offspring of 'independent' labourers led to a prohibition on the payment of school fees out of the poor rates for those on out-relief. That was only relaxed in 1855, when, at the instigation of a private Member of Parliament, unions were empowered – but not compelled – to pay the fees of these children. In practice, few chose to do so and in 1856, at a time when over two hundred thousand children were being supported on out-relief, just 3,986 were at school. Even in 1869 the position remained unsatisfactory, with 22,033 children having their fees paid from the rates, or less than a tenth of those on out-relief.[29]

Not until 1873 did the legislature finally require boards of guardians to make it a condition of receipt of outdoor relief for parents to send their offspring, aged between five and thirteen, to a public elementary school. But enforcement remained difficult, and as late as 1880 some unions were petitioning the Education Department to relax the requirement for young paupers to attend school over the age of twelve because this was 'hard on the parent, useless to the child' and led 'to "much necessary work being left undone"'.[30] No attention was given to the inadequacy of the allowances paid for their relief, or to the kind of treatment they and other youngsters received at the hands of parents and guardians. This continued to apply despite the passage of an Act in 1868 requiring unions to prosecute those who wilfully neglected to provide adequate food, clothing, medical care and lodging for any child under fourteen for whom they were responsible. Those found guilty could be imprisoned but, in practice, the cost of the exercise and the reluctance of the authorities to interfere in the delicate matter of family relationships made the legislation a virtual dead letter.[31] Also ignored were the humiliations associated with the granting of poor relief. A Bristol girl recalled that when her family applied for help one of the local guardians, who was also a doctor, visited the house to see what furniture they had: 'if you 'ad a good home you had to sell it. He even waited until my father sold the beds from under us. Then he gave him a ticket to go in the workhouse.' She herself was nearly old enough to leave school and instead of being sent to the workhouse she went to live with an aunt and uncle. While there, her uncle raped her – a traumatic event which she felt had ruined her life: 'I've never forgotten it and never forgiven it, and I never will.'[32]

For families on out-relief there was always the knowledge that this could be withdrawn without warning and the family required to enter the hated workhouse. Will Crooks's mother obtained an allowance of two or three shillings a week plus a little bread after her stoker husband lost his arm in a shipboard accident. Suddenly these small payments were stopped and she was asked to appear with her children before the guardians. There an offer was made to take the youngsters into the workhouse. At first Mrs Crooks refused, but after struggling to make ends meet she had to admit defeat. The five smallest, including eight-year-old Will, were taken to the big poorhouse near Millwall Docks, along with their father.[33]

Children on 'indoor' relief were in a minority among those supported by the poor rates, numbering around a fifth of the total of youngsters aided, compared with four-fifths on out-relief. However, once admitted to the workhouse steps were taken to segregate them from the 'contaminating' presence of adult inmates, including their own parents. Only so, it was believed, could they escape the demoralizing effects of pauperism and learn to become self-supporting. Although children were recognized as the one group of paupers not to blame for their dependent position, they were not given preferential treatment, in case that encouraged parents to renege on their responsibilities and allow their offspring to be brought up at the ratepayers' expense. A particular problem in this regard was presented by the so-called 'ins and outs', families who came in to the workhouse for a few weeks or a few days, and then left when employment offered or there was a chance of seasonal work on the land picking fruit and hops. Sometimes the youngsters came and went at parental whim, as happened to Charlie Chaplin at one period in his life. Mr Chaplin deserted his wife and two sons at an early stage and she found increasing difficulty in coping, especially when her mental condition deteriorated. Mother and sons first entered Lambeth Workhouse in 1895, when Charlie was six. They were there about three weeks before the boys were sent to a special Poor Law school at Hanwell. Charlie later described this as a 'forlorn experience' with the youngsters labelled 'inmates of the "booby hatch"' by local people, and brutal beatings administered to any boys who offended. After about a year all three Chaplins came out, only to move to another workhouse a few months later. On one occasion while they were at Hanwell, Mrs Chaplin announced her intention of taking them away, and the three of them were discharged. But it was merely a ruse to allow her to see her sons and later the same day they arrived back, to the annoyance of the workhouse officials. Their quick return not only meant further paperwork but the need to disinfect their clothing once more. Now the two boys again entered a Poor Law school, but with their mother displaying increasing signs of insanity, she was committed to an asylum. The board of guardians immediately resumed the search for Mr Chaplin and once he was located, the brothers were discharged into his care, travelling in a bread van to their new home.[34]

As a result of their migratory habits, the 'ins and outs' rarely attended school for sufficient time to receive worthwhile training. In the mid-1890s a contemporary compared them to 'buckets on a dredging machine' which passed in and out of 'all sorts of horrible places and scenes of vice'. They were thought likely to 'contaminate' the other children with whom they mixed in the workhouse.[35] The plight of some young vagrants could indeed be desperate, and this was an issue which the National Society for the Prevention of Cruelty to Children took up at the end of the century. In 1893, one mother was jailed at Burnley after tramping for three months with her wretched and ragged offspring, including a daughter suffering from consumption. Four years later, vagrant foster parents were prosecuted at Birmingham for dragging a little girl around with them and forcing her to beg. The foster parents were drunkards who beat the child and when found she was covered in mud and ravenously hungry.[36] For youngsters like these a spell in the workhouse may have been a welcome interlude in their interminable journeyings.

One means of segregating adults and children on indoor relief was for groups of unions to combine to establish district schools, capable of accommodating five hundred to a thousand pupils. They would offer a broad education, including industrial training, and avoid the stigma attached to residence in a workhouse. However, partly on administrative grounds and partly because of friction with the Poor Law Commission in London, as well as concern about the cost involved, little was done to implement the plan before the late 1840s. By 1849 only six school districts had been created, three of them in London, although elsewhere, as in Manchester, Sheffield and Liverpool, separate Poor Law schools were set up away from the workhouse. In 1898 the Manchester Union's Swinton school had nearly 800 pupils, and that at Kirkdale, Liverpool, almost 600.[37]

The scheme's disadvantages soon became obvious. The large, barrack-like institutions that resulted lacked the intimate atmosphere which the better teachers could create in individual workhouse schools, and there were chronic problems with contagious diseases (particularly ophthalmia). The young inmates were said to lack vitality and 'practical awareness', while the absence of normal domestic ties was considered especially harmful for females. An official report by Mrs Nassau Senior in the 1870s on pauper education condemned the failure to provide the 'cherishing care and individual attention' needed for the formation of the character of girls. Nor did they obtain the training required to prepare them for employment as servants or for their probable future role as wives and mothers.[38]

There were many petty restrictions, too, such as a refusal to provide toys out of the rates for smaller children. This was relaxed in 1891 and the Local Government Board (which was now responsible for Poor Law matters) also suggested that illustrated books and periodicals be supplied to young inmates. 'The question of the provision of bats, balls, skipping-ropes, etc., for the children and toys for the infants, is . . . one which the Board are desirous should receive . . . attention.'[39] Outings might be arranged and donations made to local Band of Hope societies to allow Poor Law children to participate in their activities.

Forty years earlier the attitude had been very different. When the North Surrey District School opened in November 1850, to take in children from Wandsworth, Croydon, Kingston, Lewisham and Richmond, plus the parish of St Luke in Chelsea, there were immediate problems. Two months after its inauguration the chaplain complained that if the 'slightest restraint' were exercised on the young inmates, they responded by destroying property, a trait he considered 'peculiarly workhouse'. Scarcely a day passed without some of them absconding, either to return to their respective workhouses or to 'prowl' about the countryside. The girls were 'if possible, in a lower condition than the boys'.[40] Although conditions gradually improved, even in the mid-1860s there were criticisms of the conduct of the youngest inmates, most of whom were described as the offspring of parents of the very lowest type, 'both morally and physically'.[41]

One of the benefits claimed for Poor Law education was its combination of instruction in the three R's and religion with industrial training, thereby equipping the youngsters to earn a living in later life. In reality the boys were often taught trades like carpentry, baking, tailoring and shoemaking, for which demand was limited. Some schools placed great emphasis on band music and many of the youngsters became proficient instrumentalists. They went on to join military bands. But in the skill subjects worthwhile standards were rarely attained, and frequently when the children left it was to take up quite another occupation. Employers complained of their lack of initiative and perhaps the main weakness of workhouse education was its failure to equip pupils for anything better than unskilled labouring. That meant they earned low wages and were particularly vulnerable in times of economic recession.[42] For girls, the prospect was still bleaker. Their training was normally confined to needlework, laundrywork and general domestic chores, but they had little chance to learn anything about the arrangements of a well-ordered household. This led to problems with employers.[43] Only on board the Metropolitan Asylums Board training ship *Exmouth* was real vocational instruction given, to prepare lads for a career in the Royal Navy or the merchant marine.

The harsh daily round in the district or 'barrack' schools is confirmed by former pupils. Thus when Will Crooks first entered the workhouse he was at once separated from his father and three sisters but was allowed to remain with his younger brother. But after two or three weeks, the two boys were taken with other youngsters to the Sutton district school, where the brothers were parted. 'Every day I spent in that school is burnt into my soul', Will confessed. He was unable to sleep or to play with the other lads, haunted as he was by a belief that he must have committed some dreadful sin to be taken from home in this way.

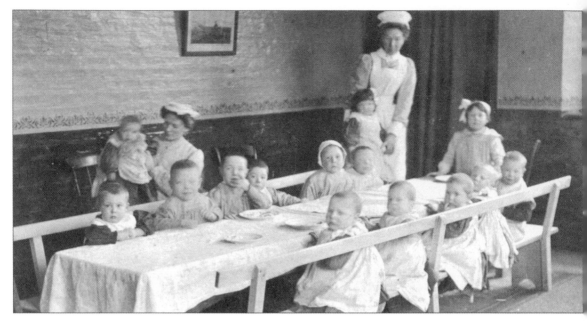

Infants in Poplar workhouse in the early twentieth century. The little girl at the head of the table seems to be acting as 'mother'. (Greater London Record Office Photograph Collection)

Sunday was particularly dreary: '. . . time could not be made more terrible to children anywhere. They had dinner at twelve and tea at six, confined during the yawning interval in the dull day-room with nothing to do but to look at the clock, and then out of the window, and then back at the clock again.' The days dragged by until one lunchtime his name was called out in the dining room and he was told to go to the tailor's shop to collect his clothes. He was going home.

> The boys crowded round him, wishing they were in his place. . . . At the gate he met his young brother and sisters again, and they were taken back to Poplar, to be welcomed with open arms by their mother. She had worked harder than ever to add to the family income in order to justify her in going before the Guardians to ask that her children be restored to her own keeping.[44]

Many children were less fortunate. In 1898, out of 50,750 youngsters in receipt of indoor relief, 33,382 were orphans or had been deserted by their parents, and of the rest, 5,759 were the illegitimate children of inmates, 8,621 were the offspring of able-bodied inmates (including the 'ins and outs'), and 2,988 were the children of non-able-bodied inmates. About half of the total were in workhouses, infirmaries or sick asylums, and nearly two-fifths were in district schools or similar institutions under the control of the guardians.[45] Shortly before this, George Lansbury, a newly appointed guardian for the borough of Poplar, described a visit to the Forest Lane district school, Stratford, which was attended by young paupers from his borough and from Whitechapel. Things seemed to have improved little from Will Crooks's days at Sutton, with the inmates housed in long dormitories and having few recreational facilities:

> at the time I first saw it the children were dressed in the old, hideous, Poor Law garb, corduroy and hard blue serge, and the girls with their hair almost shaved off, with nothing at all to make them look attractive. The food was quite coarse . . . After our first committee meeting we were taken downstairs, where a seven course dinner was to be served. It was this which made me very disgusted with the middle-class men and women who controlled the institution; they could let little girls who they knew must be starved, stand and wait on them while they ate chicken, nice soups, sweets, etc., all at the expense of the rates . . . When, later on, we bought out Whitechapel and took over the school all this sort of thing was abolished.[46]

But some situations were far worse. Indeed at Forest Lane itself a disastrous fire in 1890 led to the deaths of over twenty children. Four years later there was a scandal at Brentwood school in Essex, to which the Hackney Union sent its children. An enquiry was held when a girl inmate died from injuries sustained after being pushed downstairs by the nurse, Elizabeth Gillespie. This revealed that a regime of terror had reigned for many years, with the headmistress giving the girls black eyes and beating them with a ruler, the masters on duty at night carrying canes round the dormitories (the games master even took a cane on to the cricket field), and the entire staff conniving at Nurse Gillespie's persistent brutality. Although there was insufficient evidence to convict her of murder, she pleaded guilty to charges of cruelty and was sentenced to five years' hard labour. Reforms were instituted and it was speedily claimed that these had had the desired effect: 'we were much pleased to find, by the bright and cheery faces of the infants and their confiding manners as they pressed forward to catch hold of our hands . . . that the bitter past must already have . . . faded from their memories'.[47] How far the youngsters had, in truth, recovered from their ordeal is difficult to assess, but it is unlikely the optimistic comment that 'the bitter past' had, within a few months, 'faded from their memories' in any way matched reality.

The Brentwood case was extreme. But there is little doubt that youngsters attending many of the schools were vulnerable to ill-treatment (including sexual abuse) and yet were unable to complain. As one girl put it, when asked why she had not told of her sufferings while at school, 'We knew we should only have it worse when the gentlemen were gone, and so we bit our lips and bore it!'[48]

Perhaps more damaging to most children than outright physical punishment was the monotony of institutional life, and the lack of what Mrs Nassau Senior called '*mothering*'.[49] Already in the 1860s reformers had recognized these deficiencies and had begun taking steps to remedy them. From 1868, 'boarding out' was advocated increasingly in England and Wales for orphans and deserted children. It was a policy long applied in Scotland but its extension south of the border had its critics. In 1871, one opponent claimed that the weekly sums of 5s paid to foster parents made this tiny group of child paupers 'more eligible' than the offspring of the independent labourer. 'How many working men in this country', he asked indignantly, 'when they have to support an average mixed family, are able to devote five shillings a week to the maintenance of each of their children, besides paying for education and for all requisite medical attendance?' Another danger was that the foster parents might mistreat their young charges. To combat this in 1885 the Local Government Board appointed a lady inspector whose duty it was to visit families and examine the thousand or so children boarded out in communities beyond the area of their own union, to check for signs of neglect or abuse. After thirteen years' work she concluded that 'boarding-out' could be 'either the best or worst of systems', according to the relationship between foster parents and children. Sometimes close links were forged, with youngsters treated as family members. In one case two girls boarded out with a childless couple not only had a piano bought for them but arrangements were made for them to receive 'the best music lessons to be had in the neighbourhood'. In another instance, a girl who had been ill-treated in her first foster home (including having her hands plunged in boiling water because she had not made her bed properly), experienced great kindness from her second family. She was said to be 'literally adored' by the foster parents.[50] Elsewhere boarding out became a disguised form of outdoor relief with relatives paid to look after orphaned or abandoned youngsters. But overall the numbers involved were small. Even on 1 January 1898 only 1,896 children were in foster homes outside the area of their home union, with a further 5,191 boarded within their native area. At that time the total child pauper population, including those on both indoor and outdoor relief, was around 240,000.[51]

A variation on the 'boarding-out' theme came under legislation passed in 1889 and 1899. This empowered unions to 'adopt' children who were orphaned or deserted, or whose parents' mode of life made them unfit to assume responsibility for their offspring. In this way parental rights were overridden until the young person reached the age of eighteen, and the guardians were authorized to take decisions concerning the youngster's future. A number of boards used their new powers, and by 1 June 1902, 7,724 children had been 'adopted' in this way, 1,503 of them being over fifteen.[52] They included Arthur Carter, aged nine, who was adopted by the Portsea Union in Hampshire during October 1901. His mother was 'addicted to drink' and was frequently in and out of the workhouse, while his father was dead. Arthur was transferred to the training ship *Mercury* at Southampton, before embarking on a career in the Merchant Navy. In 1909 he joined the Union Castle line as a deck boy and was reported to be doing well.[53] Another boy adopted by the Portsea Union was subsequently sent to Canada under the auspices of the Salvation Army.[54] Such initiatives demonstrated changing public attitudes towards parental rights in the last years of the nineteenth century, as well as extending adult supervision and control over the lives of children. It was very different from the situation noted by John Stuart Mill in the late 1850s, when he declared sourly: 'One would almost think that a man's children were supposed to be literally, and not metaphorically, a part of himself, so jealous is [public] opinion of the smallest interference of law with his absolute and exclusive control over them.'[55]

An alternative adopted by some Poor Law unions was the setting up of cottage homes, with the children housed in small, village-type units, each with individual house-mothers. These had the advantage of moving youngsters from the large barrack-style institutions, but the fact that they were largely self-contained communities, with inmates educated and trained in their own 'village' meant there was little contact with the outside world. Although the organizers sought to create a 'homely' atmosphere, it often seemed artificial and lacking in any genuine feeling of 'belonging'. Nor, once a child had left the community, was there any right of return, either to find sympathy or 'to renew early affections and memories'.[56]

More attractive were the 'scattered homes' pioneered in Sheffield in 1893, whereby groups of children were settled in ordinary dwelling-houses in different parts of the city. They attended local elementary schools, along with non-paupers, and each house was presided over by a foster-mother, who cared for the inmates with the help of the older children and a charwoman. In 1897 Whitechapel and Bath unions both took up the scheme, but it remained of limited importance to the end of the century.[57]

A further option arose from a decision in the 1860s to allow guardians to make use of philanthropic institutions, such as children's homes and orphanages, that were willing to receive for payment boys and girls for whom the unions had difficulty in providing. By using 'certified schools' in this way guardians not only disposed of many physically and mentally handicapped youngsters, but of almost all their Roman Catholic, Wesleyan and Jewish charges, who were sent to denominational orphanages and boarding schools. It was a policy warmly embraced by Henry Edward Manning shortly after his consecration as Archbishop of Westminster in 1865. A year later he set up the Westminster Diocesan Educational Fund to 'rescue' as many Catholic children as possible from the workhouses and admit them to denominational institutions. In practice, this process was often lengthy, as each child had to be applied for individually, and guardians' reactions varied. Some yielded the youngsters without opposition, but others, on grounds of sectarian bias or expense, put up strong resistance. They were unwilling to pay up to 6s a week for transferred children whom they could maintain for about half that sum in the workhouse.[58] In 1898, nearly one in ten of the nation's 50,750 children on indoor relief were catered for in 'certified schools'.

Finally, for those still residing in workhouses, efforts were made at the end of the century to break the institutional mould by sending them to be educated at ordinary elementary schools. There were some initial objections because the Poor Law schools were said to give 'industrial training' and to teach 'the children to work', as well as instructing them in the three R's. But as public elementary education expanded from the 1870s this method of assimilating pauper children into the wider community became increasingly popular. By 1898, 493 Poor Law unions out of a total of 648 were using public elementary schools for their child pauper inmates. But the extent to which they were assimilated is another matter. Both in appearance and in manner they differed from non-pauper fellow pupils. Stella Davies remembered seeing long processions of youngsters from Crumpsall workhouse in Manchester being escorted to the nearby board school. They all wore 'the same drab workhouse clothes with the girls in unbleached calico aprons'. George Hewins, too, when carrying out building work at Stratford-on-Avon workhouse in about 1900, saw the children congregating to go to school.[59]

He recognized two of the girls:

> They'd had their hair chopped off, weared long holland pinnas with big red letters: STRATFORD-ON-AVON WORKHOUSE. They did some sort o' drill, then they was marched in a straight line to the National School across the road. . . . I was angry: 'There's no need for them red letters! The pauper kids is distinguished alright! You can spot em straight away – they's up against the wall watching the others play! They ain't playin – and when they marches out a-night the other kiddies is callin 'Workhus brats!' after em. '*Workus brats!*' . . . Why was you punished for being poor?

Despite the attempts to improve the lot of pauper children, therefore, as Professor Rose has noted, their position 'remained a dreary and disadvantaged one'. The acceptance of poor relief, even by 'blameless' juveniles, carried a stigma which served to reinforce their apparent lack of assertiveness and initiative.[60]

Where children leaving Poor Law institutions had no families to whom they could turn, the guardians would seek places for them. In 1895, out of 773 boys leaving the Metropolitan Poor Law schools, 174 joined army and navy bands (94 of them coming from the *Exmouth* training ship). A further 101 entered the Royal Navy in a non-band capacity, and a number of others took up baking, hairdressing, shoemaking, tailoring and domestic service, among other occupations. Out of 464 girls leaving these schools in the same year, 459 went into domestic service, and the remaining five became dressmakers or needlewomen.[61] Elsewhere, particularly in the case of rougher boys or those who came into the workhouse at the age of fourteen or fifteen and were considered unsuitable for domestic work on grounds of character, the fishing fleet was an alternative, with the ports of Brixham, Hull, Ramsgate and Grimsby among the possible destinations. As late as 1890 Grimsby had over a thousand fishing apprentices. However, the danger of the work and the seasickness experienced, particularly during winter weather, led to many absconding, especially when these conditions were combined with brutal ill-treatment. Some lads misbehaved in the hope of being released from their indentures, since they were able to earn more as non-apprenticed weekly hands. But many deserted to draw attention to grievances, including the failure of their employer to supply proper food and clothing, or in an act of desperation to escape physical and sexual abuse. Beatings were common. 'I have known cases of lads injured . . . with their eyes so swollen that they could not see out of them', confessed Isaac Miller, superintendent of the Fisher Lads' Institute at Grimsby in 1882. 'The . . . lad gets a crack with the first thing that comes sometimes if he has been saucy.'[62] About a third of the boys apprenticed in Grimsby between 1881 and 1893 were said to have absconded and the superintendent of Edmonton Poor Law schools admitted that only those 'that it would be very difficult to do anything else with' were sent to the fishing fleet. By the end of the century, as a result of technical change within the fishing industry itself, the demand for apprentices declined. Whereas 3,312 boys (including non-pauper trainees) had signed indentures at Grimsby between 1880 and 1889, that had almost halved to 1,959 between 1890 and 1899. It dropped again to 590 between 1900 and 1909.[63] In Ramsgate the number of apprentices, both pauper and non-pauper, also fell sharply, from 174 serving in 1895 to a mere 91 at work seven years later, and other ports showed a similar trend.

Even youngsters sent out as domestic workers could be badly treated, despite the passage of legislation in 1851 laying down that those hired from a workhouse as servants were to have at least two visits a year from a relieving officer or other official appointed by the union to which they belonged, up to the age of sixteen. The Act was passed in response to two highly publicized cases in 1850–1 involving the severe mistreatment (and in one case the murder) of two former workhouse girls by their employers.[64] But partly through official inertia and partly because employers failed to notify the authorities when a girl left her post, the new regulations were poorly observed. So despite the efforts to protect vulnerable, ex-workhouse servants, ill-treatment continued. As late as 1891 a fourteen-year-old former Poor Law girl was beaten to death by her mistress in South Shields.[65] It was to assist such youngsters that charitable organizations like the Metropolitan Association for Befriending Young Servants and its provincial counterpart, the Girls' Friendly Society, were set up. By 1896 the former organization had almost seven and a half thousand girls under its care in London and offered both a training home and lodging-houses where unemployed maids could gain refuge while they waited for a new place.[66]

Philanthropy also aided needy children before they reached the school-leaving age. The help varied from short-term measures, such as the provision of cheap meals and country holidays, to more permanent arrangements. Individuals could play a part, too, like the Portsmouth cobbler, John Pounds, who taught poor children in his workshop school at the start of Victoria's reign. Not only did the youngsters learn the three R's but they were offered inducements, including hot potatoes and roasted apples, to encourage attendance. Pounds even begged clothing for them and arranged for them to attend Sunday school.

However, it was the large charitable organizations, like Dr Barnardo's and the Waifs and Strays Society, which made a major contribution towards providing for the destitute and the neglected. Dr Barnardo opened his first refuge for homeless boys after teaching experience in 1867 at a ragged school. The first residential home for boys was set up in 1870, and for girls in 1873; Barnardo claimed that destitute children would be received 'at any hour of the day or night'. Within a decade his organization provided facilities for several hundred boys at its Stepney headquarters, as well as building a village home for girls in Essex, along lines similar to the cottage homes provided under the Poor Law. In addition he and specially appointed 'beadles' searched in 'low lodging-houses and other haunts of the destitute', for neglected and homeless children in need of rescue. Free schools were opened and training facilities offered to give the youngsters the skills needed to survive in adult society. Barnardo's attitude was often high-handed. He himself admitted adopting methods of dubious legality in order to take children from surroundings or parents he considered unsuitable, remarking of parents that they 'are my chief difficulty everywhere; so are relatives . . . because I have to take from a very low class'.[67] His motto was, 'Admit first: inquire afterwards'. He also insisted on transmitting his own strong Protestant faith to the young inmates, and

Technical training in the carpenters' shop at Dr Barnardo's, Stepney Causeway, London. (The author)

this caused conflict with the parents and guardians of some Roman Catholic children. But perhaps most difficult of all was the perennial lack of cash which hampered Dr Barnardo's ambitious plans for expansion. As part of his fund-raising campaigns, boys in the Home for Working and Destitute Lads were engaged for their 'industrial' training in producing firewood, brushes and other items for sale to the general public.[68] He also set up an employment agency for young city messengers and shoeblacks.[69]

Despite Barnardo's autocratic style and his character defects, the scale of his achievement was outstanding in an era which saw a multiplicity of philanthropic endeavours. Thousands of children were transformed from miserable, anti-social creatures into healthy, self-reliant young adults. By 1890, the charity claimed to have 'rescued, trained, and placed out in life' 17,122 children. In addition, meals had been provided at lodging-houses and at free schools to necessitous children, and many thousands of garments had been given away or sold at nominal prices. Just over four and a half thousand boys and girls had also been emigrated through the Barnardo homes to the colonies.[70] By 1900–1 that total of young emigrants had climbed to around one thousand per annum.[71]

Among the multiplicity of other charities caring for poor children were the National Children's Home, set up by a young Wesleyan minister in Lambeth, and the Anglican Waifs and Strays Society (later the Church of England Children's Society), also formed in Lambeth. The latter was started in 1881 at the instigation of a young civil servant, Edward Rudolf, who was the superintendent of a Lambeth Sunday school and who subsequently took holy orders. Another Mission, the Farningham Homes for Little Boys, was run on the 'cottage homes' principle, and this plan was later adopted by the Waifs and Strays Society, with some modification.[72] Efforts were made to provide something of the atmosphere and routine of ordinary family life, but overtones of 'institutionalism' survived, with inmates clad in hard-wearing rather ugly uniforms, and subjected to an austere regime of rules and regulations. The Waifs and Strays Society, for example, insisted that the girls' hair was cropped, a practice which made the child 'always [look] an untidy little guy', as one critic put it. Silence was widely enforced. At the Longwells Green Diocesan Home, for example, former inmates remembered silence being imposed on getting up, during meals, while they were walking to and from school, when they went to bed, and 'at all times outside the Home'. They were allowed to talk quietly among themselves for one hour between tea and bedtime. At another home, 'the children were bidden to complete silence for the whole of Good Friday'.[73]

Charity girls were regarded as future domestic servants, and it was seen as part of their training to condition them to accept this. In 1878 girls at Dr Barnardo's Barkingside community showed they had absorbed the message when they sang at the annual fete:

> When I go into service
> I must watch and pray
> That my Heavenly Father
> Will direct my way . . .
> I must be good-tempered,
> Always neat and clean,
> Civil in my manners,
> Never pert or mean.[74]

It is unclear whether this indoctrination process was intended to help the girls by easing their transition into domestic employment or whether it was designed to provide middle-class families with cheap and obedient maids.

A similar ambiguity occurred in respect of children sent overseas (especially to Canada) by both Poor Law and charity organizations as part of the mass emigration movement. Emigration appealed to many working with neglected children because it offered the chance of a transfer to a healthy environment where their labour was needed and where they could escape the 'contaminating' influence of English city life. For this reason the Ragged School movement adopted it in the late 1840s, with Lord Ashley requesting state aid in order to send ex-pupils to work on sheep stations in Australia. As an experiment, the government agreed to fund 150 young migrants but it then refused to renew the arrangement. The Ragged School Union tried to continue on its own, but cash shortage and other difficulties led to the scheme's abandonment in the mid-1850s.[75]

Not until the late 1860s did the main child emigration movement get under way, with Canada the prime destination. The policy was seen by supporters as having three main recommendations. First, it made room for new entrants into the often overcrowded Poor Law institutions and orphanages. Dr Barnardo, who

Child emigrants to Canada dressed in new clothes and despatched under the auspices of the Canadian Catholic Emigration Committee. They were part of a group of sixty-four youngsters (thirty-two paupers and thirty-two non-paupers) who sailed on 11 July 1889. The youngest was aged six and came from Nazareth House, Oxford. (Westminster Diocesan Archives. Father Seddon MSS)

eventually sent thousands of children away, described the process as a clearing of 'crowded hives', to enable the gates to be kept open for others in need.[76] Secondly, it reduced the burden of expenditure, since once a payment had been made to assist migration, all further maintenance costs ceased. Finally, at a time when great stress was laid on the adverse social and moral influences of urban living, the opportunity to send youngsters to a country where most people still lived in rural communities was very attractive. The fact that Canada was part of the Empire and yet, unlike Australia, was relatively near at hand added to its appeal.[77]

The first group of pauper children was taken to Canada in the autumn of 1869 by a committed Evangelical and emigration enthusiast, Maria Rye.[78] Soon others joined in the work, and by 1870–1 the Poor Law Board in London and its successor, the Local Government Board, were authorizing Poor Law guardians to participate in the scheme. But as the number of youngsters sent from unions mounted, questions were raised about the conduct of the campaign and the safeguards which existed to protect the children once they left Britain. In 1874 the Local Government Board sent an inspector to Canada to carry out a survey, and on his return he criticized the arrangements made for placing the young emigrants in their new homes and ensuring their welfare (including limiting the amount of labour they had to perform on the farmsteads where many were settled). One youngster told him sadly that for children like her 'adoption' into a Canadian farming family meant 'folks get a girl to work without wages'.[79]

As a result of this report the Local Government Board suspended all pauper child emigration in March 1875. It was not resumed until 1883 when, at a time of economic recession in Britain, a number of guardians pressed for its revival as a means of disposing of some of their young charges. However, in the interim, non-pauper children continued to be sent. Dr Barnardo alone despatched 1,181 children overseas between 1867 and 1884 and Roman Catholic charities, too, entered the field. One participant was the Canadian Catholic Emigration Committee, centred on the Westminster diocese, under the direction of Father Thomas Seddon. It began work in 1874 and within ten years had sent 463 children to the Dominion.[80] Yet, significantly, Father Seddon, despite a long-term commitment to the work (he was eventually to die on his way to Canada with a party of young migrants in 1898) was doubtful about the desirability of the policy. 'I confess the whole scheme of child emigration alarms me', he told the Local Government Board in 1884: 'I very earnestly trust that stringent regulations will be put in force . . . to keep the scheme, if it is to be carried on from degenerating into practical slavery . . . It is indeed only by compulsion, arising out of the state of the labour market in England that I send the boys out to Canadian farmers.'[81]

He was insistent that girls over nine years of age should not go. Not only might adolescents be in moral danger but those from nine to thirteen could easily become 'young slaves . . . if by chance the foster parents are exacting or unreasonable'. Even the introduction of inspections by the Canadian Department of Agriculture in 1883, following the resumption of pauper emigration, could not ensure the children were well treated. For the inspections only took place annually, and in the intervening period 'a child unhappily placed, could be ill-used, sat upon, dead and buried, and nobody be much the wiser – whether it died a natural death or not'.[82] Seddon received reports from his own representatives to supplement the official information, but even then problems arose. In March 1895, the clerk to St George's Union in London wrote to complain the guardians had learned that a former charge, sent by the Catholic Committee in 1892, was not 'very well placed' and was living with a 'rather poor farmer'. 'Boy not well clothed. Works about Farm and Stable, no wages, strong young man, should be placed where he can earn good wages, very good boy.'[83] The clerk asked for the lad's position to be looked into and it is likely that committee agents in Canada were asked to arrange for a transfer. The fact that most of the youngsters came from town workhouses and were faced with the rigours of life on an isolated farmstead among strangers, particularly during the bleak winter months, added to the pressures under which they laboured. In many cases they also lost touch with any relatives they had in England.[84]

So, although children continued to be sent overseas during the final part of the century by both Poor Law unions and charities (with Dr Barnardo's taking the leading role in the closing years, despatching 4,550 youngsters between 1896 and 1901 alone), the disadvantages were clear. Chief among them was the inability to guarantee the children's welfare once they had departed. Hence, while one enthusiast referred to emigration as a 'spring transplanting', Elaine Hadley, less romantically, has labelled it 'a life sentence of transportation into the working class' for young people without employment or prospects in their home country. A major problem was the ambivalence of many emigration organizers towards their young charges. It was unclear whether their prime objective was to benefit the children or society at large, by removing idle youngsters from areas where they posed a potential threat as criminals and troublemakers. As Joy Parr has commented: 'A programme at once severe, irrevocable and mildly palliative appealed to Victorian social conservatives and revivalist Christians for working-class children in . . . danger of drifting into the lapsed masses and the dangerous classes.'[85]

As for the children themselves, while some settled happily into their new life, others were less fortunate. One man, placed near Rapid City, Manitoba, in 1901, when he was thirteen, described the darker side. He had been sent by Barnardo's and was visited by their representative from time to time, but this did not protect him: 'I went through more than I ever want to go through again . . . I know myself that I often looked forward to the time for the man from the Homes to come . . . but when he did come I used to be too scared to say anything for fear that I got more after [he] had gone.'[86]

A similar ambiguity lay behind reformers' efforts to rehabilitate juvenile criminals. And in dealing with children who had broken the law or seemed likely to do so, the state and charitable organizations again worked in tandem, as they had done in respect of youth emigration.

In the early nineteenth century young criminals were punished in much the same way as their adult counterparts. The main differences were that up to the age of seven, children were considered incapable of criminal intent. From seven to fourteen they were presumed innocent unless the prosecution could prove their ability to distinguish between good and evil. Thereafter they were deemed fully responsible. Young offenders were tried with the full solemnity of the law, a process which Mary Carpenter, for one, considered inherently damaging.[87] If found guilty they were liable to capital punishment, transportation, or imprisonment, including solitary confinement. They had no *legal* right to be treated differently from grown-ups, although compassion might be shown by the courts because of their youth.

During the early years of Victoria's reign, however, transportation and capital conviction were increasingly replaced by imprisonment (including penal servitude) as the normal punishment for most offences, with transportation virtually ending in 1853.[88]

It was widely understood that the free association of prisoners of all ages in many gaols led to the 'contamination' of young offenders by older inmates, both in respect of criminal and moral (including sexual) matters. This was underlined in the middle of the century when the issue of juvenile delinquency came under scrutiny from official inquiries in 1847 and 1852. In the former year the Select Committee on the Execution of the Criminal Law Respecting Juvenile Offenders and Transportation concluded bleakly: 'the Contamination of a Gaol as Gaols are usually managed may often prove fatal, and must always be hurtful to Boys committed for a first Offence, . . . thus for a very trifling Act they may become trained to the worst of Crimes.'[89]

In other words, sending children to prison, far from solving the problem of juvenile crime, merely added to it. Partly as a result of pressure from penal reformers, the Summary Jurisdiction Act of 1847 recognized the special position of young offenders in respect of petty larceny (the most common juvenile crime) by laying down that those under fourteen could be tried and summarily convicted by magistrates, instead of having to appear in the higher courts. In 1850 the concession was extended to those under sixteen. The aim was to make the children liable to less severe punishments and to spare them a remand to prison to await trial at Quarter Sessions.[90] In practice, there was no immediate decline in the number of children imprisoned since many magistrates considered a short spell in gaol served both as a salutary punishment and as a warning to others tempted to commit similar offences. Among those affected in this way were two lads, aged thirteen and fifteen, convicted by the Portsmouth bench in the mid-1850s of stealing 6 oz of tobacco and a bottle of ginger beer. Each received twelve months' imprisonment and a whipping.[91] In 1856 there were nearly fourteen thousand children under sixteen in English gaols, and they formed about one in thirteen of the total prison population.[92] (See Appendix 4 for later figures.)

Occasionally strong-minded parents used the courts as a means of disciplining their offspring. In 1854, thirteen-year-old Edward Beesley of Oxford was brought before the magistrates by his mother for stealing her tea caddy. She then refused to press the charge, 'stating that it was his first offence'. She had only given him into custody 'for the purpose of frightening him'. The case was consequently dismissed.[93] A few years earlier John Parrish, aged twelve, of Portsmouth had been charged by his mother with stealing a blanket. In this case the boy was committed to gaol but was then discharged by the court.[94]

Recommittal statistics confirmed that many juveniles were undeterred by their confinement. As the chaplain of Bath prison put it in 1850, 'once in gaol, always in gaol' was a truism for boy offenders. 'They become trained to prison life.'[95] Among them were recalcitrants like ten-year-old Edward Joghill (or Joyhill), of London, who was imprisoned eight times between February 1847 and April 1849 for offences varying from simple larceny to arrest as a rogue and a vagabond. The longest term he served was three months (plus a whipping), and the shortest was one day, also with a whipping.[96] It was with such cases in mind that Charles Dickens asked rhetorically whether there was 'any earthly thing' a youngster could do when his new sentence was completed, 'but steal again, and be again imprisoned and again flogged until, a precocious human devil, [he] is shipped away to corrupt a new world'.[97] With the ending of transportation, the only world he could corrupt was that within England itself.

Faced with such blatant examples of juvenile recidivism, some reformers advocated whipping as a punishment, arguing it was better to beat a child than to send it to prison for a relatively minor transgression and thus brand it for life as a criminal. That view was confirmed by the fact that detention was normally for too brief a period to effect any permanent improvement in the young offender's character. Sentences typically ranged from one to three months. Indeed, a survey of 2,240 boys under seventeen committed to the Westminster House of Correction in 1857 reveals that 39.5 per cent of them served *less than* a month, while a mere 0.7 per cent served for a year or more. In 1859, out of 1,721 lads similarly committed, 33.6 per cent served under a month, and 1.8 per cent a year or more. Among the girls, of 330 committed in 1857 to the same prison, 53 per cent served for less than a month, and 0.6 per cent for a year and above. In 1859, when the number of girls committed had dropped to 224, 58.4 per cent served for under a month and just 1.3 per cent were committed for a year or more.[98] These brief terms did little more than give impoverished youngsters an insight into the relatively good food and shelter available in prison. Small wonder that some of those wandering the streets and sleeping rough preferred gaol. As one boy declared on his release: 'It's the most comfortable crib as ever I was in. I wish I'd got a three months 'stead o' three weeks. I'll do summat wot'll make it hot for me next time, no fear.' Scandalized critics might call this 'juvenile depravity', but it could more justly be labelled 'the instinct of survival'.[99] In winter it must have been a severe wrench to lay aside thick, sound prison clothing in favour of a young prisoner's own ragged garments, which did little to keep out the cold.

Those who had committed the most serious offences or had received the heaviest sentences were usually held in high esteem by fellow prisoners. In 1839 a contemporary wrote that lads in Newgate gaol who had been sentenced to death (which in practice, the youngsters as well as the judge knew would be commuted) conducted themselves 'as boys of a superior class to the transport lads. The boy under sentence of transportation for life is of greater consequence than the boy who is sentenced to seven years, while the lad whose sentence is a short imprisonment is not deemed worthy to associate or converse with them; in short . . . severity of punishment is by them converted into a scale of merit.'[100]

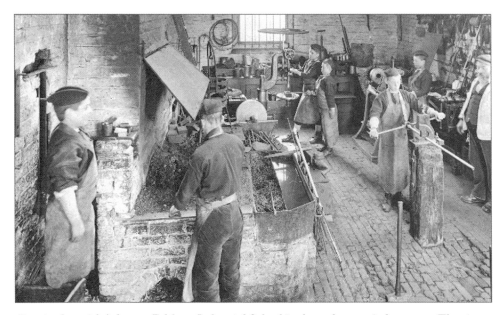

Boys in the smiths' shop at Feltham Industrial School in the early twentieth century. The aim was to teach skills and good conduct. (Greater London Record Office Photograph Collection)

Similar considerations applied to the offences committed. Pickpockets and house-breakers looked down upon shop-lifters, who in turn despised sneak thieves. The 'pudding snammers', who stole food from people leaving cookshops, were deemed the lowest class of thieves. But they considered themselves superior to those imprisoned for begging. In *Oliver Twist*, Charley Bates lamented that the Artful Dodger was to be transported not for a worthwhile theft, like that of a gold watch, chain and seals, but 'for a common twopenny-halfpenny sneeze box! . . . Oh, why didn't he rob some rich old gentleman of all his walables, and go out *as* a gentleman, and not like a common prig, without no honour nor glory!'[101]

Girls, too, had their status divisions, with the less intelligent convicted for prostitution and begging while their 'brighter sisters were primarily thieves who used prostitution merely as a means of taking strangers unawares'.[102]

As mid-century social surveys indicated the link between childhood deprivation and juvenile crime, greater emphasis was placed on the need for rescue and reform. As a first step, child prisoners were to be separated from adults. Already in 1823 early attempts at classification had led to the introduction of a separate prison hulk for youngsters. The *Euryalus* was moored at Chatham but it offered little by way of reform. Discipline was brutal and there was much bullying of younger prisoners by the bigger lads. This became so severe that some boys broke their own arms in order to escape and get into hospital. Despite repeated criticisms, the *Euryalus* remained in use until 1846. Nor did its miserable conditions prove an effective deterrent, since eight out of ten boys 'returned to their old courses, after serving their sentence'.[103]

Other efforts at classification included the establishment of a boys' penal colony at Point Puer in 1837 and, as part of a general reorganization of the transportation process, the opening of Parkhurst in 1838 as the first juvenile prison. One of its functions was to prepare young transportees for life in the Antipodes by giving instruction in farming and in trade subjects. In 1842 the first groups of lads were sent out on conditional pardon to Western Australia, where the younger ones were apprenticed to local settlers. Most of them seem to have made good.[104] But Parkhurst itself, despite its aim of reforming offenders, became characterized by harsh discipline. Nothing was to be done 'to weaken the terror of the law or . . . lessen in the minds of the juvenile population at large . . . the dread of being committed to prison'.[105] This failed to meet Mary Carpenter's requirement that child criminals should 'not be dealt with as men but as children'. Furthermore, among the tougher inmates, there were acts of defiance which solitary confinement, a bread-and-water diet, extra drill and whipping failed to check. In 1850 alone there were two instances of arson, one of which destroyed 158 cells.[106] Despite efforts to overcome these problems, Parkhurst continued to have a reputation for severity and this, combined with changing penal policy, led to the closure of its juvenile section in 1864.

More constructive in countering juvenile delinquency were the ideas of Mary Carpenter and her fellow pioneers in advocating the establishment of reformatory and industrial schools in the 1850s. Reformatories were intended for those whom Miss Carpenter labelled the 'dangerous classes', youngsters who had 'already received the prison brand, or, if the mark has not been yet visibly set upon them, are notoriously living by plunder'. Industrial schools catered for the 'perishing classes', who had 'not yet fallen into actual crime, but who are almost certain from their ignorance, destitution and the circumstances in which they are growing up, to do so, if a helping hand be not extended to raise them'.[107] In setting up reformatories, methods were applied which had already been used successfully in Germany, France and the United States of America, as well as the Philanthropic Society's Red Hill school, opened in Surrey in 1849 as an agricultural colony, where boys convicted of criminal offences could learn farming skills prior to emigrating.[108] Efforts were made to 'soften and improve' each lad's disposition, 'to instruct him thoroughly in the elements of religious truth and to accustom him to the habits of cleanliness, industry and order'. Children were referred to Red Hill from Westminster prison, and as its reputation grew, magistrates offered 'conditional pardons' to children to allow them to attend it as an alternative to prison. A similar scheme was set up at Stretton-on-Dunsmoor in Warwickshire, to take delinquent boys from the Birmingham area.[109] After completing their period of rehabilitation, boys from Red Hill were to be sent abroad immediately, to avoid any danger of 'contamination' by former associates.

Reformatory and industrial schools received legislative sanction in 1854 and 1857 respectively, with consolidating legislation passed in 1866. They were hybrid institutions, founded and partly funded by voluntary agencies, but subject to government inspection and receiving government grants. Parents, too, were expected to contribute towards their offspring's maintenance where family circumstances permitted, to ensure they did not benefit financially by the wrongdoing of their son or daughter. Reformatories catered for those under sixteen who had committed crimes punishable by imprisonment. Industrial schools were for under-fourteens who had committed less serious offences or were living in conditions likely to lead to their becoming criminals. This might be as a result of parental neglect, with no parent to be allowed to bring up a child so as to 'almost secure his becoming a criminal'. Discipline was strict, and a programme of general education was combined with vocational training and religious guidance. 'The children could expect hard labour, hard fare and a hard bed; treatment must be fair and . . . directed mainly towards deterrence.' This latter aspect was one which Mary Carpenter came to deplore.[110] A weakness of the reformatories was that future inmates had to serve a prison sentence of at least two weeks before being admitted. This was later reduced to ten days, and became optional in 1893. But not until 1899 was the prior requirement of prison with its dangers of contamination finally abolished.

By the early 1880s fifty certified reformatories were in operation in England and Wales (three of them being training ships); on 31 December 1882 they contained 5,403 inmates. At the same date there were 99 certified industrial schools (eight of them training ships), with 12,901 young inmates at the end of December 1882.[111] Contemporaries attributed the drop in juvenile crime which followed their introduction to their influence, although other factors such as increased elementary education and improved living standards were doubtless important. The fact that children were confined in reformatories for at least two years, compared with prison sentences of a month or two under the old system, was felt to give time for rehabilitation and a severing of undesirable connections. Also significant was the loss of skill by young criminals, especially pickpockets, as a result of the hard manual labour they had to perform while confined. T.B. Lloyd Baker, a powerful advocate of reformatories, claimed the tasks carried out 'ruined for ever the delicacy of touch necessary for a pickpocket'.

In 1864, Mary Carpenter argued that the work ethic instilled by the reformatories made employers eager to recruit these youngsters. That would seem an exaggeration, but even if a boy's conduct was not improved by his incarceration, the experiment was considered worthwhile by removing from society experienced child criminals likely to corrupt others. In that way, it was hoped, the ranks of juvenile delinquents would be thinned and the vicious circle perpetuating the survival of a criminal class broken. For the same reason, when youngsters left reformatories or industrial schools the authorities were anxious they should not return home. In 1880 the chaplain of Feltham Industrial School in Middlesex complained that boys who 'obstinately refused' offers of employment aid when they left, were subsequently found 'loafing about the streets under the pretence of cleaning boots, but in reality idling away their time, ready to fall into any mischief that may come in their way'. He believed some parents took their children home not from genuine affection but because they wished to be free from the small weekly payments they had to make towards their maintenance while in the institution, or because they wanted the lads to earn 'some miserable pittance to help to keep the family; if they cannot do this, they are immediately turned out . . . into the streets, to live and sleep as best they can'.[112]

Similar sentiments were expressed at the end of the century by the Inspector of Reformatory and Industrial Schools when he applauded the rising number of boys leaving reformatories to enter the armed services. Of 14,701 boys who had completed their time in the institutions between 1895 and 1897 inclusive, 1,620 had entered the army, 412 the Royal Navy, and 911 the mercantile marine. 'These boys', he declared, 'are the stuff out of which good soldiers are made; they are full of courage, reckless even to a fault, and the open-air life and steady discipline are just what suits them.' On enlistment they were 'saved from the temptation of returning to the surroundings which proved their bane in childhood. Finally, there is a fitness in boys who owe much of their education to the State repaying their debt in service to the State.'[113]

Among girls, most entered domestic service on leaving a reformatory, and every effort was made to encourage them to remain with an employer in order to establish a steady career. In Liverpool, girls who had left the Reformatory Home in Mount Vernon Green were invited back to the annual treat and those who could produce either a marriage certificate or proof they had remained in the same situation for twelve months were rewarded with 10s – a clear inducement to respectability.[114]

There were, however, complaints that the discipline in reformatories and industrial schools was over-severe, that the education given was poor, and the buildings, food and clothing supplied were unsatisfactory. On occasion chronic cash problems led to the institutions imposing heavy burdens on the inmates under the guise of industrial training, in order to raise funds. Thus lessons were sharply curtailed at the Bridge Park Farm School run by the Liverpool Juvenile Reformatory Association in the 1860s to allow for extra work chopping firewood, since this proved particularly profitable. Under the new timetable the boys rose at 5.15 a.m. in order to attend school from 6 a.m. to 7.15 a.m. They then ate breakfast and spent a quarter of an hour chanting psalms and prayers, before beginning work at 8 a.m. Apart from a break between noon and 1.15 p.m. for dinner and recreation, the rest of the day was devoted to work, until 4.45 p.m., when they washed and ate supper before attending lessons between 6 p.m. and 7 p.m. A play hour followed and there was half-an-hour of scripture and prayers before bed. But on Tuesdays and Thursdays the play period was taken up with band practice and on Friday evenings there were singing lessons.[115] Nor was this routine unusual. As late as 1889 the Inspector of Reformatory and Industrial Schools complained that in many institutions there was 'too much wood chopping and matchbox making'.[116]

The girls' routine was equally stringent. Apart from school work, inmates of the Mount Vernon Green Reformatory Home spent many hours on needlework, cooking, household duties and knitting. The older girls were employed in the laundry, to which certain local ladies sent their finery. Here equipment was limited and defective, the labour hard, and the laundry floor was constantly awash. Many girls and staff slipped and broke limbs, while complexions were 'toasted and withered from the heat of the ironing stove on which the large, heavy and cumbersome irons lined up for duty'.[117]

Nevertheless, despite the deficiencies in the reformatories and industrial schools (and a tendency for the differences between the two kinds of institution to be eroded over the years), that should not obscure their revolutionary role in dealing with deprived children. Not only were juvenile delinquents given a new legal status but their potential for reform and rehabilitation was acknowledged. This was in marked contrast to the retributive punishment administered to adult criminals and to most youngsters within the old-style prisons.

The new institutions were designed to act as 'moral hospitals', or as the commander of the Liverpool-based reformatory ship, *Akbar*, put it: 'the first great change which has to be affected [sic] . . . when they are received on board in their vagrant state is to make them "boys". They are . . . too knowing, too sharp when they come on board, too much up in the way of the world.'[118] That was not always easy to achieve. In 1887 there was a serious mutiny on the *Akbar*, during which seventeen of the ringleaders lowered a boat and enjoyed several days of freedom before being recaptured, and there were repeated attempts by some of the more daring lads to abscond individually. One youngster, William, a persistent would-be escaper, became such an expert swimmer that during the latter part of his detention he won 'acclaim and a medal' for the *Akbar* in swimming competitions with other reformatories.[119]

The *Clarence*, a reformatory ship run by the Catholic Reformatory Association and also moored in the Mersey, was twice destroyed by fires started by some of the inmates. The second attempt occurred in July 1899, after weeks of secret preparation by boys who had carried oily waste to the bowels of the ship before setting it ablaze. After this the Roman Catholics transferred to dry land, opening a nautical training school near Widnes.[120]

Not all contemporaries welcomed reformatories as an alternative to prison, and since the 1854 legislation authorizing them was only permissive, some magistrates continued to take the view that lawless youngsters needed the sharp lesson of a gaol sentence rather than the reformist approach of the new institutions. Or, like Lord Norton, they disliked the mixing of punishment with education: 'avowedly penal establishments should not have some of the enjoyments suitable and desirable for school life', Norton wrote in 1896. Otherwise the system 'became a dangerous advertisement to encourage parental neglect and give a false estimation of crime. To give a penal institution all the attractions of a Cremorne Garden, bands playing, flags flying, and holiday making, is publishing the euthanasia of juvenile crime among the endowments of the country.'[121] So even in 1895 nearly 2,000 youngsters under sixteen were still being sent to prison (1,789 of them boys and 179 girls).[122]

Occasionally in the later Victorian years minor offenders were punished by being confined in a workhouse. A Bristol lad, born in 1885, remembered going with four or five companions to rob the till in a hardware shop while the proprietor was out of the way. They spent the money on cakes and tea, and then decided to pay a second visit to the shop. This time they were caught, brought before the magistrates, and sentenced to a week in Stapleton workhouse: 'I picked oakum. . . . And they put an old pauper in charge of us. And . . . he gave us plenty of wallopings, during the week we were there . . . I was up at six and worked nearly all day, we ate bread and marge with some porridge.'[123] This lad was eleven at the time and the experience cured him of petty thieving.

In other cases, as John Gillis points out, it was non-indictable offences which often brought juveniles before the bench in the 1890s. Such activities as sliding on bridges, throwing stones, and playing street football were typical of actions which led to the arrest of gangs of youths and their subsequent court appearance. It was symptomatic of the increasing emphasis being laid by society on the need for orderly behaviour in the streets.[124]

As with many aspects of the treatment of deprived children, therefore, the Victorians were seemingly unable to decide whether their best interests were served by punishment and deterrence or by reform and rehabilitation. For many, a flimsy partition only existed between the poor but honest child and the lawbreaker. Nonetheless, if the progress made should not be overestimated, at least by the 1850s and 1860s the plight of poor children was becoming better understood and there was an assumption, through the industrial school system, that the state had a right to act *in loco parentis* where parents were failing to provide for their offspring. In this way the foundations were laid for later measures concerned with child protection and with intervention in the relationship between parent and child. This found expression in the 1880s and beyond in the establishment of Societies for the Prevention of Cruelty to Children in Liverpool and London respectively, and culminated in the setting up of the National Society for the Prevention of Cruelty to Children (NSPCC) in 1889.

The anti-cruelty societies were concerned not merely with regulating children's casual employment, as we saw in Chapter 5, but with their protection against ill-treatment and neglect by adults, including parents. To achieve this, the child's

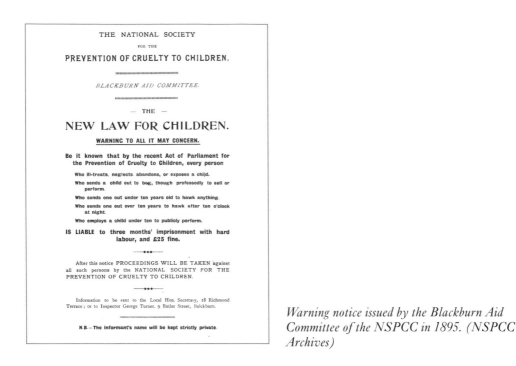

THE NATIONAL SOCIETY
FOR THE
PREVENTION OF CRUELTY TO CHILDREN.

BLACKBURN AID COMMITTEE.

— THE —

NEW LAW FOR CHILDREN.

WARNING TO ALL IT MAY CONCERN.

Be it known that by the recent Act of Parliament for the Prevention of Cruelty to Children, every person

Who ill-treats, neglects, abandons, or exposes a child.

Who sends a child out to beg, though professedly to sell or perform.

Who sends one out under ten years old to hawk anything.

Who sends one out over ten years to hawk after ten o'clock at night.

Who employs a child under ten to publicly perform.

IS LIABLE to three months' imprisonment with hard labour, and £25 fine.

After this notice PROCEEDINGS WILL BE TAKEN against all such persons by the NATIONAL SOCIETY FOR THE PREVENTION OF CRUELTY TO CHILDREN.

Information to be sent to the Local Hon. Secretary, 18 Richmond Terrace ; or to Inspector George Turner, 9 Butler Street, Blackburn.

N.B.— The Informant's name will be kept strictly private.

Warning notice issued by the Blackburn Aid Committee of the NSPCC in 1895. (NSPCC Archives)

status as an individual in its own right, rather than as an appendage to its parents, had to be established, and society educated to take seriously the mistreatment of children. All too often, the NSPCC complained, the 'base statement', 'It's only a child', underlay 'the attitude of Courts and of Parliament', and led to less serious punishments being imposed than was the case where an adult was the victim.[125]

In 1894, in a review of its work over the preceding decade, the NSPCC argued that one of the 'subtlest and most formidable of the impediments' it had had to overcome had been 'the position of children in the political sentiment of the country': 'Children were nobodies to the State. They were entitled to what their native force as children could win from their parents: that was all. The Society asserted that . . . they were . . . citizens, . . . The child once admitted to be a citizen, then action on its behalf to secure reasonable treatment is action for the extension and the enforcement of liberty.'[126]

These concepts found expression in the 1889 Prevention of Cruelty to Children Act which, for the first time, gave youngsters clearly defined rights in relation to their parents or guardians. Anyone having charge of a boy under fourteen or a girl under sixteen and wilfully ill-treating, neglecting or abandoning him or her, could now be punished. If a parent was convicted of cruelty, the courts could order a change of custody for the child to a relative or other 'fit person'. This latter included industrial schools, charitable institutions and later workhouses. And in order to ensure brutal parents did not benefit financially by the departure of the victim, weekly contributions of up to five shillings could be levied towards maintenance costs.

Much of the work involved in enforcing the 1889 'Children's Charter' and an amending Act of 1894, depended on the NSPCC and its officers. From a single inspector in 1884, the movement's 'private police force' had increased to 163 by 1900.[127] Where possible, efforts were made to protect children without bringing parents to court, but sometimes the degree of cruelty or neglect rendered prosecution necessary. One such case was highlighted by the Bradford and District branch of the National Society in 1899, when a father was committed for six weeks' imprisonment for brutality towards his two motherless children. The youngsters had threatened to drown themselves in a canal if they were forced to stay with their father. According to the Society, as a result of its intervention they were 'now in a good home' under the supervision of the Bradford Poor Law guardians.[128]

Sometimes neighbours alerted the police or the Society to ill-treatment, and by the early twentieth century the majority of examples involved neglected rather than physically abused children. Whereas physical assaults on the young had accounted for about half of the Society's complaints in four of its first five years, by 1900 such cases made up only about an eighth of its work. 'An obvious explanation for this change', comments George Behlmer, 'is that severe beating of children is apt to be noisier and therefore more likely to draw attention than, say, gradual starvation. As a result, in its early days the society naturally heard most often about public outrages; as its reputation and inspectorate grew, the discovery of child neglect grew accordingly.'[129] In the year 1898–9, the Society dealt with 28,165 cases, and prosecuted in 2,873. Of those 28,165 incidents, 21,749 involved neglect and starvation, compared with 3,748 concerned with ill-treatment and assault, and 1,080 involving abandonment and exposure.[130] 'Causing to beg, &c.' accounted for a further 574 cases.

In the light of these and other changes affecting the position of children during the Victorian years, how did their situation in the 1890s compare with that of their predecessors of sixty years before? First and foremost, concern for child welfare had extended beyond the initial concentration on working hours, schooling and juvenile criminality to cover issues of health, sexuality, legal rights and leisure pursuits, with the state playing a leading role in creating this new framework. Many of the initial measures were ineffective and had to be strengthened, and some were implemented for motives which had more to do with the protection of property rights and the discouragement of lawbreaking than with the wellbeing of the young. But they had begun a process whereby the position of the child had moved from that of being one of the least regarded members of society to one accorded a degree of protection through the vulnerable years of immaturity, and an opportunity to prepare for the responsibilities of the adult world. The fact that more youngsters were surviving, once they had negotiated the perilous months of infancy, had led to their becoming increasingly sentimental objects for the parents (and especially the mother), who could now hope that they would live to reach maturity.

Alongside this, the advent of compulsory education underlined the fact that pre-adolescent boys and girls lacked certain physical and intellectual qualities needed to cope with the demands of grown-up society. The 'minute regulation' of the school day and the introduction of a standardized elementary curriculum led to a growing desire to mould and scrutinize children's activities. Greater control was also exercised over youngsters' lives through the application of education and employment legislation. That included the setting up of special truant and day industrial schools in some towns from the late 1870s to discipline and ultimately to reform persistent absentees (see Appendix 4).

On a broader front, the growth of imperialistic sentiment influenced the curriculum in the schools and fuelled the national wish to inculcate patriotic sentiments into the future defenders of the Empire. It also affected the way children were viewed. Anxieties about the physical health of the young and their ability to fulfil their imperial mission were widely expressed. The eugenists, in particular, laid great stress on the importance of ensuring that the future parents of the race should grow up fit and strong. Even child emigration was presented partly as 'an investment in Empire' and as a means of establishing a 'living link between the Dominions and the mother country'.[131]

Within the home, meanwhile, most youngsters were subjected to strict discipline, designed to maintain order within the family. That remained true even when there were strong bonds of affection. There was what one historian has called a 'tacit mutual understanding of family roles and obligations, which "[enjoined] children to work hard, demand little, and respect the authority of the old"'.[132] Sometimes that meant parents laid down rules of conduct for their offspring which they did not themselves observe. 'One curious thing I noticed as a child', wrote Walter Southgate, 'was that although our parents and others used a great deal of swear words, even in front of their own children, yet it was a strict rule that children must not use such language on pain of dire punishment.'[133]

Appendix 1

CHILDREN IN AN URBANIZING POPULATION: ENGLAND AND WALES, 1841–1901

Percentage of Children in Total Population

Year	% of children under 15 in total population	% of children under 10 in total population	% of total population (all ages) in urban areas
1841	36.1	25.2	48.3
1851	35.5	24.8	54.0
1861	35.7	25.2	58.7
1871	36.1	25.4	65.2
1881	36.4	25.6	70.0
1891	35.0	23.9	74.5
1901	32.4	22.1	78.0

Sources: Calculated from the *Census Reports* and R.J. Morris and Richard Rodger (eds), *The Victorian City. A Reader in British Urban History* (1993), 3.

Child Employment: 1851–1901

(a) Percentage of children aged 5–9 inclusive in occupations in England and Wales, as shown in the Census Reports. *These will underestimate the position, in that many part-time, casual and seasonal child workers probably did not declare an occupation.*

	Boys %	Girls %
1851	2.0	1.4
1871	0.9	0.7

By 1881 it had become illegal for children to work full-time under the age of ten.

(b) Percentage of children aged 10–14 inclusive in occupations in England and Wales, as shown in the Census Reports. *This, too, is likely to be an underestimate (see above).*

	Boys %	Girls %
1851	36.6	19.9
1871	32.1	20.4
1891	26.0	16.3
1901	21.9	12.0

(c) Principal occupational categories of boys in 1901: 21.9 per cent of age group at work

Of those occupied:	10–14 inclusive %
Conveyance of men, goods and messages	24.6
Agriculture	13.3
Textile fabrics	11.8
Mines and quarries	9.3
Metals, machines, implements	7.8
Food, tobacco, drink & lodging	5.5
Proportion of work force	72.3

Principal occupational categories of girls in 1901: 12.0 per cent of age group at work

Of those occupied:	10–14 inclusive %
Domestic offices and services	33.8
Textile fabrics	30.7
Dress	15.3
Paper, prints, books, &c.	3.8
Food, tobacco, drink & lodging	3.5
Metal, machinery, implements	2.2
Proportion of work force	89.3

(d) Percentage of boys and girls working at various ages in 1901 Census in eleven specimen towns. Only in the textile areas, where half-time flourished, was there a high proportion of young children at work

	Boys		Girls	
	10–13 years %	*13–14 years* %	*10–13 years* %	*13–14 years* %
England and Wales	*2.3*	*34.7*	*1.3*	*17.2*
Birmingham	1.0	47.9	0.4	31.8
Birkenhead	1.5	22.3	0.2	6.5
Blackburn	15.2	74.3	16.4	69.4
Bolton	12.2	72.4	8.2	60.1
Burnley	15.6	76.4	14.3	73.3
Bradford	12.0	68.7	10.2	60.5
Halifax	17.8	71.5	14.4	68.3
Liverpool	1.1	15.8	0.2 .	3.8
London	0.6	12.7	0.2	5.1
Sheffield	0.9	49.6	0.2	21.4
West Bromwich	0.6	53.4	0.4	16.7

Appendix 2

INCOME AND HOUSEHOLD EXPENDITURE OF FAMILIES IN
DUKINFIELD IN 1836 AND THE RECESSION YEAR 1841

(a) Warehouseman and his family;
four individuals

(b) Cardroom hand and his family;
three individuals

Total income of family: per week
1836 = 16s 0d
1841 = 10s 8d

Total income of family: per week
1836 = 13s 0d
1841 = 8s 8d

Total expenditure of family: per week
1836 = 12s 9d
1841 = 14s 6d

Total expenditure of family: per week
1836 = 9s 9d
1841 = 11s 4d

| | % of Expenditure on the Total Income | | | |
	1836	*1841*	*1836*	*1841*
Rent	15.6	18.7	12.2	14.4
Flour or bread	17.2	32.8	17.3	33.6
Meat	5.0	11.7	6.1	14.4
Bacon	3.0	6.2	2.0	3.8
Oatmeal	2.0	3.9	–	–
Butter	4.7	9.4	5.8	11.4
Eggs	–	–	–	–
Milk	5.4	8.2	5.1	7.7
Potatoes	3.6	7.8	2.5	5.8
Cheese	–	–	–	–
Tea	3.1	3.9	3.2	4.3
Coffee	2.4	3.4	2.9	4.3
Sugar	4.7	9.4	5.8	11.4
Treacle	1.0	2.4	1.2	2.9
Tobacco	–	–	–	–
Soap	3.1	4.7	3.8	5.8
Salt	0.2	0.4	0.3	0.4
Candles	1.0	1.1	1.0	1.4
Coal	6.2	9.4	3.8	5.8
Yeast	1.1	2.4	2.0	2.9
Total	79.3	135.8	75.0	130.3

Both families had *underspent* in 1836 by more than 20 per cent; both were *overspending* in 1841 by over 30 per cent on their weekly income.

From: William Neild, 'Comparative Statement of the Income and Expenditure of Certain Families of the Working Classes in Manchester and Dukinfield in the Years 1836 and 1841', in *Journal of the Statistical Society of London*, Vol. IV (1841), 330, 331. Neild noted that it was 'very common, if not the general, practice for the working classes of this district to select a particular shopkeeper with whom they deal for all their provisions, and to whom they are generally in debt, and when a time of suffering comes, arising from reduced wages, want of employment, dear food, or the combination of all three, as is the case at present, they become more and more involved with the shopkeeper. This class of persons (the shopkeepers) are generally the first to feel reverses in manufacturing districts; and in all instances of considerable depression in trade numbers of them are ruined ' (p. 322).

Appendix 3

WORKING CHILDREN IN THE 1860S

(a) Child employees at Messrs Ludlow's, Legge Street, Birmingham, percussion cap manufacturers

Mary Cooper, age 7. – Does not know how long she has been here. It was warm weather when she came. 'Drops 'cussion caps' i.e. drops tinfoil in. Comes at 8; stays till 7 or 7½. 'Have us breakfast before us come.' Dinner at 1, goes home for it. Tea at about 4½, up at her work; has half an hour. Makes her tea hot by the fire. Washes under the tap sometimes. So do the big people sometimes. The master pays her and everybody else. Gets 1s 6d, or 1s 3d. Went to a week-day school till she came here. 'A catholic school.' Paid 1d a week. Used to go to night school with her sister. Paid 2d at one. Goes to a Sunday school now in the morning, and from there to church ('not catholic') and to school again in the afternoon. Her sister works with her here, and has the same hours for work and meals. Thinks London is a town. Good people go to heaven. (Spells words of 3 or 4 letters).

Esther Bubb, age 6. – Her sister thinks she is under 7, but said, 'she would look at the Bible when she went home and let you know'. Has only lately come. 'Drops in.' All leave work at the same time. Some stay to dinner, not so many. Is not ever poorly. Likes this better than school. Gets 1s 4d a week, or less. 'Sometimes get my 18 pence.' Mother has it for her clothes. Father works at barrels (gun). He comes home at 8. He makes her brother hear them 'say and spell'. Sometimes says it every night out of a spelling book. Went to a week-day school till she came here. Paid 3d a week for it. Can read the Testament. Can write. Never 'writed' on a paper. Wrote down sums that teacher put down. Could not count them up. Teacher told them how. Father reads the Testament on Sundays to her mother. Sometimes her brother has a large Bible and reads it to her father. It is a 'large Bible what has us names in, when we was born'. 'Christ is God. Calls the people to die. Takes the good up into heaven. Puts (the bad) 'em in the fire.'

Mary Ann Adderley, age 8. – Can tell me [the Assistant Commissioner] now how old she is. Has just asked mother. 'Bands' i.e. puts green tickets on cartridges. Licks the back of each ticket to stick it on. The stuff tastes in her mouth. When she first came she had her lips bad with it. Makes her sick sometimes; not only feel sick, but really sick. Makes her feel sick every day, chiefly towards dinner time, and about 7 in the evening. Did not feel sick ever till she came here. Has been here two months. Sometimes she tells mother of it, and she gives her some 'magnesia'. 'I never have no tea, nor no breakfast now.' When she did not go to work, could eat two rounds off a big loaf. At dinner can sometimes eat a length off a little loaf, or sometimes a round. A little loaf costs 2¼d now. Dinner at 1. Generally has it in the shop, but goes home sometimes. Tea about 4½. Often washes her hands at the tap; must do so, because 'it makes my thumb and finger so green'. It makes her thumb gather. It hurts her (shows a fester half an inch long by the nail). The other girls lick their bands the same as she does. There are only two besides. Gets 2*s* or 2*s* 3*d* a week sometimes. Went to a school before she came here 'but I didn't learn anything. It was only an old lady's school.' Could not read or write. 'All as I could say was my A, B, C.' Does not know what the Bible is about at all. The Testament is about the 'Lord and Jesus Christ'. He died for us.

(b) Lucifer Match Manufactory, Lincoln's, Bull Close, Norwich

Walter Thacker, age 12. At the work two years. Empties the frames when the matches are dry, and boxes. Also stirs the [phosphorus] composition for two hours a day at four or five different times.

Hours of work are from 6 to 7. Has breakfast at 8½, half an hour. Looks at a neighbour's clock or guesses. Dinner at 1, an hour. Goes outside or eats on the stove here. The composition gets on his hands, but he washes it off in the pot (in the water outside like that of a glue pot) every time. Sometimes when he is stirring the stuff catches alight round the edges. The smoke does not take away his hunger. Has not a cough. His teeth have ached, but only once.

Gets 3*s* 3*d* a week. Mother allows him 3*d*. He puts that in the bank. Begun this year. Will have it out at Christmas and buy a new coat.

Went to a week school till he came to work. Goes every Sunday now, and on Tuesday evening from 7 till 9. Can read and write big and little hand on paper and do multiplication. A whale is a large fish.

(c) Mr Joseph Broadbent's, Door-bolt Manufacturer, Brick-kiln Street, Wolverhampton

Charles Smith. – I am going 12. I live in Church Street. My father is a locksmith. I have been here six years. When I first came I got victuals and no wages. I stopped because I liked to be here. I got meat here, and I only got bacon and taties at home. I now get 3*s* 6*d*. I come at 7, sometimes not till nearly 8, and I go home at 8. I get my breakfast at 9. I have half-an-hour for breakfast. I stop at 1 for dinner; I go home for dinner. It is very seldom that we have meat for dinner. I come back at 2. I never begin work before 2. I stop at 5 for tea. I have 35 minutes for tea. I know how long I have by the clock. I always go away at 8. I have stopped to 9 about 12 times since I have been here. I have stayed away and played some days. It was wrong. When I go home I wash, have my supper, and go to bed. I am often tired. It is not hard work I have to do. I often get a box on the ears; but I was never hit with a stick or anything of that kind. I got a box on the ears the other day for not doing my stint. Sometimes my stint is too much to do. (Reads a little.) I went to school for six months before I came to work. I go to Sunday school now. I have got two testaments given me at Sunday school. Mother reads the testament. I have three brothers and two sisters. I am the oldest.

[*Mr J. Broadbent*, his employer, noted that four boys were employed: 'Poor people often send their boys here at seven or eight years of age, that they may earn a little money, and learn the trade. Then when they have been here for three or four years the parents will take them away, and get them into a large manufactory, and apprentice them. . . . Sometimes the mothers will come for the money, where the lads spend their wages. It is a common thing for boys to get 2*s* 6*d* and pay their parents only 2*s*; but I attribute this a good deal to the parents' fault, in not taking proper care of their children. The children who come very young are all the children of very poor parents. We have one case of a boy, who has been here for a long time. He came and worked for the men for nothing but his meals, because he liked the meals they gave him better than what he had at home. He was between six and seven when he came; now he is going 12, and he is earning 3s 6d a week. He is going to be bound apprentice to me. He will have 4s a week when he begins in June. Then his wages will rise 1s every year till he is 21. . . . The boys will not work beyond the regular hours except to earn extra wages for themselves. The boys generally work overtime before the holidays, to get a little money for themselves. There are three days holidays at Easter, Whitsuntide, and Christmas, and also at the fair and races. They generally have a week at the races.']

Sources: Evidence in the *First* and *Third Reports of the Children's Employment Commission*, PP 1863, Vol. XVIII and PP 1864, Vol. XXII, respectively.

Appendix 4

CHILD OFFENDERS IN GREAT BRITAIN, 1865–1900

(a) Year	Total number of offenders under order of detention in reformatories	Total number of children detained in industrial schools (including truant schools)	Total number of children attending day industrial schools
1865	4.508	1,952	–
1870	5,433	8,788	–
1875	5,615	12,682	–
1880	5,927	16,446	1,005
1885	6,241	20,250	2,324
1890	5,854	22,735	3,698
1895	5,633	24,577	3,223
1900	5,611	24,718	3,253

(b) Number of juveniles under sixteen committed to prison (England and Wales)

Year	Boys	Girls	Total
1865	8,350	1,290	9,640 *
1870	8,619	1,379	9,998
1875	6,319	893	7,212
1880	4,786	793	5,579
1885	4,245	568	4,813
1890	3,456	416	3,872
1895	1,789	179	1,968
1900	1,295	58	1,353 *

* *Adult* commitments to prison in 1865 were 116,398 and in 1900, 144,964.

Sources: Forty-second Annual Report of the Inspector of Reformatory and Industrial Schools in Great Britain, PP 1899, Vol. XLIV; Forty-fifth Annual Report of the Inspector of Reformatory and Industrial Schools in Great Britain, PP 1902, Vol. XLVIII.

(c) Children convicted of indictable offences: 1894–1900

Year	Number between ages 12 and 16
1894	6,604
1895	5,330
1896	5,773
1897	5,625
1898	6,104
1899	5,715
1900	6,550

Source: *Forty-fifth Annual Report of the Inspector of Reformatory and Industrial Schools.* The inspector concluded (p. 15): 'For what these figures are worth as a measure of juvenile crime, they certainly do not show any alarming tendency to increase.'

Appendix 5

CHILDHOOD DEPRIVATION IN LIVERPOOL IN 1883

(a) Two girls of 11 and 7. Father in prison. Stepmother sends them out at night to beg, and with the understanding that they must not return home without a certain sum be the hour what it may; found shivering and crying by a lady at 11.0 p.m. and brought to the Shelter. Subsequently Superintendent and Matron appeared before the Stipendiary with the lady to prefer a charge of begging, and the girls were committed to an Industrial School until they are 16 years of age.

(b) Boy of eight habitually selling papers at 10.30 at night and later. Visitation proved the case to be one of poverty, as the mother was a widow in bad health, with only 4*s* from the parish, and left with five children to support, the ages are 14, 9, 8, and twins 4. Being the widow of a seaman, application was made for help to the Seamen's Orphanage. The application resulted in a grant of 20*s* per month. The gentleman who reported this case was so gratified with results that he became a subscriber, and promises to look after the boy.

(c) Two motherless girls, aged 8 and 10, have had to fly from the cruelty of a drunken father, and have been known to wander in the streets nearly the whole night. Neither fines nor imprisonment would meet this case, but relations have interfered, and have undertaken to provide for both girls.

(d) A complete gutter child of seven was brought at midnight. She was frightened when put into a bath, and very much astonished to see her hard black hands become white under the influence of soap and water. Her mother was dead, her father had deserted her, her sisters and brothers had drifted away, and she just dropped into the houses of neighbours for her bite of food. If a neighbour would let her lie on the floor, well and good, if not closets or cellars had to do. She was admitted to Shaw Street Emigration Home.

(e) A boy and girl of the ages of 12 and 13 were brought by a School Board visitor from a house of ill-fame, were sheltered for one night, taken next morning before a magistrate, and eventually both sent to Industrial Schools . . .

From: *First Report of the Liverpool Society for the Prevention of Cruelty to Children for 1883*, H.179.2 LIV. at Liverpool Record Office.

Notes

PP = Parliamentary Papers

1   Victorian Towns

1. J.A. Banks, 'The Contagion of Numbers' in H.J. Dyos and Michael Wolff (eds), The Victorian City, Vol. I (1973), 105; John Saville, Rural Depopulation in England and Wales 1851–1951 (1957), 61.
2. Nigel Morgan, *Vanished Dwellings. Early Industrial Housing in a Lancashire Cotton Town: Preston* (1990), 15, 39.
3. *Schools Inquiry Commission*, PP 1867–8, Vol. XXVIII, Pt VIII, Report by Mr J. Bryce on Schools in Lancashire, 749–50.
4. W.E. Marsden, 'Education and the Social Geography of Nineteenth-century Towns and Cities' in D.A. Reeder (ed.), *Urban Education in the Nineteenth Century* (1977), 49.
5. [Anonymous], *Work about the Five Dials* (1878), 46.
6. Marsden, 'Education and Social Geography' in Reeder, 56.
7. Asa Briggs, 'The Human Aggregate' in Dyos and Wolff, 93.
8. George Sturt, *A Small Boy in the Sixties* (1982), 111, 118, 148.
9. Gustave Doré and Blanchard Jerrold, *London. A Pilgrimage* (1970), 62–3. The book was first published in 1872.
10. Thomas Hardy, *The Mayor of Casterbridge* (1953 Pan pbk edn), 206. The book was first published in 1886.
11. P.J. Keating, 'Fact and Fiction in the East End' in Dyos and Wolff, Vol. II, 596–7.
12. H.J. Dyos and D.A. Reeder, 'Slums and Suburbs' in Dyos and Wolff, Vol. I, 362.
13. Gertrude Himmelfarb, 'The Culture of Poverty' in Dyos and Wolff, Vol. II, 718; see also Michael Wolff and Celina Fox, 'Pictures from the Magazines' in Dyos and Wolff, Vol. II, 569.
14. H.J. Dyos, 'The Slums of Victorian London', *Victorian Studies*, Vol. XI, No. 1 (September 1967), 14–15.
15. D.A. Reeder, 'Predicaments of City Children: Late Victorian and Edwardian Perspectives on Education and Urban Society' in Reeder, 77.
16. John Garwood, *The Million-peopled City; or, One-half of the People of London Made Known to the Other Half* (1853), 16–17.
17. *Hansard*, 3rd Ser., Vol. XCIX (29 May–30 June, 1848), col. 446.
18. Quoted in Reeder, 'Predicaments of City Children', in Reeder, 76.
19. Stephen Humphries, *Hooligans or Rebels? An Oral History of Working-class Childhood and Youth 1889–1939* (1983 edn), 22–3; D.A. Reeder, 'History, Education and the City: a Review of Trends in Britain' in Ronald K. Goodenow and William E. Marsden (eds), *The City and Education in Four Nations* (1992), 30.
20. L.C.B. Seaman, *Life in Victorian London* (1973), 62–3.
21. Barbara Finkelstein, 'Redoing Urban Educational History' in Goodenow and Marsden, 173.
22. Alice Foley, *A Bolton Childhood* (1990 edn), 15.
23. Walter Southgate, *That's the Way It Was. A Working Class Autobiography 1890–1950* (1982), 22–3.
24. Robert Roberts, *The Classic Slum. Salford Life in the First Quarter of the Century* (1971), 3–4.
25. Roberts, *The Classic Slum*, 5–9.
26. Thea Thompson, *Edwardian Childhoods* (1981), 11. Tommy was born in 1892 and left home when he was about thirteen. He was then sent to a charity school.
27. University of Essex, Oral Archives Transcript No. QD1/FLWE/65.

28. Bristol People's Oral History Project, Transcript No. R.019 at Bristol Local History Library.

29. William E. Marsden, 'Social Stratification and Nineteenth-century English Urban Education' in Goodenow and Marsden, 118, 123.

30. Per Bolin-Hort, *Work, Family and the State. Child Labour and the Organization of Production in the British Cotton Industry, 1780–1920* (1989), 151–2, 213.

31. Carl Chinn, *They Worked All Their Lives. Women of the Urban Poor in England, 1880–1939* (1988), 67.

32. Southgate, *That's the Way It Was*, 50.

33. James Walvin, *A Child's World. A Social History of English Childhood 1800–1914* (1982), 12.

34. *Child's Guardian*, May 1889, 73. Copies of the *Child's Guardian* may be seen in NSPCC Archives.

35. *Charity Organisation Review*, December 1889, 468.

36. London School Board: Report of Sub-Committee on Underfed Children Attending School 1898–99, SBL.1469 at Greater London Record Office.

37. *Charity Organisation Review*, June 1885, 263. See also Helen Bosanquet, *Social Work in London. A History of the Charity Organisation Society* (1914), 255–6.

38. Robert H. Sherard, *The Child-Slaves of Britain* (1905), 11, 58.

39. Sherard, *Child-Slaves*, 19, 57.

40. Hugh Cunningham, *The Children of the Poor. Representations of Childhood since the Seventeenth Century* (1991), 217.

41. Report of the Medical Officer of Health for 1893 in *Proceedings of the Council of the City of Liverpool for 1893–94*, 20, H.352.COU. at Liverpool Record Office.

42. Report of the Medical Officer of Health for 1901 in *Proceedings of the Council of the City of Liverpool for 1901–02*, 26–7, H.352.COU. at Liverpool Record Office.

43. Report of the Medical Officer of Health for 1901, 149.

44. *Report of the Medical Officer of Health for Bolton for 1892*, 32, B.352–4 BOL. at Bolton Local History Library and Archives.

45. Carol Dyhouse, *Girls Growing up in Late Victorian and Edwardian England* (1981), 89–92.

46. Helen Dendy, 'The Children of Working London' in Bernard Bosanquet (ed.), *Aspects of the Social Problem* (1895), 33.

47. Cunningham, *Children of the Poor*, 153.

48. The Revd E. Bans and Arthur Chilton Thomas, *Catholic Child Emigration to Canada* (1902), 3–4 in Westminster Diocesan Archives. Documents in the archives are quoted by permission of His Eminence the Cardinal Archbishop of Westminster.

49. E.J. Urwick, 'Conclusion' in E.J. Urwick (ed.), *Studies of Boy Life in Our Cities* (1904), 265–6.

50. Log Book of All Saints Boys' School, 1863–88 at Greater London Record Office, EO/DIV.8/ALL/LB/1, entries for 20 June, 4 July, 6 July, 22 August 1865, for example; Log Book for Christ Church Boys' School, 1863–86, at Greater London Record Office, EO/DIV.8/CHC/LB/1, entry for 6 January 1863.

51. A.P. Wadsworth, 'The First Manchester Sunday Schools' in M.W. Flinn and T.C. Smout (eds), *Essays in Social History* (1974), 118.

52. Southgate, *That's the Way It Was*, 26–7.

53. Foley, *A Bolton Childhood*, 17, 21–2.

2   *Middle-class Children*

1. W.J. Reader, *Professional Men. The Rise of the Professional Classes in Nineteenth-century England* (1966), 211.

2. *Schools Inquiry Commission*, PP 1867–8, Vol. XXVIII, Part VIII, Report by Mr J. Bryce on Schools in Lancashire, 751.

3. Reader, *Professional Men*, 202. Anne Digby, 'New Schools for the Middle Class Girl' in Peter Searby (ed.), *Educating the Victorian Middle Class* (1982), 2.

4. W.E. Marsden, 'Social Stratification and Nineteenth-century English Urban Education' in Ronald K. Goodenow and William E. Marsden (eds), *The City and Education in Four Nations* (1992), 114.

5. Harold Perkin, *The Rise of Professional Society. England since 1880* (1989), 81.

6. Katharine Chorley, *Manchester Made Them* (1950), 21–2.

7. Charles Dickens, *Dombey and Son*, Alan Horseman (ed.), (1974 edn), 3, 134.

8. Molly Hughes, *A London Family 1870–1900* (1991 edn), 7, 30, 33.

9. Gwen Raverat, *Period Piece. A Cambridge Childhood* (1952), 53–4.

10. Margaret Fletcher, *O, Call Back Yesterday* (1939), 5.

11. Fletcher, *O, Call Back*, 6–7.

12. Perkin, *Professional Society*, 96.

13. Linda A. Pollock, *Forgotten Children. Parent–Child Relations from 1500 to 1900* (1988 edn), 123, 186–7.

14. *General Report of the Royal Commission on Secondary Education*, PP 1895, Vol. XLIII, 74.

15. Perkin, *Professional Society*, 28.

16. Maria Cadbury, 'The Happy Days of Our Childhood', manuscript autobiography in Birmingham Archives, BRL.466/344, 20–1. Catherine Hall, 'The Butcher, The Baker, The Candlestickmaker: The Shop and Family in the Industrial Revolution' in R.J. Morris and Richard Rodger (eds), *The Victorian City. A Reader in British Urban History 1820–1914* (1993), 311.

17. Chorley, *Manchester Made Them*, 155.

18. Thea Thompson, *Edwardian Childhoods* (1981), 125.

19. Chorley, *Manchester Made Them*, 172–3.

20. Robert Graves, *Goodbye to All That* (1960 edn), 19.

21. *General Report of the Royal Commission on Secondary Education*, 74.

22. C. Stella Davies, *North Country Bred. A Working-class Family Chronicle* (1963), 54–8, 66.

23. Paul Thompson, 'Voices from Within' in H.J. Dyos and Michael Wolff (eds), *The Victorian City*, Vol. I (1973), 63.

24. Davies, *North Country Bred*, 63–4.

25. Fletcher, *O, Call Back*, 45–6.

26. University of Essex, Oral Archives Transcript No. QD1/FLWE/188.

27. Thompson, *Edwardian Childhoods*, 129.

28. Elizabeth Gladstone to Margaret Gladstone, PRO.30/69/874 at the Public Record Office.

29. Isabella Gladstone to Margaret Gladstone, 8 and 13 August 1882, PRO.30/69/874 at the Public Record Office.

30. Winifred Gérin, *Elizabeth Gaskell* (1976), 52–4.

31. J.A.V. Chapple and Arthur Pollard (eds), *The Letters of Mrs Gaskell* (1966), 57.

32. Gérin, *Elizabeth Gaskell*, 72.

33. Chapple and Pollard, *Letters of Mrs Gaskell*, 259.

34. Hughes, *A London Family*, 41–3, 58, 148.

35. See, for example, Margaret Gladstone's diary entry for 26 April 1885, PRO.30/69/909 at the Public Record Office. J. Ramsay Macdonald, *Margaret Ethel Macdonald* (1929 edn), 18, 46–7.

36. Margaret Gladstone to Florence Gladstone, 15 March 1882 and 18 April 1883, PRO.30/69/869 at the Public Record Office.

37. V.E. Stack (ed.), *Oxford High School* (1963), 6. Digby, 'New Schools', 18.

38. Cadbury, 'The Happy Days', 47. Maria Cadbury to her parents, 19 October 1853, MS.466/341/2, at Birmingham Archives.

39. Richard Cadbury to Maria Cadbury, 28 March 1846, MS.466/285/1, at Birmingham Archives.

40. Richard Cadbury to Maria Cadbury, 11 April 1855, MS.285/9–10, at Birmingham Archives.

41. *Children's League of Pity Paper*, Vol. I, No. 4 (November 1893), 28. *Child's Guardian*, December 1891, 130, at the headquarters of the National Society for the Prevention of Cruelty to Children, London.

42. *Children's League of Pity Paper*, Vol. I, No. 1 (August 1893), 1–2. George K. Behlmer, *Child Abuse and Moral Reform in England 1870–1908* (1982), 188.

43. Silas K. Hocking, *Her Benny* (1890), 140–3, 157, 288. The book was first published in 1880.

44. Chorley, *Manchester Made Them*, 175–6.

45. Pollock, *Forgotten Children*, 123.

46. Hughes, *A London Family*, 183–4.

47. Perkin, *Professional Society*, 95.

48. Jean E. McCann, *Thomas Howell and the School at Llandaff 1860–1890* (1972), 66, 86.

49. Sarah E. Fox (ed.), *Edwin Octavius Tregelles. Civil Engineer and Minister of the Gospel* (1892), 118–19. Pollock, *Forgotten Children*, 123.

50. Gillian Avery, *The Best Type of Girl. A History of Girls' Independent Schools* (1991), 99–100.

51. *Schools Inquiry Commission*, PP 1867–8, Vol. XXVIII, Part VI, Report by Mr D.R. Fearon on the Metropolitan District, 343.

52. *Royal Commission on Secondary Education*, PP 1895, Vol. XLVIII, Mr Massie's Report on Warwickshire, 70.

53. H.J. Foster, 'Private, Proprietary and Public Elementary Schools in a Lancashire Residential Town: A Contest for the Patronage of the Lower Middle Classes

1870–1900' in Searby, *Educating the Victorian Middle Class*, 76. *Royal Commission on Secondary Education*, PP 1895, Vol. XLVIII, Mr Kitchener's Report on Lancashire, 235.

54. Raverat, *Period Piece*, 61.
55. Brian Heeney, *Mission to the Middle Classes. The Woodard Schools 1848–1891* (1969), 10.
56. Michael Sanderson, *Education, Economic Change and Society in England 1780–1870* (1983), 33.
57. T.J.H. Bishop and Rupert Wilkinson, *Winchester and the Public School Elite* (1967), 103–9.
58. J.L. Garvin, *The Life of Joseph Chamberlain*, Vol. 1 (*1836–85*) (1935), 30–6. David Dutton, *Austen Chamberlain. Gentleman in Politics* (1985), 15. Sanderson, *Education, Economic Change*, 38.
59. James Walvin, *A Child's World. A Social History of English Childhood 1800–1914* (1982), 82.
60. *Schools Inquiry Commission*, Report by Mr J. Bryce on Schools in Lancashire, 752–3.
61. Reader, *Professional Men*, 111.
62. J. Stuart Maclure, *Educational Documents. England and Wales 1816–1968* (1969 edn), 94.
63. Asa Briggs, *Social Thought and Social Action. A Study of the Work of Seebohm Rowntree 1871–1954* (1961), 9.
64. Edmund Knowles Muspratt, *My Life and Work* (n.d. [1917]), 10–12.
65. *Christ's College, Blackheath. Magazine*, January 1895, 23. At this date there were sixty scholars at the school, fifty-two of them boarders. See *Magazine* at the Church of England Record Centre, NS/SR/MISC.1/1/1.
66. Margaret E. Bryant, *The London Experience of Secondary Education* (1986), 157–9.
67. *Royal Commission on Secondary Education*, Mr Kitchener's Report on Lancashire, 224–7.
68. Maclure, *Educational Documents*, 95.
69. W.E. Marsden, 'Schools for the Urban Lower Middle Classes . . .' in Goodenow & Marsden, 47.
70. *Schools Inquiry Commission*, Report by Mr J. Bryce on Schools in Lancashire, 734–6.
71. W.E. Marsden, 'Education and the Social Geography of Nineteenth-century Towns and Cities' in D.A. Reeder (ed.), *Urban Education in the Nineteenth Century* (1977), 67.

72. *Royal Commission on Secondary Education*, Mr Kitchener's Report on Lancashire, 119. Marsden, 'Education and Social Geography' in Reeder, 67.
73. *Schools Inquiry Commission*, Report by Mr D.R. Fearon on the Metropolitan District, 246.
74. *Royal Commission on Secondary Education*, Mr Kitchener's Report on Lancashire, 236.
75. Marsden, 'Education and Social Geography' in Reeder, 68.
76. Heeney, *Mission to the Middle Classes*, 12.
77. *Royal Commission on Secondary Education*, Mr Kitchener's Report on Lancashire, 234. Mr Massie's Report on Warwickshire, 51–3.
78. Carl Chinn, 'Was Separate Schooling a Means of Class Segregation in Late Victorian and Edwardian Birmingham?', *Midland History*, Vol. XIII (1988), 102–3.
79. Chinn, 'Separate Schooling', 104.
80. Stuart Maclure, *One Hundred Years of London Education 1870–1970* (1970), 57.
81. Marsden, 'Education and Social Geography' in Reeder, 65–6.
82. Marsden, 'Social Stratification' in Goodenow and Marsden, 119.
83. Gillian Sutherland, *Policy-making in Elementary Education 1870–1895* (1973), 201. *Education in Bradford since 1870* (Bradford Corporation, 1970), 19.
84. *General Report of the Royal Commission on Secondary Education*, 53.
85. *Education in Bradford*, 23–5.
86. *Schools Inquiry Commission*, Report by Mr J. Bryce on Lancashire, 791.
87. Digby, 'New Schools', 3.
88. Jane E. Sayers, *The Fountain Unsealed. A History of the Notting Hill and Ealing High School* (1973), 102.
89. Diary of Margaret Gladstone for 1885, PRO.30/69/909 at the Public Record Office.
90. *General Report of the Royal Commission on Secondary Education*, 76. Digby, 'New Schools', 1. *General Report of the Schools Inquiry Commission*, PP 1867–8, Vol. XXVIII, Part I, 554.
91. Digby, 'New Schools', 1.
92. Digby, 'New Schools', 3.
93. Digby, 'New Schools', 3.
94. Digby, 'New Schools', 18.
95. Fletcher, *O, Call Back*, 54–5.

96. Sayers, *The Fountain Unsealed*, 71. Stack, *Oxford High School*, 64. According to one former pupil, who attended Oxford High School at the end of the 1890s, even at that late date some 'parents still thought games unladylike'.
97. R.M. Scrimgeour (ed.), *The North London Collegiate School 1850–1950* (1950), 122–3.
98. Marsden, 'Education and Social Geography' in Reeder, 69. Avery, *Best Type of Girl*, 69. Sayers, *The Fountain Unsealed*, 73.
99. Stack, *Oxford High School*, 5.
100. Hughes, *A London Family*, 169, 173, 179.
101. Sayers, *The Fountain Unsealed*, 30–1. Avery, *Best Type of Girl*, 60.
102. Stack, *Oxford High School*, 52.
103. Avery, *Best Type of Girl*, 57.
104. Sayers, *The Fountain Unsealed*, 58, 59, 60, 67, 73.
105. Fletcher, *O, Call Back*, 47, 51–2.
106. Digby, 'New Schools', 21.
107. *General Report of the Royal Commission on Secondary Education*, 50, 51.
108. Michael J. Winstanley, *The Shopkeeper's World 1830–1914* (1983), 144–7.
109. Winstanley, *Shopkeeper's World*, 148–9.
110. Winstanley, *Shopkeeper's World*, 162.
111. Winstanley, *Shopkeeper's World*, 162.
112. Chorley, *Manchester Made Them*, 189–90, 196–205. Carol Dyhouse, *Girls Growing up in Late Victorian and Edwardian England* (1981), 42.

3 Working-class Home Life

1. Old People's Reminiscences at Lancashire Record Office, DDX.9783/3/13.
2. *Royal Commission on Population*, Cmnd. 7695 (HMSO, 1949), 24.
3. *Royal Commission on Population*, 28. Michael Anderson suggests that for marriages in the early 1880s, men in professional occupations like barristers, solicitors, and medical practitioners, whose wives were aged between 20 and 24, were having between three and four children. Miners with wives in the same age group at marriage were averaging more than seven children per marriage. Michael Anderson, 'The Social Implications of Demographic Change' in F.M.L. Thompson (ed.), *The Cambridge Social History of Britain 1750–1950*, Vol. 2 (1990), 44.
4. Michael Anderson, *Family Structure in Nineteenth Century Lancashire* (1971), 44.
5. Margaret Llewelyn Davies (ed.), *Life as We Have Known It* (1977 edn), 1. The book was first published in 1931.
6. Charles Booth, *Life and Labour of the People in London*, First Series: Poverty, Vol. 1 (1902), 158–9.
7. Bristol People's Oral History Project, transcript R.019 at Bristol Reference Library.
8. Alice Foley, *A Bolton Childhood* (1990 edn), 9.
9. Geoffrey Trodd, *Political Change and the Working Class in Burnley, 1880–1914* (University of Lancaster PhD thesis, 1978), 259.
10. Carl Chinn, 'Was Separate Schooling a Means of Class Segregation in Late Victorian and Edwardian Birmingham?', *Midland History*, Vol. XIII (1988), 97.
11. Richard Dennis, *English Industrial Cities of the Nineteenth Century* (1986 edn), 75.
12. *Health of Towns Commission*, PP 1844, Vol. XVII, Evidence of Thomas Ashton of Hyde, 332, Qu. 5509.
13. Quoted in Nigel Morgan, *Vanished Dwellings. Early Industrial Housing in a Lancashire Cotton Town. Preston* (1990), 18, 63.
14. Brian R. Law, *Fieldens of Todmorden. A Nineteenth Century Business Dynasty* (1995), 170–1.
15. *Twenty-seventh Annual Report of the Registrar General for Births, Deaths and Marriages for 1864*, PP 1866, Vol. XIX, 1.
16. *Report of an Inquiry held by Messrs D. Cubitt Nichols and Shirley F Murphy as to the Immediate Sanitary Requirements of the Parish of St Matthew, Bethnal Green, 1888*, PP 1889, Vol. LXV, 5.
17. John Burnett, *A Social History of Housing* (1986 edn), 175.
18. *Sixth Annual Report of the Work of the Public Health and Housing Department for Bethnal Green by the Chief Inspector, for the year ending December 1901* (1902), 6, at the British Library, A.R.859.
19. *Fifth Annual Report on the Work of the Sanitary Department for Bethnal Green for the Year ending December 1900* (1901), 12, at the British Library, A.R.859.
20. Calculated from the 1891 Census Return for Digby Walk at the Public Record Office, RG.12.272.
21. *First Report of the Royal Commission on the Housing of the Working Classes*, PP 1884–5, Vol. XXX, 13.

22. K.F. Carpenter, *Public Health in Portsmouth 1873–1900* (typescript dissertation, 1979, at Portsmouth Record Office), 20. John Burnett, *Plenty and Want* (1968 edn), 241, 259, 263.

23. Davies, *Life as We Have Known It*, 21.

24. Davies, *Life as We Have Known It*, 22.

25. Foley, *A Bolton Childhood*, 3. Hugh Cunningham, *The Children of the Poor. Representations of Childhood since the Seventeenth Century* (1991), 191–2.

26. Foley, *A Bolton Childhood*, 5.

27. Foley, *A Bolton Childhood*, 5.

28. Foley, *A Bolton Childhood*, 6–8.

29. Angela Hewins, *A Stratford Story* (1994 edn), 122.

30. Hewins, *Stratford*, 122.

31. David R. Green and Alan G. Parton, 'Slums and Slum Life in Victorian England: London and Birmingham at Mid-century' in S. Martin Gaskell (ed.), *Slums* (1990), 25.

32. Gaskell, 'Introduction' in Gaskell, 13.

33. J.D.A. Stanford, *Working-class Children in Mid-nineteenth Century Portsmouth* (typescript dissertation, November 1971, 1591A/1, at Portsmouth Record Office), 27. Mrs Jean Stanford and Professor A. Temple Patterson, *The Condition of the Children of the Poor in Mid-Victorian Portsmouth* (Portsmouth Papers No. 21, March 1974), 6.

34. Eric Hopkins, *Childhood Transformed. Working-class Children in Nineteenth-century England* (1994), 106.

35. Burnett, *A Social History of Housing*, 173.

36. Walter Southgate, *That's The Way It Was. A Working Class Autobiography 1890–1950* (1982), 67.

37. University of Essex, Oral Archives Transcript No. QD1/FLWE/78.

38. University of Essex, Oral Archives Transcript No. QD1/FLWE/237.

39. William Neild, 'Comparative Statement of the Income and Expenditure of Certain Families of the Working Classes in Manchester and Dukinfield, in the Years 1836 and 1841', *Journal of the Statistical Society of London*, Vol. IV (1841), 321, 322, 331, 332.

40. *Twenty-sixth Annual Report of the Registrar General for Births, Deaths and Marriages for 1863*, PP 1865, Vol. XIV, xxiii. Law, *Fieldens of Todmorden*, 116–17.

41. Margaret Hewitt, *Wives and Mothers in Victorian Industry* (1958), 116–17.

42. Joseph Stamper, *So Long Ago* (1960), 51–2, 75.

43. 'A Lancashire Parson', 'Home Life amongst the Lancashire Operatives' in *Good Words*, December 1882, 806. 'The Education of Girls' in the *Guardian*, 19 January 1996, quoting from the *Manchester Guardian*, 16 January 1864.

44. *Health of Towns Commission*, Evidence of Dr Southwood Smith, 74, Qu.945.

45. *First Report of the Royal Commission on the Housing of the Working Classes*, 11.

46. Annie Macpherson, *The Little Matchbox-Makers* (n.d. [1870]), 13.

47. Macpherson, *Little Matchbox-Makers*, 47.

48. George Haw, *From Workhouse to Westminster. The Life Story of Will Crooks, MP* (1911), 3, 5.

49. Haw, *Workhouse to Westminster*, 6, 8, 12, 16.

50. Anderson, *Family Structure*, 74.

51. *Report on the Health of Bolton for 1874 by the Medical Officer of Health*, 7, at Bolton Local History Library.

52. Grace M. Belfiore, *Family Strategies in Essex Textile Towns 1860–1895: The Challenge of Compulsory Elementary Schooling* (Oxford University DPhil thesis, 1986), 117. A survey of Burnley in the 1890s showed that out of 165 children left by their mothers when they went to work in the mills, about a quarter were left with grandparents and a quarter with other relatives; just under half were left with neighbours and about one-twentieth had no care at all. Belfiore, *Family Strategies*, 118.

53. *Third Report of the Children's Employment Commission*, PP 1864, Vol. XXII, Evidence of Mrs Waring, 95.

54. Marguerite W. Dupree, *Family Structure in the Staffordshire Potteries 1840–1880* (Oxford University DPhil thesis, 1981), 137.

55. Hopkins, *Childhood Transformed*, 104.

56. University of Essex, Oral Archives Transcript No. QD1/FLWE/87.

57. Elizabeth A.M. Roberts, 'Women's Strategies, 1890–1940' in Jane Lewis (ed.), *Labour and Love. Women's Experience of Home and Family 1850–1940* (1986), 230.

58. Charles Booth, *Life and Labour of the People in London*, First Series: Poverty, Vol. 2 (1902), 49.

59. Stanford, *Working-class Children*, 23. *Annual Report of the Portsea Free Ragged Schools for 1868* in Minute Book of the Ragged Schools DS/37/1A/1 at Portsmouth Record Office. The soup kitchen was financed from special funds, separate from those used to finance the schools themselves.

60. Raphael Samuel (ed.), *East End Underworld. Chapters in the Life of Arthur Harding* (1981), 24–5.

61. School Board for London: *Report of a Special Committee on Underfed Children Attending School*, SBL.1468 at the Greater London Record Office; Evidence of Mrs Marian Leon, a manager of the Vere Street Clare Market School, 7 November 1895, 29.

62. *Charity Organisation Review*, Vol. 7 (September 1891), 359.

63. Bristol People's Oral History Project, Transcript No. R.001 at Bristol Local History Library.

64. Helen Bosanquet, *The Standard of Life and Other Studies* (1898), 77–8.

65. University of Essex, Oral Archives Transcript No. QD1/FLWE/94.

66. University of Essex, Oral Archives Transcript No. QD1/FLWE/61.

67. University of Essex, Oral Archives Transcript No. QD1/FLWE/61.

68. Anderson, 'The Social Implications of Demographic Change' in Thompson, 49. Anderson, *Family Structure*, 148. In some cases neighbours brought up a child, perhaps helped by payments from the Poor Law authorities.

69. Belfiore, *Family Strategies*, 76.

70. Hewins, *Stratford*, 12, 14, 16, 38, 40, 46.

71. Lynn Hollen Lees, *Exiles of Erin. Irish Migrants in Victorian London* (1979), 132–3.

72. Henry Mayhew, *London Labour and the London Poor*, Vol. 1 (1968 edn), 135. The first full edition of this book was published in 1861–2.

73. Paul Thompson, 'Voices from Within' in H.J. Dyos and Michael Wolff (eds), *The Victorian City*, Vol. 1 (1973), 77–8.

74. Thompson, 'Voices from Within', 77–8.

75. Stanford, *Working-class Children*, 29. *Hampshire Telegraph*, 22 April 1848.

76. Thompson, 'Voices from Within', 74.

77. Foley, *A Bolton Childhood*, 8.

78. Bristol People's Oral History Project, Transcript No. R.001.

79. University of Essex, Oral Archives Transcript No. QD1/FLWE/34.

80. Haw, *Workhouse to Westminster*, 19.

81. Foley, *A Bolton Childhood*, 25–6.

82. Thompson, 'Voices from Within', 73.

83. E.J. Urwick (ed.), *Studies of Boy Life in Our Cities* (1904), 33.

84. Arthur Morrison, *A Child of the Jago* (1971 pbk edn), 49, 186–7. The book was first published in 1896.

85. Samuel, *East End Underworld*, 9, 42–3, 44–5.

86. Charles Booth, *Life and Labour of the People in London*, First Series: Poverty, Vol. 1, 160.

87. Robert R. Dolling, *Ten Years in a Portsmouth Slum* (1896), 20.

88. School Board for London: *Special Report of the General Purposes Committee on Underfed Children Attending School*, SBL.1469 at the Greater London Record Office; Evidence of Mrs Burgwin on 30 January 1899.

89. Foley, *A Bolton Childhood*, 32.

90. Hopkins, *Childhood Transformed*, 280.

4 *The Growth of Mass Schooling*

1. Old People's Reminiscences at Lancashire Record Office, DDX.9783/3/13.

2. Stephen Lassonde, 'Learning and Earning: Schooling, Juvenile Employment, and the Early Life Course in Late Nineteenth Century New Haven', *Journal of Social History*, Vol. 29, No. 4 (Summer 1996), 840.

3. Edmund Frow and Ruth Frow, *The Half-time System in Education* (1970), 21–2, 30–1. Harold Silver, 'Ideology and the Factory Child: Attitudes to Half-time Education' in Phillip McCann (ed.), *Popular Education and Socialization in the Nineteenth Century* (1977), 148, 159.

4. Pamela Horn, *Children's Work and Welfare, 1780–1890* (1995 edn), 65–6.

5. J.S. Hurt, *Elementary Schooling and the Working Classes 1860–1918* (1979), 28–9.

6. Hurt, *Elementary Schooling*, 33.

7. David Rubinstein, *School Attendance in London, 1870–1904: A Social History* (1969), 12.

8. *Report of the Committee of Council for 1872–3*, PP 1873, Vol. XXIV, Report by the Revd F. Watkins, HMI, on South Yorkshire, 213.

9. W.B. Stephens, 'Illiteracy and Schooling in the Provincial Towns, 1640–1870: A Comparative Approach' in D.A. Reeder (ed.), *Urban Education in the Nineteenth Century* (1972), 31–2.

10. Stephens, 'Illiteracy' in Reeder, 34.

11. National illiteracy rates calculated from Eric Hopkins, *Childhood Transformed. Working-class children in Nineteenth-century England* (1994), 138.

12. Brian Simon, *Education and the Labour Movement 1870–1920* (1965), 131.

13. *Minutes of the Committee of Council for 1845* (HMSO, 1846), Report by the Revd F.C. Cook, HMI, on the Eastern District, 153–4.

14. Rubinstein, *School Attendance*, 7.

15. *Royal Commission on the State of Popular Education in England: Reports of the Assistant Commissioners*, PP 1861, Vol. XXI, Part II, Report by Mr J.S. Winder on the Rochdale and Bradford Districts, 192.

16. Quoted in Rubinstein, *School Attendance*, 5.

17. Log Book of the Beneficial Girls' School, Portsmouth, 536A/18/2 at Portsmouth City Record Office, entries for 5 September 1864 and 6 November 1865. See also 11 September and 6 November 1865.

18. *Third Report of the Children's Employment Commission*, PP 1864, Vol. XXII, Report by Mr J.E. White upon the Metal Manufactures of the Birmingham District, 65.

19. Report by Mr J.E. White, loc. cit., 66.

20. Report by Mr J.E. White, loc. cit., 60–1.

21. *Report of the Royal Commission on the State of Popular Education in England*, PP 1861, Vol. XXI, Part I, 55.

22. Michael Sanderson, *Education, Economic Change and Society in England 1780–1870* (1983), 18.

23. *Report of the Committee of Council on Education for 1877–8*, PP 1878, Vol. XXVIII, xiii.

24. *Report of the Committee of Council for 1877–8*, Report by W. Scott Howard, HMI, on the Wigan District of Lancashire, 449.

25. John Burnett, *Destiny Obscure* (1984), 158. David Wardle, *Education and Society in Nineteenth-century Nottingham* (1971), 91, comments that by 1880 'there was still far to go before the syllabus could be said to be anything but narrow'.

26. Log Book of the Beneficial Girls' School, Portsmouth, entry for 21 April 1868.

27. Pamela Horn, *School Log Books* (The Historical Association, Short Guides to Records No. 44, 1994 edn), 1.

28. Log Book of the Beneficial Girls' School, Portsmouth, entry for 28 August 1865.

29. Log Book for St Peter's Mixed School, Burnley, 1863–1890, SM.By.34/1 at Lancashire Record Office, entries for 10 February and 1 May 1873. On 21 August 1871, the head had noted: 'Very vexed at Massey Layfield's striking a boy. Repeatedly prohibited any teacher whipping any boy.'

30. Bristol People's Oral History Project, Transcript No. R.003 at Bristol Local History Library.

31. University of Essex, Oral Archives Transcript No. QD1/FLWE/94.

32. Log Book for St James's National School, Bolton, SLB.57/1 at Bolton Local History Library, entries for 9 and 20 March 1865.

33. Log Book of the Beneficial Girls' School, Portsmouth, entries for 20 January 1870, 9 December 1871, and HMI Report for July 1873. Correspondence of Beneficial Society School, Portsmouth, at Portsmouth Record Office 536A/4/2, letter dated 8 March 1897. Laurence V. Gatt, *The Portsmouth Beneficial School 1755–1939* (Portsmouth Papers No. 46, November 1986), 11, 15.

34. Log Book of the Beneficial Girls' School, Portsmouth, entries for 17 May 1865 and 7 September 1870.

35. *Report of the Committee of Council on Education for 1872–3*, Report by S.N. Stokes, HMI, on Southwark, 174.

36. Phil Gardner, *The Lost Elementary Schools of Victorian England* (1984), 254.

37. Reports by HM Inspectors on schools in Chelsea in 1871, ED.3.1. at the Public Record Office.

38. Charles Shaw, *When I Was a Child* (1977 edn), 4–5. The book was first published in 1903.

39. Gillian Sutherland, 'Education' in F.M.L. Thompson (ed.), *The Cambridge Social History of Britain 1780–1950* (Vol. 3) (1990), 128.

40. *Report of the Committee of Council on Education for 1872–3*, Report by Mr Brodie, HMI, on Lancashire, 54–5.

41. *Report of the Royal Commission on the State of Popular Education in England*, Part I, 90, 96.

42. University of Essex, Oral Archives Transcript No. QD1/FLWE/59.

43. Gardner, *Lost Elementary Schools*, 206–7.

44. Quoted in William E. Marsden, 'Social Stratification and Nineteenth-century English Urban Education' in Ronald K. Goodenow and William E. Marsden (eds), *The City and Education in Four Nations* (1992), 118, 120.

45. *Report of the Committee of Council on Education for 1872–3*, Report by the Revd J.G.C. Fussell, HMI, on Finsbury, 84.

46. Quoted in Richard Johnson, 'Educational Policy and Social Control in Early Victorian England', *Past and Present*, No. 49 (November 1970), 96.

47. Sanderson, *Education, Economic Change*, 17–18.

48. Horn, *Children's Work and Welfare*, 47.

49. *Tenth Report of the Church Street Ragged School, Chelsea*, 1870, in ED.3.1 at the Public Record Office. Rubinstein, *School Attendance*, 21.

50. *Hansard*, 3rd Ser., Vol. XCIX (29 May to 30 June 1848), col. 448.

51. Horn, *Children's Work and Welfare*, 48–9.

52. Annual Report of the Portsea and Portsmouth Free Ragged Schools for 1877 in Minutes of Meetings of the Subscribers and Managing Committee, 1863–1883, DS/37/1A/1 at Portsmouth City Record Office.

53. Horn, *Children's Work and Welfare*, 49.

54. Portsea Free Ragged Schools: Shoe Black Station Account Book, DS/37/3A/1/2 at Portsmouth City Record Office. An entry for April 1865 shows one boy made a down payment of 8*d* on clogs and 1*s* 4*d* for a waistcoat out of his earnings. Notes were given to be taken to local shopkeepers, as in May 1865, when a shoemaker was advised to 'supply the bearer with Boots to the amt. of 12*s* 4*d*.'

55. Thomas Walter Laqueur, *Religion and Respectability. Sunday Schools and Working Class Culture 1780–1850* (1976), xi, 147, 246.

56. Laqueur, *Religion and Respectability*, xi.

57. *Report of the Royal Commission on the State of Popular Education in England*, Part I, 55.

58. Quoted in Hopkins, *Childhood Transformed*, 149.

59. Shaw, *When I Was a Child*, 7–9.

60. Burnett, *Destiny*, 98.

61. Quoted in E.G. West, *Education and the State* (1970), 135. See also E.G. West, *Education and the Industrial Revolution* (1975), 108.

62. J. Stuart Maclure, *Educational Documents. England and Wales. 1816–1968* (1969 edn), 104.

63. Horn, *Children's Work and Welfare*, 61.

64. Log Book of the Beneficial Girls' School, entry for 14 February 1871. See also 1 March 1871.

65. Log Book of the Kent Street School, DS/23/3/A/1 at Portsmouth City Record Office, entries for 23 March and 13 April 1874.

66. Log Book of the Kent Street School, entry for 6 December 1872.

67. Grace M. Belfiore, *Family Strategies in Essex Textile Towns 1860–1895: The Challenge of Compulsory Elementary Schooling* (Oxford University DPhil thesis, 1986), 255.

68. Bristol People's Oral History Project, Transcript No. R.001 at Bristol Local History Library.

69. Log Book of the Kent Street School, entry for 9 July 1873, noted, for example, that 70 children fewer were in attendance in the afternoon than in the morning because of a local 'Band of Hope Demonstration'.

70. Report of the London School Board School Accommodation and Attendance Committee for the Year ending Lady-day 1892, vi, SBL.1520 at the Greater London Record Office.

71. Calculated from Kent Street, Swan Street and Green Row Visitation Committee records, G/SB.6/1 at Portsmouth City Record Office. Rubinstein, *School Attendance*, 48–9.

72. Calculated from Kent Street, Swan Street and Green Row Visitation Committee records. The tradesmen and small businessmen prosecuted included shoemakers, engineers, a carpenter, a baker and a shipwright.

73. Mrs Hudson's name appeared on the list repeatedly in June, September, October and November 1876, for example.

74. Quoted in Christine M. Heward, 'Compulsion, Work and Family: a Case Study from Nineteenth-century Birmingham' in Goodenow and Marsden, 150.

75. *The Twenty-Second Report of the Children's Aid Society for 1898*, H.362.72 CHI. at Liverpool Record Office noted that there had been several cases 'in which repayment

has been resumed after a suspension of more than a year, and clothes and boots long since worn out cheerfully paid for when better times returned'.

76. Rubinstein, *School Attendance*, 102.
77. Walter Southgate, *That's the Way It Was. A Working Class Autobiography 1890–1950* (1982), 56.
78. Southgate, *That's the Way It Was*, 57.
79. Horn, *Children's Work and Welfare*, 63.
80. Bristol People's Oral History Project, Transcript No. R.001 at Bristol Local History Library.
81. *School Board for London: Report of a Special Committee on Underfed Children Attending School, 1895*, SBL.1468 at Greater London Record Office, Evidence of Mr W.H. Libby, 10–13. According to Hugh Cunningham, *The Children of the Poor. Representations of Childhood since the Seventeenth Century* (1991), 204, by 1895 only about 10 per cent of feeding associations still tried to collect payments for the meals they offered.
82. Managers' Yearly Report for the year ending January 1894, for Nichol Street Boys' School, EO/PS/12/N15/28 at the Greater London Record Office.
83. Horn, *Children's Work and Welfare*, 63.
84. *Public Health*, Vol. 1 (1888–9), 198.
85. *Public Health*, Vol. 1, 200.
86. *The Lancet*, 8 December 1883, 1005.
87. *The Lancet*, 21 June 1884, 1133.
88. Quoted in Heward, 'Compulsion', 154–5.
89. Pamela Horn, 'Changing Attitudes to the Welfare of Elementary Schoolchildren in the 1880s' in Richard Aldrich (ed.), *In History and in Education. Essays presented to Peter Gordon* (1996), 42–4.
90. Sydney C. Buxton, 'Over-Pressure', *Nineteenth Century*, Vol. 16 (1884), 806. Horn, 'Changing Attitudes to the Welfare of Elementary Schoolchildren', 44.
91. *Western Mail*, 9 October 1889. Tony Taylor, 'As the Old Cocks Crow, the Young Ones Learn: the School Strikes of 1889 and the New Union Movement', *History of Education*, Vol. 23, No. 1 (1994), 89.
92. *Western Daily Press*, 5 October 1889.
93. *Western Mail*, 9 October 1889.
94. *Liverpool Echo*, 9 October 1889.
95. Taylor, 'As the Old Cocks Crow', 105.
96. Wardle, *Education and Society*, 106–7. Horn, *Children's Work and Welfare*, 64.
97. Wardle, *Education and Society*, 107.

98. J.S. Hurt, *Outside the Mainstream. A History of Special Education* (1988), 104, 105, 124, 134. Horn, *Children's Work and Welfare*, 64–5.
99. Harry Hendrick, *Child Welfare. England 1872–1989* (1994), 87.
100. Bristol People's Oral History Project, Transcript No. R.019 at Bristol Local History Library.
101. Southgate, *That's the Way It Was*, 32.
102. *St Matthew's School Magazine*, Denmark Hill, December 1899, 276. See also the issue for January 1900, 4: 'Stories of brave deeds and noble self-sacrifice are dear to the heart of every boy and girl'. The magazines are at the Church of England Record Centre, NS/SR9/1/1.
103. Alice Foley, *A Bolton Childhood* (1990 edn), 37.
104. J.S. Hurt, 'Drill, Discipline and the Elementary School Ethos' in McCann, *Popular Education*, 187.
105. Hurt, 'Drill, Discipline' in McCann, 181.
106. *General Reports of the Divisional Inspectors for 1897*, PP 1898, Vol. XXIII, Report by the Revd T.W. Sharpe on the Metropolitan Division, 5–6.
107. Southgate, *That's the Way It Was*, 54.
108. Quoted in Marsden, 'Social Stratification' in Goodenow and Marsden, 116.
109. W.E. Marsden, 'Education and the Social Geography of Nineteenth-century Towns and Cities' in D.A. Reeder (ed.), *Urban Education in the Nineteenth Century* (1977), 64.

5   At Work

1. Reminiscences of James Holt at Lancashire Record Office, DDX/978/1/8/9.
2. Michael Anderson, *Family Structure in Nineteenth Century Lancashire* (1971), 116.
3. Census return for Burnley for 1891, RG.12.3365, at the Public Record Office. Elizabeth was aged thirteen.
4. Marguerite W. Dupree, *Family Structure in the Staffordshire Potteries 1840–1880* (1995), 153.
5. Census return for the Farnworth area of Bolton for 1891, RG.12.3093 at the Public Record Office.
6. *Report of the Royal Commission on Popular Education in England*, PP 1861, Vol. XXI, Part I, 188.
7. Pamela Horn, *Children's Work and Welfare, 1780–1890* (1995 edn), 45.

8. Allen Clarke, *The Effects of the Factory System* (1899), 105–6.

9. *Report of the Interdepartmental Committee on the Employment of School Children*, PP 1902, Vol. XXV, 19.

10. Michael J. Childs, *Labour's Apprentices. Working-class Lads in Late Victorian and Edwardian England* (1992), 20.

11. Childs, *Labour's Apprentices*, 19.

12. Noel Streatfeild (ed.), *The Day Before Yesterday* (1956), 62–3.

13. Horn, *Children's Work*, 72.

14. Alice Foley, *A Bolton Childhood* (1990 edn), 49.

15. Foley, *A Bolton Childhood*, 47.

16. Childs, *Labour's Apprentices*, 54–5.

17. Standish Meacham, *A Life Apart. The English Working Class 1890–1914* (1977), 182. Eric Hopkins, *Childhood Transformed. Working-class Children in Nineteenth-century England* (1994), 24.

18. Hopkins, *Childhood Transformed*, 24.

19. *Appendix to the Second Report of the Children's Employment Commission*, PP 1843, Vol. XIV, Report by Major J.G. Burns on Lace-making, a53.

20. Walter Besant, *East London* (1901), 167. Michael Winstanley (ed.), *Working Children in Nineteenth-century Lancashire* (1995), 101, 104.

21. Letter to John Ellison, aged thirteen, from a Mr Ackerley, 2 West Side, George's Dock, Liverpool, 26 August 1853, in Museum of Liverpool Life.

22. University of Essex, Oral Archives Transcript No. QD1/FLWE/262.

23. J.R. Clynes, *Memoirs. 1869–1924* (1937), 29–30.

24. Marjorie Cruickshank, *Children and Industry. Child Health and Welfare in North-west Textile Towns during the Nineteenth Century* (1981), 97.

25. *Second Annual Report of the Bolton and District Card Blowing, Ring and Throstle Room Operatives' Provincial Association*, FT/7/6/2 at Bolton Local History Library and Archives. See also the Association's Minute Book, FT/7/1/3, meeting on 28 January 1894, when it was agreed that Maria Bowers, aged fifteen, should receive 'the permanent accident benefit' of £30 for amputation of the right arm. She was a card tenter.

26. Harry Hendrick, *Child Welfare. England 1872–1989* (1994), 72.

27. Hugh Cunningham, *The Children of the Poor. Representations of Childhood since the Seventeenth Century* (1991), 78.

28. Cunningham, *Children of the Poor*, 79.

29. John Burnett (ed.), *Useful Toil* (1974), 306.

30. Clark Nardinelli, *Child Labor and the Industrial Revolution* (1990), 11.

31. *Report of the Interdepartmental Committee on the Employment of Children*, 19.

32. Nardinelli, *Child Labor*, 105.

33. Per Bolin-Hort, *Work, Family and the State. Child Labour and the Organization of Production in the British Cotton Industry, 1780–1920* (1989), 81.

34. Cruickshank, *Children and Industry*, 85.

35. Clarke, *Effects of the Factory System*, 152.

36. Ben Turner, *About Myself. 1863–1930* (1930), 36–7.

37. *Reports of the Inspectors of Factories for the Half-year ending 31 October, 1874*, PP 1875, Vol. XVI, 56.

38. Cruickshank, *Children and Industry*, 97.

39. Log book of St James's National Mixed School at Bolton Local History Library and Record Office, SLB.57/1. In a further entry on 9 March 1876, it was noted that T.W. Heaton & Sons had declared they were sending their half-timers to three schools, 'viz. the Board School, Roman Catholic School, or St George's'. The reason given was 'that confusion arises in consequence of having so many mill books to examine'.

40. On 6 March 1874, for example, came the entry: 'Five girls have had to leave and go to other schools this week through getting employment at Barlow & Jones's mill.' Log book of St James's National Mixed School, Bolton.

41. Obituary in *Bolton Evening News*, 29 May 1912. Edmund Frow and Ruth Frow, *The Half-time System in Education* (1970), 64, 71.

42. Horn, *Children's Work*, 41. Nardinelli, *Child Labor*, 105.

43. See also Clynes, *Memoirs*, 61. He noted that when the inspector arrived 'word went round from mouth to mouth, and a good many flagrant defiances of the law were discreetly hidden for the time being'.

44. George Smith, *The Cry of the Children from the Brick-yards of England*, (6th edn, 1879), 148.

45. Geoffrey Trodd, *Political Change and the Working Class in Burnley, 1880–1914* (University of Lancaster PhD thesis, 1978), 229–31.

46. Harry Pollitt, *Serving My Time. An Apprenticeship to Politics* (1940), 26–7.
47. Pollitt, *Serving My Time*, 28.
48. University of Essex, Oral Archives Transcript No. QD1/FLWE/78.
49. University of Essex, Oral Archives Transcript No. QD1/FLWE/61.
50. Stephen Lassonde, 'Learning and Earning: Schooling, Juvenile Employment, and the Early Life Course in Late Nineteenth-century New Haven' in *Journal of Social History*, Vol. 29, No. 4 (Summer 1996), 840. Winstanley, *Working Children*, 60–1.
51. Cruickshank, *Children and Industry*, 94.
52. *Reports of the Inspectors of Factories for the Half-year Ending 30 April, 1875*, PP 1875, Vol. XVI, Report by Sub-inspector Cramp on the Bolton, Blackburn and Accrington area, 66.
53. Nardinelli, *Child Labor*, 106.
54. *Reports of the Inspectors of Factories for the Half-year Ending 31 October, 1864*, PP 1865, Vol. XX, 68.
55. Charles Shaw, *When I Was a Child* (1977 edn), 13–16. The book was first published in 1903.
56. B.L. Hutchins and A. Harrison, *A History of Factory Legislation* (1966 edn), 154–5.
57. *Fifth Report of the Royal Commission on Labour*, PP 1894, Vol. XXXV, Summary of Evidence, Group A, Part II, 135.
58. Horn, *Children's Work*, 44.
59. *Factory and Workshop Acts Commission*, PP 1876, Vol. XXIX, Appendix D, no. 86, 181.
60. *Factory and Workshop Acts Commission*, Appendix D, no. 86, 182.
61. *Factory and Workshop Acts Commission*, Appendix C, no. 40, 99–100 and Appendix C, no. 32, 73.
62. Horn, *Children's Work*, 44–5.
63. Calculated from Clarke, *Effects of the Factory System*, 107–8. Bolin-Hort, *Work, Family, State*, 161–2, 228–9.
64. *Fifth Report of the Royal Commission on Labour*, Summary of Evidence, Group C, Part I, 247.
65. Quoted in *Child's Guardian*, July 1891, 73.
66. *Hansard*, 3rd Ser., Vol. 354 (18 June 1891), cols. 873–5 and col. 870 for the comments of the Home Secretary.
67. *Child's Guardian*, July 1891, 72.
68. Quoted in *Child's Guardian*, July 1891, 73.
69. Henry Edward, Cardinal Manning, 'Child Labour: Minimum Age for Labour of Children', *Contemporary Review*, Vol. 59 (1891), 796.
70. Henry Dunckley, 'The Half-Timers', *Contemporary Review*, Vol. 59 (1891), 799–800.
71. Margaret Llewelyn Davies (ed.), *Life as We Have Known It* (1977 edn), 20–2. The book was first published in 1931.
72. Llewelyn Davies, *Life as We Have Known It*, 25.
73. *Report of the Royal Commission on Popular Education in England*, Part I, 186.
74. Henry Mayhew, *London Labour and the London Poor*, Vol. I (1968 edn), 471. The book was first published in four volumes in 1861–2.
75. James Walvin, *A Child's World. A Social History of English Childhood 1800–1914* (1982), 69.
76. *Proceedings of Manchester City Council for 1877–8*, 173–4, at Manchester Central Library and Record Office.
77. George K. Behlmer, *Child Abuse and Moral Reform in England 1870–1908* (1982), 90.
78. Pamela Horn, 'English Theatre Children, 1880–1914: a Study in Ambivalence', *History of Education*, Vol. 25, No. 1 (1996), 49–50.
79. Horn, 'English Theatre Children', 47.
80. Sir John B. Gorst, *The Children of the Nation* (1907 edn), 101.
81. Thomas Burke, 'The Street-trading Children of Liverpool', *Contemporary Review*, Vol. 78 (November 1900), 721. *Liverpool Corporation Act 1898*: section on Street Trading, para. 8.
82. Frederic Keeling, *Child Labour in the United Kingdom* (1914), 261, 264.
83. Edith F. Hogg, 'School Children as Wage Earners', *The Nineteenth Century*, Vol. 42 (August 1897), 239–40.
84. Minute by the Chief Inspector of Factories, 10 February 1898, HO.45.9929.B.25717 at the Public Record Office. See also *Women's Industrial Council Report on Home Work* and associated correspondence at this reference.
85. *Elementary Schools (Children Working for Wages) Return*, Cmnd. 205, Part I (HMSO, 1899), 13. Pamela Horn, 'Aspects of Child Employment, 1890–1914: Continuity and Change' in V. Alan McClelland (ed.), *Children at Risk* (1994), 128.
86. *Report of the Interdepartmental Committee on the Employment of School Children*, 17.
87. Horn, 'Aspects of Child Employment', 135.
88. Childs, *Labour's Apprentices*, 17. Winstanley, *Working Children*, 110–12.

89. University of Essex, Oral Archives Transcript No. QD1/FLWE/87.
90. Reminiscences of Mr J. Hummer at Lancashire Record Office, DDX.978/1/6/1.
91. B. Seebohm Rowntree, *Poverty. A Study of Town Life* (1903 edn), 39–40, 59, 131, footnote 1.
92. O. Jocelyn Dunlop, with Richard D. Denman, *English Apprenticeship and Child Labour* (1912), 309–10, 348.
93. Horn, 'Aspects of Child Employment', 128. S. Webb and B. Webb, *Industrial Democracy* (1902 edn), 483.
94. Childs, *Labour's Apprentices*, 80.
95. Hopkins, *Childhood Transformed*, 226.

6 *Surviving*

1. Old People's Reminiscences at Lancashire Record Office, DDX/9783/3/13.
2. [Anon.], *A Short History of the Hospital for Sick Children, Great Ormond Street* (n.d. [1907]), 11, at the British Library, 07306.df.37(1).
3. Ellen Ross, *Love and Toil. Motherhood in Outcast London 1870–1918* (1993), 183
4. *Report of the Medical Officer of Health for Liverpool for 1880*, 20, H.352.COU at Liverpool Record Office, and *Report of the Medical Officer of Health for Portsmouth for 1887*, 30, CCR/VI/2 at Portsmouth Record Office.
5. *Thirty-fourth Report of the Registrar-General of Births, Deaths and Marriages in England for 1871*, PP 1873, Vol. XX, 'Causes of Death in 1871: Supplement to Dr Farr's Letter', 227, 229.
6. *Report of the Interdepartmental Committee on Physical Deterioration*, PP 1904, Vol. XXXII, Appendix V, 133, 134. There were over 130,000 illegitimate births in London in 1902.
7. James Walvin, *A Child's World. A Social History of English Childhood 1800–1914* (1982), 43.
8. Irina Stickland (ed.), *The Voices of Children 1700–1914* (1973), 204.
9. Walter Southgate, *That's the Way It Was. A Working-class Autobiography 1890–1950* (1982), 12, 71, 74.
10. Alice Foley, *A Bolton Childhood* (1990 edn), 37–8.
11. Ross, *Love and Toil*, 189.
12. F.B. Smith, *The People's Health 1830–1910* (1979), 65.
13. *Report of the Interdepartmental Committee on Physical Deterioration*, Appendix V, 131, calculated from table.
14. Marjorie Cruickshank, *Children and Industry. Child Health and Welfare in North-west Textile Towns during the Nineteenth Century* (1981), 65–6.
15. *Report of the Interdepartmental Committee on Physical Deterioration*, 51, 53.
16. *Report of the Medical Officer of Health for Bolton for 1891*, 15, at Bolton Local History Library.
17. Cruickshank, *Children and Industry*, 117.
18. Ross, *Love and Toil*, 185.
19. Lady Bell, *At the Works. A Study of a Manufacturing Town (Middlesbrough)* (1969 edn), 193, 199. The book was first published in 1907.
20. Lara V. Marks, *Model Mothers. Jewish Mothers and Maternity Provision in East London, 1870–1939* (1994), 72–3.
21. Cruickshank, *Children and Industry*, 72. Eric Hopkins, *Childhood Transformed. Working-class Children in Nineteenth Century England* (1994), 113.
22. J.A.V. Chapple and Arthur Pollard (eds), *The Letters of Mrs Gaskell* (1966), 12–13.
23. Joseph Stamper, *So Long Ago* (1960), 62–4.
24. Cruickshank, *Children and Industry*, 103.
25. *Minutes of Evidence of the Interdepartmental Committee on Physical Deterioration*, PP 1904, Vol. XXXII, Appendix XX, 81.
26. Stamper, *So Long Ago*, 62.
27. Southgate, *That's the Way It Was*, 80.
28. Maria Cadbury to her parents, 2 November 1853, 466/341/5 at Birmingham Archives.
29. Bristol People's Oral History Project, Transcript No. R.001, at Bristol Local History Library.
30. Ross, *Love and Toil*, 177.
31. Cruickshank, *Children and Industry*, 73. Bristol People's Oral History Project, Transcript No. R.019.
32. Smith, *The People's Health*, 97.
33. Cruickshank, *Children and Industry*, 67.
34. *Report of the Medical Officer of Health for Liverpool for 1901*, 149, H.352.COU at Liverpool Record Office. Jane Lewis, 'The Social History of Social Policy: Infant Welfare in Edwardian England', *Journal of Social Policy*, Vol. 9, No. 4 (1980), 474.
35. Lewis, 'Social History of Social Policy', 474.
36. [Anon.], *A Short History of the Hospital for Sick Children*, 10. Lewis, 'Social History of Social Policy', 478.

37. *Report of the Interdepartmental Committee on Physical Deterioration*, 58.
38. Lewis, 'Social History of Social Policy', 469.
39. Ross, *Love and Toil*, 168–9.
40. Bristol People's Oral History Project, Transcript No. R.003.
41. *Appendix to the Second Report of the Commissioners of Inquiry into the State of Large Towns and Populous Districts*, PP 1845, Vol. XVIII, 52.
42. Cruickshank, *Children and Industry*, 68. Smith, *The People's Health*, 137.
43. Smith, *The People's Health*, 138.
44. Cruickshank, *Children and Industry*, 68, 116.
45. Smith, *The People's Health*, 136.
46. Smith, *The People's Health*, 143 5.
47. Smith, *The People's Health*, 146.
48. Cruickshank, *Children and Industry*, 74.
49. *Report of the Medical Officer of Health for Portsmouth for 1891*, 6, CCR/VI/2 at Portsmouth Record Office.
50. Gwendoline M. Ayers, *England's First State Hospitals and the Metropolitan Asylums Board 1867–1930* (1971), 122.
51. Smith, *The People's Health*, 151.
52. Ayers, *England's First State Hospitals*, 110, 122.
53. *Minutes of the Metropolitan Asylums Board*, Vol. IX (1875–6), 291, 292, 311, 349–50, 439, 442 at the Greater London Library.
54. *Minutes of the Metropolitan Asylums Board*, Vol. XV (1881–2), 149.
55. Anthony S. Wohl, *Endangered Lives. Public Health in Victorian Britain* (1983), 138–9.
56. Wohl, *Endangered Lives*, 138.
57. *Queen Mary's Hospital for Children, Carshalton, Surrey: The First Sixty Years* (Typescript, n.d. *c.* 1970), 1–2, at the Greater London Library.
58. Quoted in K.F. Carpenter, *Public Health in Portsmouth 1873–1900* (Dissertation, 1979), 58, at Portsmouth Record Office.
59. Carpenter, *Public Health in Portsmouth*, 59.
60. *Report of the Medical Officer of Health for Portsmouth for 1876*, 24 CCR/VI/1 at Portsmouth Record Office.
61. Carpenter, *Public Health in Portsmouth*, 61 and Table 6. *Report of the Medical Officer of Health for Portsmouth for 1887*, 27, CCR/VI/2, at Portsmouth Record Office.
62. Wohl, *Endangered Lives*, 132–3.
63. Wohl, *Endangered Lives*, 133.
64. Wohl, *Endangered Lives*, 134.
65. Barrie Trinder, *Victorian Banbury* (1982), 151. Among those fined or imprisoned for non-compliance in October 1876 were two carpenters, a brickmaker and an iron moulder.
66. Trinder, *Victorian Banbury*, 151.
67. Ben Turner, *About Myself 1863–1930* (1930), 70–3.
68. Turner, *About Myself*, 73–4.
69. Wohl, *Endangered Lives*, 135.
70. Beneficial Girls' School Log Book, 1863–1876, 536A/18/2 at Portsmouth Record Office.
71. *School Board for London: Report by the Medical Officer on an Outbreak of Diphtheria at Lewisham in 1896* (January 1897), 10–11, SBL.1464 at the Greater London Record Office.
72. Gillian Avery, *The Best Type of Girl. A History of Girls' Independent Schools* (1991), 332–3.
73. Avery, *Best Type of Girl*, 50.
74. Ruth G. Hodgkinson, *The Origins of the National Health Service* (1967), 550–1.
75. Hodgkinson, *Origins of the NHS*, 553–4.
76. Wohl, *Endangered Lives*, 260.
77. Thomas E. Jordan, *The Degeneracy Crisis and Victorian Youth* (1993), 54.
78. *Fourth Report of the Children's Employment Commission*, PP 1865, Vol. XX, Mr J.E. White's Report on the Sheffield District, 9–10.
79. Cruickshank, *Children and Industry*, 70.
80. *Third Report of the Children's Employment Commission*, PP 1864, Vol. XXII, Mr J.E. White's Report on the Birmingham District, 148.
81. *Third Report of the Children's Employment Commission*, Mr J.E. White's Report on the Birmingham District, 148.
82. Cruickshank, *Children and Industry*, 133. Thomas Twistington Higgins, *Great Ormond Street 1852–1952* (n.d. [1952]), 10. Smith, *The People's Health*, 152.
83. Cruickshank, *Children and Industry*, 77.
84. Twistington Higgins, *Great Ormond St*, 5, 7–24.
85. Calculated from the *Fourteenth Annual Report of the Hospital for Sick Children, Great Ormond Street* (1866), Table of Outpatients admitted 1 January to 31 December 1865. A.R.580 at the British Library.
86. Ibid. Twistington Higgins, *Great Ormond St*, 18.

87. Twistington Higgins, *Great Ormond St*, 33.
88. *Fraser's Magazine*, Vol. XLIX (January 1854), 'A Visit to the Hospital for Sick Children', 65, 66, 67.
89. Cruickshank, *Children and Industry*, 77–8.
90. Cruickshank, *Children and Industry*, 78–9.
91. Smith, *The People's Health*, 155. Valentine A.J. Swain, 'East London Hospital for Children, Shadwell, 1868–1963. Queen Elizabeth Hospital for Children, Shadwell', *British Medical Journal*, 14 December 1968, 696–7.
92. Evelina Hospital Case Register, H9/EV/B1/1 at the Greater London Record Office. H.E. Priestley, *The Evelina. The Story of a London Children's Hospital, 1869–1969* (1969), 7, 8, 10.
93. Priestley, *The Evelina*, 15.
94. Southgate, *That's the Way It Was*, 74.
95. *The Bristol Royal Hospital for Sick Children* (1960), 9, 10, 14, 18, H9/EV/Lib./11 at the Greater London Record Office.
96. Cruickshank, *Children and Industry*, 82.
97. Cruickshank, *Children and Industry*, 82.
98. Stickland, *Voices of Children*, 156.
99. *Life, Journals and Letters of Henry Alford, D.D. Late Dean of Canterbury*, edited by his widow (1873), 183–4.
100. *Life, Journals and Letters of Henry Alford*, 187.
101. Charles Dickens, *Oliver Twist* (Hazell, Watson & Viney edn, n.d.), Chapter 17, 108–9. The book was first published in 1837–8.
102. Silas K. Hocking, *Her Benny* (1890 edn), 120, 129.
103. Bell, *At the Works*, 192. Walvin, *A Child's World*, 31.
104. Walvin, *A Child's World*, 32.
105. Walvin, *A Child's World*, 41.
106. Southgate, *That's the Way It Was*, 70–1.
107. University of Essex, Oral Archives Transcript No. QD1/FLWE/143.
108. J.D.A. Stanford, *Working-class Children in Mid-nineteenth Century Portsmouth* (Dissertation, November 1971), 30, at Portsmouth Record Office, 1591A/1.
109. Bell, *At the Works*, 83.
110. Stamper, *So Long Ago*, 65. Smith, *The People's Health*, 67–8, noted that in the larger towns old midwives had understandings with local cemetery officials to bury small coffins with no questions asked beyond, perhaps, a pencilled note from the doctor or midwife that the child was believed to have been 'stillborn' or 'prematurely born' or to have suffered 'fatal convulsions'.
111. Stickland, *Voices of Children*, 182.
112. Lionel Rose, *Massacre of the Innocents. Infanticide in Great Britain 1800–1939* (1986), 146–7.
113. Rose, *Massacre of the Innocents*, 150–1.
114. Ross, *Love and Toil*, 172.
115. Rose, *Massacre of the Innocents*, 151.
116. Ross, *Love and Toil*, 189.
117. Bell, *At the Works*, 194.
118. George K. Behlmer, *Child Abuse and Moral Reform in England 1870–1908* (1982), 20–2. Smith, *The People's Health*, 78. Rose, *Massacre of the Innocents*, 110–11.
119. Rose, *Massacre of the Innocents*, 159. Smith, *The People's Health*, 78.
120. Smith, *The People's Health*, 79.
121. Rose, *Massacre of the Innocents*, 151–2. Smith, *The People's Health*, 79.
122. Rose, *Massacre of the Innocents*, 162.
123. Rose, *Massacre of the Innocents*, 177–8.
124. *Sixty-second Annual Report of the Registrar General of Births, Deaths, and Marriages in England, 1899*, PP 1900, Vol. XV, lxvi–lxviii.
125. Cruickshank, *Children and Industry*, 148.
126. *Minutes of Evidence to the Interdepartmental Committee on Physical Deterioration*, 258, Qu.6484.
127. Jordan, *The Degeneracy Crisis*, 148.
128. Jordan, *The Degeneracy Crisis*, 14–15.
129. Charles Booth, *Life and Labour of the People in London, First Series: Poverty*, Vol. 3 *Blocks of Buildings, Schools and Immigration* (1902), 207.
130. Pamela Horn, *The Victorian and Edwardian Schoolchild* (1989), 84.
131. Harry Hendrick, *Child Welfare. England 1872–1989* (1994), 4, 34.
132. Francis Warner, *The Children: How to Study Them* (1887), 72–3, 80. Francis Warner, *The Study of Children and their School Training* (1897), vii, 79.
133. D.G. Pritchard, *Education and the Handicapped, 1760–1960* (1963), 118. See also David Mills Daniel, '"Education, or Care and Control?": The Development of Provision for Mentally Handicapped Children in England and Wales, 1870 to 1914 – An Examination of Legislation, Reports, Theory and Practice', *History of Education Society Bulletin*, No. 57 (Spring 1996), 20. Warner, *The Study of Children*, 69.

134. Memorandum by the Chairman of the School Management Committee of the London School Board, 28 June 1900, in SBL.1462 at the Greater London Record Office.

135. Ibid. See also the *First Annual Report of the Medical Officer of the School Board for London for 1902–3*, which lamented there were 'no trustworthy measurements of the development of London children'. It called for these to be provided. SBL.1462 at the Greater London Record Office.

136. Jordan, *The Degeneracy Crisis*, 173.

7 *At Leisure*

1. James Walvin, *A Child's World. A Social History of English Childhood 1800–1914* (1982), 79.

2. Quoted in Pamela Horn, 'Aspects of Child Employment, 1890–1914: Continuity and Change' in V. Alan McClelland (ed.), *Children at Risk* (1994), 130.

3. *Appendix to First Report of the Children's Employment Commission*, PP 1842, Vol. XVII, Evidence of James Essex, surgeon, 622.

4. Henry Mayhew, *London Labour and the London Poor*, Vol. I (1968 edn), 151–2.

5. *Appendix to Second Report of the Children's Employment Commission*, Part I, PP 1843, Vol. XV, evidence of Thomas Massey, c. 76; see also evidence of James Perry, aged 12, c. 85: 'I play Mondays unless mother wants to send me anywhere.'

6. J.D.A. Stanford, *Working-class Children in Mid-nineteenth Century Portsmouth* (Dissertation, November 1971), 28 at Portsmouth Record Office, 1591A/1. This is based on a report in the *Hampshire Telegraph*, 3 March 1849. For *Punch*, Walvin, *A Child's World*, 95–6.

7. Stanford, *Working-class Children*, 28. This took place in 1851.

8. *Grimsby Observer and Humber News*, 19 January 1876.

9. Pamela Horn, 'English Theatre Children, 1880–1914: a Study in Ambivalence', *History of Education*, Vol. 25, No. 1 (1996), 37.

10. Nina Auerbach, *Ellen Terry. Player in Her Time* (1989 edn), 41. Edith Craig and Christopher St John (eds), *Ellen Terry's Memoirs* (1933), 11.

11. University of Essex, Oral Archives Transcript No. QD1/FLWE/118.

12. Diary of Hastings Rashdall for 1873, MS.Eng.Misc.e.361 at the Bodleian Library, Oxford.

13. Diary of Hastings Rashdall, Summary of his 'Midsummer holidays'.

14. John Springhall, *Coming of Age: Adolescence in Britain 1860–1960* (1986), 117.

15. Margaret Fletcher, *O, Call Back Yesterday* (1939), 17–18.

16. Paul Thompson, 'Voices from Within' in H.J. Dyos and Michael Wolff (eds), *The Victorian City*, Vol. 1 (1973), 63–4.

17. University of Essex, Oral Archives Transcript No. QD1/FLWE/407.

18. S. Humphries, '"Hurrah for England": Schooling and the Working Class in Bristol, 1870–1914', *Southern History*, Vol. 1 (1979), 187.

19. Walter Southgate, *That's the Way It Was. A Working-class Autobiography 1890–1950* (1982), 46.

20. Irina Stickland (ed.), *The Voices of Children 1700–1914* (1973), 154.

21. Stickland, *Voices of Children*, 203. Edwin Pugh, 'Some London Street Amusements' in George R. Sims (ed.), *Living London*, Vol. III (1903), 266.

22. W. Macqueen-Pope, *Give Me Yesterday. A Backward Glance down the Years* (1957), 62.

23. Log Book for All Saints Boys' School at Portsmouth Record Office, D/55/2/A/1.

24. Log Book for Kent Street School at Portsmouth Record Office, D.23/3/A/1, entries for 23 March, 8 and 14 July 1874; see also 15 June 1875: 'There was a small attendance in consequence of the Circus and the Agricultural Show.'

25. Beneficial Girls' School Log Book at Portsmouth Record Office, 536A/18/2, entries for 10 March and 14 April 1863. Stuart Maclure, *One Hundred Years of London Education 1870–1970* (1970), 56.

26. Pamela Horn, *The Victorian and Edwardian Schoolchild* (1989), 150.

27. Southgate, *That's the Way It Was*, 25.

28. Southgate, *That's the Way It Was*, 32.

29. Alice Foley, *A Bolton Childhood* (1990 edn), 18.

30. University of Essex, Oral Archives Transcript No. QD1/FLWE/34.

31. Bristol People's Oral History Project, Transcript No. R.032 at Bristol Local History Library.

32. Advertisement at the Bethnal Green Museum of Childhood, London.

33. University of Essex, Oral Archives Transcript No. QD1/FLWE/94.
34. Reginald A. Bray, 'The Boy and the Family' in E.J. Urwick (ed.), *Studies of Boy Life in Our Cities* (1904), 71.
35. Joseph Stamper, *So Long Ago* (1960), 47.
36. E.P. Thompson and Eileen Yeo (eds), *The Unknown Mayhew. Selections from the Morning Chronicle 1849–1850* (1984), 339.
37. Mayhew, *London Labour*, 445. Ruth Bottomley, *Rocking Horses* (1994 edn), 6.
38. Pauline Flick, *Old Toys* (1995 edn), 9, 18.
39. Flick, *Old Toys*, 14.
40. Flick, *Old Toys*, 23.
41. Margaret Llewelyn Davies (ed.), *Life as We Have Known It* (1977 edn), 16.
42. Flick, *Old Toys*, 19–20.
43. Flick, *Old Toys*, 21–22.
44. Flick, *Old Toys*, 20.
45. See, for example, *Twenty-second Report of the Children's Aid Society for the Year ending 31 December, 1898* (1899), 10-11, H.362.72 CHI. at Liverpool Record Office.
46. L. Cope Cornford, *London Pride and London Shame* (1910), 93–5.
47. Thomas Walter Laqueur, *Religion and Respectability. Sunday Schools and Working-class Culture 1780–1850* (1976), xi, 116–19.
48. F.J. Harvey Darton, *Children's Books in England* (1958), 220, 247, 253.
49. Michael Wheeler, *English Fiction of the Victorian Period 1830–1890* (1994 edn), 178.
50. E.S. Turner, *Boys Will Be Boys* (1957 edn), 46.
51. Wheeler, *English Fiction*, 107. G. Salmon, 'What Boys Read', *Fortnightly Review*, No. 230, New Ser. (February 1886), 250–1. Nina Auerbach, 'Alice and Wonderland: A Curious Child', *Victorian Studies*, Vol. XVII, No. 1 (September 1973), 33, 35.
52. John Springhall, Brian Fraser and Michael Hoare, *Sure and Stedfast* [*sic*]. *A History of the Boys' Brigade 1883 to 1983* (1983), 21, 25.
53. Edward G. Salmon, 'What Girls Read', *The Nineteenth Century*, Vol. XX (October 1886), 516–17.
54. Salmon, 'What Girls Read', 527. 'Young people cannot read too much biography', was Salmon's conclusion. 'Fiction should lend relief to girl-life, biography should impart right principle, and poetry grace.'
55. Hugh Cunningham, *The Children of the Poor. Representations of Childhood since the Seventeenth Century* (1991), 137–40.
56. Salmon, 'What Boys Read', 249.
57. Turner, *Boys Will Be Boys*, 46.
58. Turner, *Boys Will Be Boys*, 59–60.
59. Turner, *Boys Will Be Boys*, 67–8. Springhall, *Coming of Age*, 129.
60. Turner, *Boys Will Be Boys*, 70. Springhall, *Coming of Age*, 129.
61. Salmon, 'What Boys Read', 255.
62. Patrick A. Dunae, 'Penny Dreadfuls: Late Nineteenth-century Boys' Literature and Crime', *Victorian Studies*, Vol. XXII, No. 2 (Winter 1979), 144.
63. Springhall, *Coming of Age*, 129.
64. Springhall, *Coming of Age*, 131. Turner, *Boys Will Be Boys*, 100–4.
65. Dunae, 'Penny Dreadfuls', 149.
66. Salmon, 'What Girls Read', 523.
67. *The Girl's Own Paper*, Vol. III (2 December 1882), 132–4.
68. Salmon, 'What Girls Read', 520.
69. Kirsten Drotner, *English Children and Their Magazines, 1751–1945* (1988), 115, 121.
70. Mayhew, *London Labour*, 40.
71. John Springhall, '"Corrupting the Young"? Popular Entertainment and "Moral Panics" in Britain and America since 1830' in McClelland, 97–8.
72. Springhall, *Coming of Age*, 125, 127–8.
73. Eric Hopkins, *Childhood Transformed. Working-class Children in Nineteenth-century England* (1994), 301.
74. Angela Hewins, *A Stratford Story* (1994), 46.
75. Jack Jones, 'The Not So Good Old Days' in Noel Streatfeild (ed.), *The Day before Yesterday* (1956), 69.
76. F. Gordon Roe, *The Victorian Child* (1959), 126.
77. Flick, *Old Toys* (1977 edn), 19 (not included in 1995 edn).
78. *Interdepartmental Committee on Physical Deterioration*, PP 1904, Vol. XXXII, Evidence of Mr Douglas Eyre, 154, Q.3605, and 155–7, Q.3608, 3680 and 3682.
79. Transcript of Tape 003, Miss Ashton of Dukinfield, at Tameside Local Studies Library, Stalybridge.
80. Steven Fielding, *Class and Ethnicity. Irish Catholics in England, 1880–1939* (1993), 74–5.
81. Laqueur, *Religion and Respectability*, 177.
82. Laqueur, *Religion and Respectability*, 178.
83. Laqueur, *Religion and Respectability*, 236.
84. Alan Delgado, *The Annual Outing and Other Excursions* (1977), 109.
85. Lillian Lewis Shiman, 'The Band of Hope Movement: Respectable Recreation for

Working-class Children' in *Victorian Studies*, Vol. 17, No. 1 (September 1973), 49, 54, 59–60.

86. Lewis Shiman, 'The Band of Hope', 66–7, 73.

87. Bristol People's Oral History Project, Transcript No. R.001 at Bristol Local History Library.

88. Laqueur, *Religion and Respectability*, 246.

89. Laqueur, *Religion and Respectability*, 248.

90. *The Charity Organisation Review*, Vol. VI (June 1890), 253–4. Helen Bosanquet, *Social Work in London* (1914), 242.

91. Southgate, *That's the Way It Was*, 69–70.

92. *Interdepartmental Committee on Physical Deterioration*, Appendix XXII, submitted by Mr T.C. Horsfall, 84.

93. *Third Report of the Children's Employment Commission*, PP 1864, Vol. XXII, 57.

94. *Third Report of the Children's Employment Commission*, Evidence of Mr Charles Iles, 106.

95. Old People's Reminiscences at Lancashire Record Office, DDX.978/1/6/1. Hopkins, *Childhood Transformed*, 305.

96. Molly Hughes, *A London Family 1870–1900* (1991 edn), 85, 102–3, 104, 124.

97. J.A.V. Chapple and Arthur Pollard (eds), *The Letters of Mrs Gaskell* (1966), 119.

98. *Report of the Public Schools Commission*, PP 1864, Vol. XX, 41.

99. *Christ's College, Blackheath Magazine*, November 1896, 125, 126, at Church of England Record Office, NS/SR/MISC.1/1/1.

100. *Interdepartmental Committee on Physical Deterioration*, Evidence of Dr Niven, 252, Q.6307 and 6310. Hopkins, *Childhood Transformed*, 302.

101. Log Book of Malmesbury Road Boys' School, EO/DIV.5/MAL/LB/1 at Greater London Record Office, 12 March 1888, and illuminated address, dated 21 November 1888.

102. Log Book of Malmesbury Road Boys' School, letter dated 12 October 1888.

103. Hopkins, *Childhood Transformed*, 257. Stuart Maclure, *100 Years*, 66, 69.

104. Springhall et al., *Sure and Stedfast*, 23–4.

105. Springhall et al., *Sure and Stedfast*, 25.

106. Sharman Kadish, *'A Good Jew and a Good Englishman': The Jewish Lads' and Girls' Brigade 1895–1995* (1995), 1.

107. Springhall et al., *Sure and Stedfast*, 48, 50.

108. Southgate, *That's the Way It Was*, 39.

109. Springhall et al., *Sure and Stedfast*, 56.

110. Springhall et al., *Sure and Stedfast*, 57.

111. Springhall et al., *Sure and Stedfast*, 65.

112. John Springhall, *Youth Empire and Society* (1977), 27, 37–8. Springhall et al., *Sure and Stedfast*, 68–9.

113. Springhall, *Youth, Empire and Society*, 38–9, 48.

114. Kadish, *'A Good Jew'*, 2.

115. Kadish, *'A Good Jew'*, 11–12.

116. *Royal Commission on Alien Immigration*, PP 1903, Vol. IX, Evidence of Captain E.W. Denniss, 271–2, Q.18,273 and 18,280.

117. Kadish, *'A Good Jew'*, 13.

118. Kadish, *'A Good Jew'*, 15.

119. Springhall, *Youth, Empire and Society*, 43.

120. Springhall, *Youth, Empire and Society*, 44–5. Springhall et al., *Sure and Stedfast*, 70.

121. Springhall, *Youth, Empire and Society*, 88.

122. For an examination of this mood see Kathleen Woodroofe, *From Charity to Social Work in England and the United States* (1962), 64–5.

123. Springhall, *Coming of Age*, 148–50.

124. Roger Bryant, *Don't Touch the Holy Joe. Father Dolling's Battle for Landport and St Agatha's* (1995), 18–19.

125. Charles Booth, *Life and Labour of the People in London. First Series: Poverty*, Vol. 3 (1902), 219. Children also went into public houses. Not until 1872 was the sale of spirits to under-sixteens forbidden, while liquor could be sold to the under-eighteens until 1923. In 1933 under-fourteens were forbidden to enter the bar areas of licensed premises. Hopkins, *Childhood Transformed*, 311.

8   Rescue and Reform

1. Quoted in Hugh Cunningham, 'The Rights of the Child from the Mid-eighteenth to the Early Twentieth Century' in V. Alan McClelland (ed.), *Children at Risk* (1994) 6.

2. R.J.W. Selleck, 'Mary Carpenter: A Confident and Contradictory Reformer', *History of Education*, Vol. 14, No. 2 (1985), 101.

3. *Select Committee on Criminal and Destitute Juveniles*, PP 1852, Vol. VII, Evidence of Mary Carpenter, 119, Q.935.

4. Pamela Horn, *Children's Work and Welfare, 1780–1890* (1995 edn), 50. Lionel Rose, *Crime and Punishment* (1977), 82.

5. Deborah Gorham, 'The "Maiden Tribute of Modern Babylon" Re-examined: Child Prostitution and the Idea of Childhood in Late-Victorian England', *Victorian Studies*, Vol. 21, No. 3 (1978), 371.
6. Kellow Chesney, *The Victorian Underworld* (1970), 207, 325. Judith R. Walkowitz, *City of Dreadful Delight. Narratives of Sexual Danger in Late-Victorian London* (1992), 123.
7. Rose, *Crime and Punishment*, 76–7.
8. Joan Rimmer, *Yesterday's Naughty Children. Training Ship, Girls' Reformatory and Farm School* (1986), 47.
9. Quoted in Cunningham, 'The Rights of the Child', 10.
10. *Hansard*, 3rd Ser., Vol. XCIX (29 May to 30 June 1848), cols 431–2.
11. *Night and Day*, 15 January 1877, 3. Lionel Rose, *The Erosion of Childhood. Child Oppression in Britain 1860–1918* (1991), 80.
12. Jo Manton, *Mary Carpenter and the Children of the Streets* (1976), 6.
13. Harry Stone (ed.), *The Uncollected Writings of Charles Dickens. Household Words 1850–1859*, Vol. II (1968), 424.
14. Horn, *Children's Work*, 46.
15. Joseph Stamper, *So Long Ago* (1960), 74.
16. Manton, *Mary Carpenter*, 5.
17. Charles Dickens, *Oliver Twist* (1966 edn), 50–7, for examples of Fagin's activities. William Augustus Miles, *A Letter to Lord John Russell Concerning Juvenile Delinquency* (1837), 7, 8289.bb.37(4) at the British Library.
18. Quoted in Selleck, 'Mary Carpenter', 104. Horn, *Children's Work*, 46.
19. Quoted in Horn, *Children's Work*, 48.
20. J.J. Tobias, *Crime and Industrial Society in the 19th Century* (1967), 57.
21. Selleck, 'Mary Carpenter', 112.
22. Stone, *Uncollected Writings*, Vol. I, 263.
23. Selleck, 'Mary Carpenter', 113.
24. *Twenty-eighth Annual Report of the Local Government Board for 1898–9*, PP 1899, Vol. XXXVII, 324.
25. Pamela Horn, 'Changing Attitudes to the Welfare of Elementary Schoolchildren in the 1880s' in Richard Aldrich (ed.), *In History and in Education* (1996), 52.
26. Mary C. Tabor, 'The Rights of Children', *Contemporary Review*, Vol. 54 (1888), 410, 414.
27. Sidney Webb and Beatrice Webb, *English Poor Law History*, Part II, *The Last Hundred Years*, Vol. 1 (1929), 246.
28. Sidney Webb and Beatrice Webb, *English Poor Law Policy* (1910), 183.
29. Francis Duke, 'Pauper Education' in Derek Fraser (ed.), *The New Poor Law in the Nineteenth Century* (1976), 82. Webb and Webb, *English Poor Law History*, 250.
30. Webb and Webb, *English Poor Law History*, 252.
31. Webb and Webb, *English Poor Law Policy*, 180. *Poor Relief Act, 1868*, 31 & 32 Victoria, c. 122, sect. 37.
32. Bristol People's Oral History Project, Transcript No. R.003 at Bristol Local History Library.
33. George Haw, *From Workhouse to Westminster. The Life Story of Will Crooks, MP* (1911), 9.
34. Charles Chaplin, *My Early Years* (1981 edn), 19–26. David Robinson, *Chaplin, His Life and Art* (1985), 24–6.
35. Webb and Webb, *English Poor Law History*, 278.
36. Lionel Rose, *'Rogues and Vagabonds'. Vagrant Underworld in Britain 1815–1985* (1988), 134.
37. *Twenty-eighth Annual Report of the Local Government Board*, Report for 1898 by Mr J.R. Mozley, Inspector of Poor Law Schools for the Northern District and Wales, 183. Webb and Webb, *English Poor Law History*, 263.
38. *Report of Mrs Nassau Senior as to the Effect on Girls of the System of Education at Pauper Schools*, PP 1874, Vol. XXV, 319–20. Ivy Pinchbeck and Margaret Hewitt, *Children in English Society*, Vol. II (1973), 516–19.
39. Webb and Webb, *English Poor Law Policy*, 190.
40. *A Short History of the North Surrey District School by the Superintendent* (n.d. [c. 1908]), 16–19, NSSD/94 at the Greater London Record Office.
41. *Annual Report of the North Surrey District School for 1865–6*, 31, NSSD/88 at the Greater London Record Office.
42. M.A. Crowther, *The Workhouse System 1834–1929. The History of an English Social Institution* (1983 edn), 220.
43. Fanny Fowke (ed.), *Children of the State* by Florence Davenport-Hill, 2nd edn (1889), 23.
44. Haw, *From Workhouse to Westminster*, 11–13.
45. *Twenty-eighth Annual Report of the Local Government Board*, 324.

46. Raymond Postgate, *The Life of George Lansbury* (1951), 67.
47. Norman Longmate, *The Workhouse* (1974), 179–80.
48. Fowke, *Children of the State*, 17.
49. *Report of Mrs Nassau Senior*, 320.
50. *Twenty-eighth Annual Report of the Local Government Board*, Miss Mason's Report on Boarding Out, 194–5. Webb and Webb, *English Poor Law History*, 274–5. Pinchbeck and Hewitt, *Children in English Society*, 519–23.
51. *Twenty-eighth Annual Report of the Local Government Board*, lxxxvii.
52. Webb and Webb, *English Poor Law Policy*, 206.
53. Portsea Union: Register of Children under the Control of the Guardians, BG/AY/1/1 at Portsmouth Record Office.
54. Portsea Union: Register of Children under the Control of the Guardians, case of George Duffey.
55. Quoted in Horn, *Children's Work*, 4.
56. Fowke, *Children of the State*, 90–1.
57. Webb and Webb, *English Poor Law History*, 288–9.
58. V. Alan McClelland, 'Child Emigration to Canada in Late Victorian and Edwardian England: A Denominational Case Study' in McClelland, 39–40. Webb and Webb, *English Poor Law History*, 267–8.
59. Angela Hewins, *A Stratford Story* (1994 edn), 101–2. C. Stella Davies, *North Country Bred. A Working-class Family Chronicle* (1963), 73.
60. Eric Hopkins, *Childhood Transformed. Working-class Children in Nineteenth-century England* (1994), 188.
61. William Chance, *Children under the Poor Law. Their Education, Training and After-care* (1897), 256–7, 284.
62. Pamela Horn, 'Youth Migration – the Fisher Boy Apprentices of Grimsby 1870–1914', *Genealogists' Magazine* (September 1995), 103. See also Registers of Indentures of Fisherboys at Archive Office, Grimsby. David Boswell, *Sea Fishing Apprentices of Grimsby* (1974), *passim*.
63. Horn, 'Youth Migration', 103–4. In 1913, just thirty-one boys signed apprenticeship indentures at Grimsby, of whom twenty came from Poor Law unions and other public bodies. Two decades before the annual total had been 282, with 882 apprentices serving at Grimsby at the end of that year. Chance, *Children under the Poor Law*, 279, 281.
64. Pamela Horn, *The Rise and Fall of the Victorian Servant* (1995 edn), 138.
65. Rose, *Erosion of Childhood*, 43.
66. Rose, *Erosion of Childhood*, 48–50.
67. Harry Hendrick, *Child Welfare. England 1872–1989* (1994), 79.
68. *Night and Day*, 15 January, 15 March and 16 May 1877. June Rose, *For the Sake of the Children. Inside Dr Barnardo's: 120 Years of Caring for Children* (1987), 15, 18, 30, 37, 40–8.
69. June Rose, *For the Sake of the Children*, 47.
70. *Twenty-fifth Annual Report of 'Dr Barnardo's Homes' for Orphan and Destitute Children for 1890*, 23.
71. 'These Forty Years'. *Fortieth Annual Report of Dr Barnardo's Homes for 1905*, 34.
72. Gertrude M. Tuckwell, *The State and Its Children* (1894), 58. John Stroud, *Thirteen Penny Stamps. The Story of the Church of England Children's Society (Waifs and Strays) from 1881 to the 1970s* (1971), 94–101. James Walvin, *A Child's World. A Social History of English Childhood 1800–1914* (1982), 154. Entry for Edward Rudolf in the *Dictionary of National Biography*.
73. Stroud, *Thirteen Penny Stamps*, 104, 112–13.
74. Rose, *Erosion of Childhood*, 44–5.
75. Horn, *Children's Work*, 50–1.
76. *Fortieth Report of Dr Barnardo's Homes for 1905*, 29.
77. *Porcupine*, 27 May 1871, 137.
78. *Porcupine*, 9 July 1870, 146. Joy Parr, *Labouring Children* (1980), 30.
79. *Report to the President of the Local Government Board by Andrew Doyle*, PP 1875, Vol. LXIII, 12–13.
80. Thomas Seddon to Walter J. Sendall, 13 November 1884, in Westminster Diocesan Archives, WDA, Box I. This and other documents in the Westminster Diocesan Archives are quoted by permission of His Eminence, the Cardinal Archbishop of Westminster.
81. Thomas Seddon to Walter J. Sendall, 17 October 1884, WDA, Box I.
82. Thomas Seddon to Major-General Fremantle, 7 January 1884, WDA, Box I.
83. Clerk to St George's Poor Law Union to Thomas Seddon, 19 March 1895, WDA, Box XI.

84. Parr, *Labouring Children*, 72.
85. Parr, *Labouring Children*, 40. *Fortieth Annual Report of Dr Barnardo's Homes*, 34. By the turn of the century around seven thousand workhouse children had emigrated, mainly to Canada. Pinchbeck and Hewitt, *Children in English Society*, 579.
86. Parr, *Labouring Children*, 106.
87. *Report from the Select Committee on Criminal and Destitute Juveniles, 1852*, Evidence of Mary Carpenter, 119, Q.935.
88. Tobias, *Crime and Industrial Society*, 213. Margaret May, 'Innocence and Experience: the Evolution of the Concept of Juvenile Delinquency in the Mid-nineteenth Century', *Victorian Studies*, Vol. XVIII, No. 1 (September 1973), 8–9.
89. *Second Report of the Select Committee on the Execution of the Criminal Law, Especially Respecting Juvenile Offenders and Transportation*, PP 1847, Vol. VII, 5.
90. John Springhall, *Coming of Age: Adolescence in Britain 1860–1960* (1986), 163.
91. F.H. Edwards, *Crime and Law and Order in Mid-Victorian Portsmouth* (Portsmouth Papers No. 55, February 1989), 11.
92. Lionel Rose, *Young Offenders and the Law* (1984), 26.
93. John R. Gillis, 'The Evolution of Juvenile Delinquency in England 1890–1914', *Past and Present* (May 1975), 108.
94. Borough of Portsmouth Police Report, 1843–9, entry for 8 March 1844, in Portsmouth Record Office, DF/P1/1/1.
95. May, 'Innocence and Experience', 11.
96. *Select Committee on Criminal and Destitute Juveniles, 1852*, Evidence of Mr Serjeant Adams, assistant judge in the Middlesex quarter sessions, 215, Q.1872. Tobias, *Crime and Industrial Society*, 82.
97. Stone, *Uncollected Writings*, Vol. I, 263–4.
98. Calculated from a return of the number and description of prisoners committed to the House of Correction at Westminster during the years ending Michaelmas 1856–9, 5, at Greater London Record Office, WA/GP/1859/6.
99. Manton, *Mary Carpenter*, 7. Tobias, *Crime and Industrial Society*, 206.
100. Tobias, *Crime and Industrial Society*, 65.
101. Charles Dickens, *Oliver Twist*, 295.
102. Tobias, *Crime and Industrial Society*, 67.
103. Pinchbeck and Hewitt, *Children in English Society*, 449. Hopkins, *Childhood Transformed*, 196–7, 198.
104. Julius Carlebach, *Caring for Children in Trouble* (1970), 25–8. *First Report of the Select Committee on the Execution of the Criminal Law*, Evidence of Captain Hall, Governor of Parkhurst Prison, 242, Q.2198. May, 'Innocence and Experience', 11.
105. Quoted in Horn, *Children's Work*, 55.
106. Rose, *Young Offenders*, 25. Pinchbeck and Hewitt, *Children in English Society*, 464.
107. Quoted in Tobias, *Crime and Industrial Society*, 54.
108. Rose, *Young Offenders*, 30, 33. Carlebach, *Caring for Children*, 4, 22–5.
109. Rose, *Young Offenders*, 33.
110. Joan Rimmer, *Yesterday's Naughty Children*, 6. Manton, *Mary Carpenter*, 164–7. J.A. Stack, 'Interests and Ideas in Nineteenth Century Social Policy: The Mid-Victorian Reformatory School', *Journal of Educational Administration and History*, Vol. XIV, No. 1 (January 1982), 42–3. Contributions from parents were difficult to collect; in 1866, of 1,315 offenders admitted to reformatories, there were 22 per cent of cases in which no proceedings were taken because parents or step-parents could not be located and 29 per cent in which proceedings were initiated, but the parents or step-parents were excused because of poverty; in 49 per cent of cases parents were placed under orders of payment.
111. *Report of the Commissioners on Reformatories and Industrial Schools*, PP 1884, Vol. XLV, ix, xliii.
112. *Twenty-second Annual Report of the Committee of Visitors of the Industrial School at Feltham (1881)*, Chaplain's Report for 1880, 28–9, MA/RS/2/92 at the Greater London Record Office. Tobias, *Crime and Industrial Society*, 215.
113. *Forty-second Report of the Inspector of Reformatory and Industrial Schools*, PP 1899, Vol. XLIV, 44–5.
114. Rimmer, *Yesterday's Naughty Children*, 46.
115. Rimmer, *Yesterday's Naughty Children*, 79–80.
116. *Report of the Departmental Committee on Reformatory and Industrial Schools*, PP 1896, Vol. XLV, 45.
117. Rimmer, *Yesterday's Naughty Children*, 52–4.

118. Quoted in May, 'Innocence and Experience', 28–9.
119. Rimmer, *Yesterday's Naughty Children*, 13.
120. Rimmer, *Yesterday's Naughty Children*, 41–3.
121. *Report of the Departmental Committee on Reformatory and Industrial Schools*, Appendix L, 343–4.
122. *Forty-second Report of the Inspector of Reformatory and Industrial Schools*, 22. This compares with 101,599 adult males and 39,874 adult females in prison in the same year. Stack, 'Interests and Ideas', 39–40.
123. Bristol People's Oral History Project, Transcript No. R.003 at Bristol Local History Library.
124. Gillis, 'Evolution of Juvenile Delinquency', 99, 103, 124.
125. *Child's Guardian*, May 1895, 62, 69.
126. *Justice to Children. A Ten Years' Review. Annual Report of the National Society for the Prevention of Cruelty to Children for 1893–4*, 43–4, at NSPCC headquarters in London. Alan Brack, *All They Need is Love. The Story of the Liverpool Society for the Prevention of Cruelty to Children 1883–1983* (1983), 14.
127. George K. Behlmer, *Child Abuse and Moral Reform in England, 1870–1908* (1982), 162.
128. *Fourth Annual Report of the Bradford and District Branch of the NSPCC* (1899), 10, at NSPCC headquarters.
129. Behlmer, *Child Abuse*, 181.
130. *The Power of the Parent: A Factor of the State, Being the Annual Report of the National Society for the Prevention of Cruelty to Children for 1898–9*, Appendix B, 73.
131. Hendrick, *Child Welfare*, 82.
132. Stephen Lassonde, 'Learning and Earning: Schooling, Juvenile Employment, and the Early Life Course in Late Nineteenth-century New Haven', *Journal of Social History*, Vol. 29, No. 4 (Summer 1996), 840.
133. Walter Southgate, *That's the Way It Was. A Working Class Autobiography 1890–1950* (1982), 22.

Bibliography

Official Papers

PP = Parliamentary Papers

Children's Employment Commission, First Report of, PP 1842, Vol. XVI; *Second Report of*, PP 1843, Vols XIV and XV.
Children's Employment Commission, Third Report of, PP 1864, Vol. XXII; *Fourth Report of*, PP 1865, Vol. XX.
Criminal and Destitute Juveniles, Select Committee on, PP 1852, Vol. VII.
Education, Royal Commission on the State of Popular, in England, PP 1861, Vol. XXI, Pts I and II.
Elementary Schools (Children Working for Wages) Return, Cmnd. 205 (1899).
Interdepartmental Committee on the Employment of School Children, Report of, PP 1902, Vol. XXV.
Public Schools Commission, PP 1864, Vol. XX.
Reformatory and Industrial Schools, Report of Departmental Committee on, PP 1896, Vol. XLV.
Schools Inquiry Commission, PP 1867–8, Vol. XXVIII, Pts I, VI and VIII.
Secondary Education, Royal Commission on, PP 1895, Vols XLIII and XLVIII.
Hansard

Printed Books and Articles

Anderson, Michael, *Family Structure in Nineteenth Century Lancashire* (1971).
Avery, Gillian, *The Best Type of Girl. A History of Girls' Independent Schools* (1991).
Ayers, Gwendoline M., *England's First State Hospitals and the Metropolitan Asylums Board 1867–1930* (1971).
Behlmer, George, *Child Abuse and Moral Reform in England 1870–1908* (1982).
Bolin-Hort, Per, *Work, Family and the State. Child Labour and the Organization of Production in the British Cotton Industry, 1780–1920* (1989).
Bosanquet, Bernard (ed.), *Aspects of the Social Problem* (1895).
Booth, Charles, *Life and Labour of the People in London*, First Series, *Poverty* (1902).
Burnett, John, *A Social History of Housing* (1986 edn).
Burnett, John, *Destiny Obscure* (1984).
Burnett, John, *Useful Toil* (1974).
Carlebach, Julius, *Caring for Children in Trouble* (1977).
Childs, Michael J., *Labour's Apprentices. Working-class Lads in Late Victorian and Edwardian England* (1992).
Chinn, Carl, 'Was Separate Schooling a Means of Class Segregation in Late Victorian and Edwardian Birmingham?', *Midland History*, Vol. XIII (1988).
Chorley, Katharine, *Manchester Made Them* (1950).
Clarke, Allen, *The Effects of the Factory System* (1899).
Clynes, J.R., *Memoirs 1869–1924* (1937).
Crowther, M.A., *The Workhouse System 1834–1929. The History of an English Social Institution* (1983 edn).
Cruickshank, Marjorie, *Children and Industry. Child Health and Welfare in North-west Textile Towns during the Nineteenth Century* (1981).
Cunningham, Hugh, *The Children of the Poor. Representations of Childhood since the Seventeenth Century* (1991).

Doré, Gustave and Jerrold, Blanchard, *London. A Pilgrimage* (1970 edn).

Dunae, Patrick A., 'Penny Dreadfuls: Late Nineteenth Century Boys' Literature and Crime', *Victorian Studies*, Vol. XXII, No. 2 (1979).

Dupree, Marguerite W., *Family Structure in the Staffordshire Potteries 1840–1880* (1995).

Dunlop, O. Jocelyn with Denman, Richard D., *English Apprenticeship and Child Labour* (1912).

Dyos, H.J. and Wolff, Michael (eds), *The Victorian City* (2 vols) (1973).

Fletcher, Margaret, *O, Call Back Yesterday* (1939).

Flick, Pauline, *Old Toys* (1977 and 1995 edns).

Foley, Alice, *A Bolton Childhood* (1990 edn).

Fowke, Fanny (ed.), *Children of the State* by Florence Davenport-Hill, 2nd edn (1889).

Fraser, Derek (ed.), *The New Poor Law in the Nineteenth Century* (1976).

Frow, Edmund and Frow, Ruth, *The Half-time System in Education* (1970).

Gardner, Phil, *The Lost Elementary Schools of Victorian England* (1984).

Gillis, John R., 'The Evolution of Juvenile Delinquency in England 1890–1914', *Past and Present* (1975).

Goodenow, Ronald K. and Marsden, William E. (eds), *The City and Education in Four Nations* (1992).

Gorham, Deborah, 'The "Maiden Tribute of Modern Babylon" Re-examined: Child Prostitution and the Idea of Childhood in Late-Victorian England', *Victorian Studies*, Vol. XXI, No. 3 (1978).

Haw, George, *From Workhouse to Westminster. The Life Story of Will Crooks, MP* (1911).

Hendrick, Harry, *Child Welfare. England 1872–1989* (1994).

Hopkins, Eric, *Childhood Transformed. Working-class Children in Nineteenth-century England* (1994).

Horn, Pamela, *Children's Work and Welfare, 1780–1890* (1995 edn).

Horn, Pamela, *The Victorian and Edwardian Schoolchild* (1989).

Humphries, Stephen, *Hooligans or Rebels? An Oral History of Working-class Childhood and Youth 1889–1939* (1983 edn).

Hurt, J.S., *Elementary Schooling and the Working Classes 1860–1918* (1979).

Jordan, Thomas E., *The Degeneracy Crisis and Victorian Youth* (1993).

Keeling, Frederic, *Child Labour in the United Kingdom* (1914).

Laqueur, Thomas Walter, *Religion and Respectability. Sunday Schools and Working Class Culture 1780–1850* (1976).

Lewis, Jane, 'The Social History of Social Policy: Infant Welfare in Edwardian England', *Journal of Social Policy*, Vol. 9, No. 4 (1980).

Longmate, Norman, *The Workhouse* (1974).

McCann, Phillip (ed.), *Popular Education and Socialization in the Nineteenth Century* (1977).

Maclure, J. Stuart, *Educational Documents. England and Wales 1816–1968* (1969 edn).

Manton, Jo, *Mary Carpenter and the Children of the Streets* (1976).

Marks, Lara, *Model Mothers. Jewish Mothers and Maternity Provision in East London, 1870–1939* (1994).

May, Margaret, 'Innocence and Experience: The Evolution of the Concept of Juvenile Delinquency in the Mid-nineteenth Century', *Victorian Studies*, Vol. XVIII, No. 1 (1973).

Mayhew, Henry, *London Labour and the London Poor* (4 vols) (1968 edn).

Nardinelli, Clark, *Child Labor and the Industrial Revolution* (1990).

Parr, Joy, *Labouring Children* (1980).

Perkin, Harold, *The Rise of Professional Society. England since 1880* (1989).

Pinchbeck, Ivy and Hewitt, Margaret, *Children in English Society*, Vol. II (1973).

Pollock, Linda A., *Forgotten Children. Parent–Child Relations from 1500 to 1900* (1988 edn).

Pritchard, D.G., *Education and the Handicapped, 1760–1960* (1963).

Reader, W.J., *Professional Men. The Rise of the Professional Classes in Nineteenth-century England* (1966).

Reeder, D.A. (ed.), *Urban Education in the Nineteenth Century* (1977).

Rose, June, *For the Sake of the Children. Inside Dr Barnardo's* (1987).

Rose, Lionel, *Massacre of the Innocents. Infanticide in Great Britain 1800–1939* (1986).

Rose, Lionel, *The Erosion of Childhood. Child Oppression in Britain 1860–1918* (1991).

Ross, Ellen, *Love and Toil. Motherhood in Outcast London 1870–1918* (1993).

Rubinstein, David, *School Attendance in London, 1870–1904: A Social History* (1969).
Searby, Peter (ed.), *Educating the Victorian Middle Class* (1982).
Shaw, Charles, *When I Was a Child* (1977 edn).
Sherard, Robert, *The Child-slaves of Britain* (1905).
Smith, F.B., *The People's Health 1830–1910* (1979).
Southgate, Walter, *That's the Way It Was. A Working Class Autobiography 1890–1950* (1982).
Springhall, John, *Coming of Age: Adolescence in Britain 1860–1960* (1986).
Springhall, John, Fraser, Brian and Hoare, Michael, *Sure and Stedfast. A History of the Boys' Brigade 1883 to 1983* (1983).
Springhall, John, *Youth, Empire and Society* (1977).
Stamper, Joseph, *So Long Ago* (1960).
Stickland, Irina (ed.), *The Voices of Children 1700–1914* (1973).
Tabor, Mary, 'The Rights of Children', *Contemporary Review*, Vol. 54 (1888).
Taylor, Tony, 'As the Old Cocks Crow, the Young Ones Learn: the School Strikes of 1889 and the New Union Movement', *History of Education*, Vol. 23, No. 1 (1994).
Thompson, F.M.L. (ed.), *The Cambridge Social History of Britain 1750–1950* (3 vols) (1990).
Tobias, J.J., *Crime and Industrial Society in the 19th Century* (1967).
Tuckwell, Gertrude M., *The State and its Children* (1894).
Turner, E.S., *Boys Will Be Boys* (1957 edn).
Urwick, E.J. (ed.), *Studies of Boy Life in Our Cities* (1904).
Walvin, James, *A Child's World. A Social History of English Childhood 1800–1914* (1982).
Wardle, David, *Education and Society in Nineteenth-century Nottingham* (1971).
Webb, Sidney and Webb, Beatrice, *English Poor Law History, Part II, The Last Hundred Years* (1929).
Webb, Sidney and Webb, Beatrice, *English Poor Law Policy* (1910).
Wheeler, Michael, *English Fiction of the Victorian Period 1830–1890* (1994 edn).
Winstanley, Michael (ed.), *Working Children in Nineteenth-century Lancashire* (1995).
Wohl, Anthony S., *Endangered Lives. Public Health in Victorian Britain* (1983).

Index